THE SPECIAL ARTIST'S HANDBOOK

Art Activities and Adaptive Aids
for Handicapped Students

Susan Rodriguez

Photographs by Paul Blumenthal

DALE SEYMOUR PUBLICATIONS

Printed in the United States of America. Published simultaneously in Canada.

Order number DS11907
ISBN 0-86651-476-7 (formerly ISBN 0-13-826355-8)

DALE
SEYMOUR
PUBLICATIONS
P.O. BOX 10888
PALO ALTO, CA 94303

9 10 -ML- 99 98

*This book is dedicated to the memory of Elaine Dubrow,
a gifted teacher and an inspired artist.*

ACKNOWLEDGMENTS

I would like to extend my thanks to the many people who have helped in the production of *The Special Artist's Handbook.* My family, friends, colleagues, and students deserve a large personal note of appreciation. For their direct assistance, I would like to thank: Leora Chwalow, early childhood teacher; Pearl Olanoff, teacher of the deaf, Martin School, Philadelphia, Pennsylvania; and Esther Chwalow, consultant for deaf education, Tel Aviv, Israel. The Moss Rehabilitation Center in Philadelphia, Pennsylvania; the Please Touch Museum of Philadelphia; the Philadelphia Regional Chapter of the Epilepsy Foundation of America; Bette Ann Lawrence of the Philadelphia Museum of Art; and Dr. Mike McCann, Director of the Center for Occupational Hazards in New York are acknowledged for their cooperation. For photographic credits: Jamie Watson, Will Brown, Janet Keyser of the Tyler School of Art, and Amy Schaeffer of the Philadelphia College of Art.

Kip Simons, of Imagery Photography studio, is recognized for his valuable technical assistance. I am also grateful to the editorial advice I received at Prentice-Hall through editors Tom Power and Evelyn Fazio.

A very special note of gratitude is extended to Marilyn Moller, principal of the Philadelphia School District's Overbrook Educational Center in Philadelphia, Pennsylvania. Her total support has helped to make *The Special Artist's Handbook* possible.

ABOUT THE AUTHOR

Susan Rodriguez currently teaches art in the Philadelphia public schools. She has more than 18 years of experience with both regular and special needs classes, and has taught students of all ages. She has also held teaching positions at the Philadelphia Museum of Art, Temple University, and the Philadelphia College of Art at the University of the Arts where she remains on the faculty and directs their Saturday School for Children.

Susan has been teaching blind, visually impaired—and sighted—children within the Philadelphia public school system. A strong advocate for the arts and the handicapped, she has lectured widely at colleges, museums, conferences, and in the community. She has published articles and makes frequent appearances on television, radio, and the news media addressing these topics. She is the repeated recipient of grants and honors for her work with special children.

An exhibiting artist who combines her love of painting with teaching, Susan considers her visually impaired students to be a source of continual inspiration. She says, "It is my blind students who have taught me how to see—not with my eyes, but with my heart."

Susan Rodriguez earned her Bachelor of Fine Arts and Master of Education degrees from the Tyler School of Art. She also completed the art appreciation and philosophy program at the Barnes Foundation in Merion, Pennsylvania, and holds an honorary doctorate in Fine Arts from the Moore College of Art. She is a member of the Authors' Guild in New York, and the National Art Education Association.

ABOUT THE PHOTOGRAPHER

Paul Blumenthal, B.A., M.Ed., has educational expertise in special education, and has originated adaptive materials for his special needs students. He has a background and an ongoing interest in both art and photography, with experience in photographing children. Most recently, his work was published as a photographic essay.

(Note of interest: Paul is the grandnephew of the internationally known artist, Man Ray.)

PREFACE

The art room door slams behind you. You are an art teacher meeting a new class. One child is deaf. Three children are blind. A few appear "normal."

All are handicapped.

Perhaps you have years of experience as an art educator, or maybe you are beginning your career. Whatever the extent of your background, you will likely be teaching students with exceptionalities similar to those just described. Either now—or in the near future—your role as an art teacher will be shaped by this reality.

Since Public Law 94-142 granted to the handicapped the right to education in the least restrictive environment, special needs students are very much a part of school populations. Either in the classroom or in special programs, the handicapped student has arrived.

Are art teachers prepared to respond to this challenge as sensitive and effective educators?

University art education programs have rarely required that teachers be trained for teaching art to exceptional students. Not until recently have courses been offered that attempt to fill the gap between special education and art education. While special education degrees are not generally expected of art educators, the teaching of special students most definitely *is* expected—by law. This clearly leaves the art teacher with an urgent need for information and guidance.

It is in response to this need that *The Special Artist's Handbook* was written.

In recognizing your special students, you will be accepting their abilities along with their disabilities. You do this when you set realistic goals. The art teacher should be aware that students may be more capable than they may appear. So while you adjust your expectations to include modest results, you may also be surprised by considerable accomplishments. Working with handicapped students often produces the unexpected—which can go either way. There is always the unpredictable element, which is why your lessons should be structured with room for individual creative growth.

In turn, art therapists understand modest results. The emphasis in art therapy is usually placed on the "process"—all that occurs within the art experience. The "product" or final outcome is secondary to the process itself, which holds the real therapeutic aspect. The intrinsic sensory qualities of art materials are indeed a joy for any artist, while their manipulation can teach cognitive skills as well. Even if a final product is not of a recognizable nature, learning and enjoyment are occurring.

All this is important to remember because we as art teachers look forward to a final product that communicates an idea. When that does not happen, professional frustration can set in. Keep in mind that development may be slower in many special students, but it is still taking place.

As an art educator, no one has to convince you of the importance of art. You teach it because you believe in it, and you fully understand the extent of the value of art. Your students' work touches you; when that stops happening, you have a real concern. Although the business of teaching may have its trying moments, you manage to keep finding new sources of strength and inspiration—and *all* your students benefit.

TO THE TEACHER

I once faced a class of students with visual, hearing, and "hidden" handicaps. After surveying the newly assigned group on that day, I decided to use my ever-popular "Torn Paper Collage" lesson, since it is among the most simple and basic of activities.

What happened after I announced the lesson and handed out brightly colored paper squares could easily be called a lesson in "How Paper Does Not Tear." Pounding, crushing, waving, and ignoring paper are all effective techniques to not tear paper—which is what my new class taught me on that day.

Where did I go wrong? Was that lesson a classified failure? One basic flaw in my presentation was that I had overlooked an important fact—this group had no proficiency in tearing! The absence of that motor control skill did, however, suggest that clay would be a better choice for a lesson. Successful paper tearing came later.

This art room drama illustrates the importance of recognizing your students' developmental levels when selecting projects. Identifying and understanding the students' exceptionalities are integral parts of making a fair assessment. Your own professional experience may help, too, as well as common sense. But you may need some additional guidance.

The Special Artist's Handbook can help. It is an art activities reference manual for art teachers of exceptional children or for those teachers who have handicapped children in their classroom. The *Handbook* is divided into four major sections, with "Art Activities" representing the heart of the book. The other sections—"The Handicaps," "Adaptive Aids and Materials," and "The Art Classroom"—exist for the successful implementation of the art activities.

The Handicaps It is important that you become familiar with "The Handicaps" section. Learning to identify the characteristic traits of the handicaps is the key to knowing how to select the appropriate projects and approaches. The more you know about your students, the more likely you are to both meet their needs and be satisfied with the outcome.

Art Activities The activities are presented in an uncomplicated step-by-step format. Each activity is designed as a lesson unit that would be appropriate for *any* student, whether handicapped or nonhandicapped. Specific adaptations and recommendations for each exceptionality appear with every lesson unit. In addition, plans indicate special skill requirements, as well as advance teacher preparation.

The activities are meant to engage the students' interest. You will find that lessons are geared toward student independence. Many times the interaction is placed between students, rather than between student and teacher. The *Handbook*, therefore, is student-centered, which encourages students to find their own style.

The *Handbook* acknowledges every student's need for self-esteem, particularly the exceptional youngster's, because this student may already have many difficulties to overcome. This is why the projects will often be confidence builders. Lessons are meant to improve self-concepts and overall awareness.

Finally, the activities are often "imagination tickling," which will captivate attention. The point is to get the student engaged in his or her work. A satisfied student means a satisfied teacher, so both parties are winners.

Adaptive Aids and Materials This section serves two main functions. The aids are easy-to-construct devices made from ordinary materials that will enable many students to participate in lessons from which they might otherwise be excluded. The aids can compensate for missing skills and help students cope with physical losses.

The real value of the adaptive aids is that they give students independence. Teachers may not have to intervene in a technical process, which places the student in charge of his or her own work.

The "Materials" part of this section is almost a recipe file of media that can enhance the art experience for exceptional students. Although the media recipes are written for students with sensory losses, they can add "spice" to any art lesson.

The Art Classroom "The Art Classroom" section looks at the environment in which school art is taking place. The removal of possible barriers and making art activities more accessible are important concerns for teachers of handicapped students. Overall room arrangements, as well as the potential for activity centers should be considered. Since internal dynamics have great impact on students, a checklist is included that raises teacher awareness.

Using materials in the art room can pose problems for any student, but especially for the handicapped. Since safety in the art room concerns both student and teacher, this section will point out ways to maintain a healthier and safer art room.

Glossary The language used by special educators and art therapists is largely unfamiliar to the art teacher, so the *Handbook* also includes a glossary of terms and their definitions. The knowledge of these terms will give you better insight toward your students' needs.

A Final Word The purpose of this book is never to limit any one special group to one activity based on a definition. While you need to know about your students' conditions, avoid limiting activities on that basis. Stereotyping, like the notion that blind artists can only make clay objects, should be put aside in your students' best interests. Remember, you are teaching *students*, not handicaps. Let your students show you what they *can* do.

Susan Rodriguez

CONTENTS

SECTION THREE: ADAPTIVE AIDS AND MATERIALS   227

SECTION FOUR: THE ART CLASSROOM   249

GLOSSARY   272

INDEX   275

ONE

THE HANDICAPS

- **Recognizing the Handicap**
- **Myths, Prejudices, and Misconceptions**
- **Handicaps Reference Guide:**
  Definitions of Exceptionalities and Their Identifying Characteristics
  - Mentally Retarded
  - Socially and Emotionally Disturbed
  - Physically Handicapped
  - Learning Disabled
  - Sensory Losses
    Hearing Impaired
    Visually Handicapped/Blind
  - Gifted
- **Sign Language Guide**

Recognizing the Handicap

A handicap may range from mild to severe, be temporary or permanent. It may be physical, intellectual, or emotional. It can occur as one handicap or as a combination of several impairments. Handicaps can be congenital, or acquired through disease or injury. Some handicaps are easy to recognize, other are hidden. Causes may not always be clear.

When the disability interferes with learning, a special placement may be recommended for the student according to the *dominant* handicap. For example, a visually handicapped child with a hearing loss would be placed in a program for the visually handicapped if the vision loss interferes more with learning than the hearing impairment.

Because there is such a wide spectrum of student needs, a variety of placements are available. Mainstreaming, which is the blending of special students into the regular classroom, is perhaps the most common placement today. This includes the integration of special classes into the neighborhood school. Both these junctions are where classroom and specialist teachers are likely to encounter the handicapped student. Other settings are special schools or centers, resource rooms, hospitals, and the children's own homes, where they receive homebound instruction.

Enrichment programs and special classes are also available to gifted students. (Gifted students are considered exceptional because of their special educational needs.) Literally millions of students have been diagnosed as exceptional.

Since the passage of Public Law 94-142, which grants an "education in the least restrictive way" to the handicapped, teachers are meeting students with a wide variety of special needs. Since not all teachers are trained in special education, and not all needs are easy to identify, the "Handicap Reference Guide" beginning on page 7 provides basic information that will help you know more about special students. Special education teachers, art teachers, classroom teachers, recreational therapists, parents, and anyone else who is involved with educating exceptional children, will find pointers and guidelines in this guide.

Art is an area of abundance for the special student. But before pinpointing what characterizes and affects exceptional students, let's consider some commonly held beliefs that can be obstacles to achievement.

Myths, Prejudices, and Misconceptions

"All of the handicapped are retarded. They're just not as smart as normal people."

There are only two exceptionalities that primarily involve intelligence. One is *gifted,* the other, *mentally retarded.* Mental retardation encompasses the range from severely and profoundly impaired to educable (mildly) retarded. Diagnosis is made essentially on the basis of I.Q. levels and functional development.

The gifted are above the normal I.Q. range, although performance on test scores does not always accurately reflect intelligence. When potential and ability appear to exceed the developmental level, the student is considered gifted.

"Mentally retarded people are too slow to know what's going on—and they don't care anyway. They are a burden to society."

Mentally retarded people have the same feelings that all people share, and those feelings can certainly be hurt by insensitive treatment and thoughtless remarks. This is particularly true among the educable (mildly) mentally retarded, who are aware that they are not on the same level with their peers, yet are powerless to change that fact.

Being retarded does not mean leading a wasted life. For those not able to enter the job world, sheltered workshops are a means of productivity. Many retarded students learn skills at vocational centers and are capable of efficiency at simple tasks. The educable mentally retarded person *is* capable of learning and growing—that's why the term "educable" applies.

Perhaps the impairment most often confused with retardation and intelligence level is the learning disability.

"Doesn't a learning disability affect a person the same way as retardation? It adds up to the same thing—slow thinking."

Learning disabilities are unrelated to intelligence levels. The learning disabled can in fact have superior intelligence. Consider: Albert Einstein was learning disabled!

Often, the learning disabled are confused by simple information. They can easily misjudge situations and be poorly coordinated. Some are dyslexic. Repetition of directions is often required. But all of this is the result of a breakdown in the brain's ability to process information. It is not an intelligence deficiency.

Another condition which is thought to directly reduce intellectual capacity is cerebral palsy.

"People who can't control their bodies—the ones who walk and talk in an other-than-normal way—must not be able to *think* clearly either."

Motor impairments (such as cerebral palsy) that are marked by slurred speech, stumbling gait, etc. are often thought to negatively affect mental abilities. This is not true. These are *physical* impairments that often slow people down— but they are unrelated to intelligence.

Adults with cerebral palsy have even been mistaken for being intoxicated on occasion. The characteristics of the condition, along with the speech difficulties, have caused this regrettable confusion.

"You know, I always thought that deaf and dumb go together—if you're deaf, you're mute too."

The two do not necessarily go together. Being hearing impaired is not synonymous with absence of speech. Certainly, language and speech development are affected by hearing—but the deaf have voices!

Also, the term "dumb" is obsolete in the professional vocabulary—probably for both its incorrect usage, and for the implication of "stupidity" that the word "dumb" brings to mind.

"If you want a deaf person to hear you better, speak as loud as you can. Better yet, shout."

Raising your voice does *not* help the hearing handicapped to hear you better. In fact, shouting distorts the face so much that normal facial expression cannot be interpreted. Hearing impaired children could in fact be frightened by shouting— and wonder what they did to cause someone to shout at them!

If hearing impaired and blind people are with other nonhandicapped persons, people who meet them will often not address them directly. Referring to the hearing impaired or blind person, they might turn to their companions and ask, "Does *he* want to join us?"

Here's another common myth in dealing with blind people....

"I am so embarrassed! I just asked that blind woman if she 'saw' my point!"

Most blind people live in the real world. The expression "Do you see?" or any other use of the verb "see" should not upset them. Do not avoid using it.

Have you ever heard this one?

"Blind people should not strain their eyes. They need to save whatever vision they have left."

The "sight conservation" theory was believed long ago. Today, progressive programs for the blind and visually handicapped encourage the development of residual vision through use of special techniques and stimulating materials. The contemporary philosophy in educating the visually handicapped is that the student should maximize the usage of whatever eyesight he or she has.

There are also prejudices about the blind and deaf that surround their participation in the arts.

"Why invite a blind person to a museum, unless he is allowed to touch the sculpture?"

Total blindness is a rare thing. Degrees of visual impairment can vary greatly; it is almost impossible to judge just what another person sees, with or without glasses—or even with a white cane.

There is more to appreciation than perfect visual acuity. The museum, like other experiences, calls on many senses. The visually impaired are fully capable of appreciating art and creating it. And not every visually impaired person prefers clay—many enjoy painting, too!

"Why invite a deaf person to a concert?"

Again, deafness can be partial to severe and can change with varying environmental conditions (weather, allergies, etc.). Music can be experienced through vibrations, particularly when there is a wooden floor through which sound resonates. Percussion instruments are particularly good for the hearing impaired to understand.

And who said the hearing impaired cannot create music? After all, Beethoven was deaf in his later years.

And finally, the "tragedy" of being handicapped....

"The poor, helpless handicapped. We should protect them and not expect too much."

The healthiest attitude toward handicapped students and adults is to give the same fair and considerate treatment that you would afford anyone. Handicapped students, just like nonhandicapped students, are responsible for their actions and should not be excused from reasonable behavior on the sole basis of their handicaps.

Certainly, support should be offered when it is needed. But the most appreciated effort is in helping the handicapped student toward independence so that he or she can reach and grow.

Handicaps Reference Guide

DEFINITIONS AND CHARACTERISTICS OF
MAJOR HANDICAPPING CONDITIONS AND EXCEPTIONALITIES

MENTALLY RETARDED

Retardation is an intelligence impairment, causing a student to function below developmental level.

Severely and Profoundly Impaired

The severely retarded student has limited experience with his or her environment. Art activities should focus on sensory interaction between the student and the materials. The student is generally responsive to the physical movement and textural qualities that are intrinsic to art experiences.

May Lack:	*May Require:*
1. ABILITY TO UNDERSTAND DIRECTIONS. Attention span is short.	One-step directions. Student needs steps broken down—he or she cannot understand more than one thing at a time.
	When instructing, turn student's head in the direction of the task. Student will need lots of time on any activity. Keep it simple. Give physical and verbal prompting. Reinforce repeatedly.
2. BASIC CONCEPTS. May not understand simple concepts like in/out, up/down, etc.	Demonstrate with concrete objects and movement; i.e., produce both a big object and small object when showing size differences.
3. SENSORY DEVELOPMENT AND DISCRIMINATION. May be tactilely defensive.	Concrete experience to point out differences, as in rough/smooth (i.e., providing sample of sandpaper and of satin). Use desensitizing techniques for tactual aversions to paint, clay, etc. For example, introduce clay to student in small amounts, and allow student to get acquainted with the material. If student appears to be repelled by the clay don't force him or her to continue. Remove the material and present it again at a later time.
4. MOBILITY AND KINESTHETIC SENSE. Poor coordination. Not able to move one or more parts of the body in a functional way. Has difficulty walking, running, jumping, etc.	Use functional body parts over nonfunctional body parts. Projects should be adapted so that student can carry them out. Teacher can get student to physically understand a larger movement such as the kind that an art activity might require. Teacher actually gets behind student and guides him or her through motions much like a golf instructor. Teacher uses *physical prompting and verbal cues,* i.e., "We are *pounding* the clay." Teacher assists in activity and "fades out" once student learns the motion.

5. Awareness of body parts, spatial relationships. May not have bilaterality (movement of two hands together). May be spastic or athetoid, or lack ability to cross arms past "midline" of body to opposite side.	Gently ease student into movements by hand-over-hand method. Place student's hands in directions desired for activity, having student use one hand.
6. Fine grasping technique, fine motor skill (pincer grasp).	Work *into* smaller movements progressively from larger movements.
7. Appropriate group behaviors and self-awareness. May "rock," make noises and gestures that are incongruous in the classroom. May exhibit "blindisms"—rocking, flicking fingers in front of face, banging, etc. May keep head down.	Use student's name frequently; i.e., "Ms. Jones is helping Billy make a building." Use touch and eye contact to back up verbal communication. Limit socially unacceptable behavior by placing hand on student's shoulder, firmly reminding him or her *not* to rock, bang the desk, etc. *Remember, inappropriate behavior is often the result of lack of outside stimulation. Offer alternatives to unacceptable behavior—bring student's attention into activity. Recognize positive behaviors with praise!*

NOTE: Many S.P.I. students have seizures on occasion. See page 270 for "First-Aid for Seizures."

Trainable Mentally Retarded

Generally should be able to do matching, sorting, random brush and crayon work, clay pounding, paper tearing, building parts, and replication of simple forms.

May Lack:	*May Require:*
1. DEDUCTIVE REASONING, ABSTRACT THINKING. Cannot usually draw own conclusions based on information given by teacher.	No more than two to three steps at a time. Care should be taken not to overload with information, as it will overwhelm the student.
2. CONCEPTS DEVELOPMENT.	Concrete examples, i.e., "stop/go," "in/out," "over/under" can be demonstrated to students. These are useful concepts for daily living.
3. REFINED GROSS MOVEMENT. May appear awkward, have difficulty navigating body spatially. May not handle art materials well.	Art lessons that involve gross movement (such as "Faces and Traces," page 69) will create greater body awareness. Offer simple art materials and techniques (clay, paint, crayons) until student seems ready for more complex projects. *Teach* proper materials usage.
4. SOCIALIZATION SKILLS. Often unwilling to participate. May display stubborness, refusal to join group. May be tactually defensive.	Group activities that allow for positive "teamwork." Sharing experiences (such as the exploration of shell, page 161) help to improve class interaction. Desensitization should be used for tactual defensiveness.

5. INDEPENDENCE, SELF-HELP.	Give student work that he or she will succeed in because it is at *his or her skill level*. For example, if a student can sort objects well, let him or her sort out crayons. Give praise and support for a job well done.
6. ABILITY TO COMMUNICATE IDEAS IN A DIRECT WAY.	Listen to students' ideas with interest. Give them a chance to express themselves, without judging "correctness" of expression.

Educable Mentally Retarded

Often capable of some abstract thinking, and can sometimes do problem solving. Ability to follow and understand more complex directions varies with age levels and life experiences.

May Lack:	*May Require:*
1. ABILITY TO FOLLOW COMPOUNDED DIRECTIONS.	Break down multifaceted lessons into manageable chunks. Student can usually handle three or four steps, but attending to instruction depends on how many variables exist (motivation, interest, age, etc.). Repetition is often needed. Reminders and reinforcements are helpful.
2. SELF-ESTEEM. Often more easily frustrated. E.M.R. students have greater awareness of their shortcomings, which can make self-acceptance difficult. Display of anger is not uncommon.	Make sure student understands what a job requires in order to be done successfully. Goals should be clear and reasonable. Offer praise and encouragement whenever it is indicated.
3. LIFE EXPERIENCES. Information and enrichment gathered through travel, general participation. May have limited opportunities to learn about world outside of their immediate environment.	Bring in outside reference materials frequently. Share travel slides, talk about events of interest. Neighborhood walks, museum visits are helpful. Use media—filmstrips, films, books— to expand awareness. Holiday lessons complement student's own experiences and are pleasant to recall.

SOCIALLY AND EMOTIONALLY DISTURBED

Behavior disorder that interferes with learning. Inappropriate behaviors may range from withdrawal to aggression.

The socially and emotionally disturbed student can come from any social-economic background, but often the life and events outside of school have contributed to the difficulties the student is undergoing. NOTE: Students whose behavior is extreme enough to threaten their own safety or the safety of others would probably suggest a clinical or institutional placement. Other conditions inappropriate for the classroom setting include symptoms of serious mental illness, such as psychotic or schizophrenic behaviors.

May Lack:	May Require:
1. ABILITY TO CONCENTRATE. May not be able to focus on the task—may be restless or appear uninterested. May refuse to work, often getting out of seat and wandering around the room.	High interest material. Projects that elicit personal involvement. Learning new techniques can provide challenges and force students to get involved with their work. Students need accomplishments and appreciate using their skills. Students should be encouraged to carry out all steps of an activity and complete it.
2. SELF-ESTEEM. May be withdrawn into own world and be isolated, with lack of interest in self and others. On the other side, may be attention-seeking, overreactive and ill-tempered. Mood swings are common.	Building better self-image. Projects that "accent the positives" help (pages 65, 97, 137). Studio experiences often create opportunities for self-expression and self-exploration (pages 168, 189) without placing rigid expectations on students. Reassurance and praise should be given whenever indicated.
3. NORMAL INTERPERSONAL RELATIONSHIPS. May be distrustful, negative, and rebellious. Often unresponsive or hostile toward authority (parents, teachers, etc.). Poor attitudes may range from uncooperative to malicious.	Providing opportunities for productive interaction. Group projects and "buddy" projects are excellent. Encourage group discussion, sharing ideas and thoughts in a nonjudgmental atmosphere. Teacher needs to be accessible and approachable—it's not necessary to be the ultimate disciplinarian at *all* times (just when it seems needed).
4. SELF-CONTROL. Unable to manage own behavior. May be poorly motivated with no confidence in ability to make decisions. May disregard classroom order with disruptive, challenging behaviors.	Firm guidelines. Make expectations clear and stick to them. *Avoid* confrontations that go nowhere, i.e., let reaction to unacceptable behavior be known, but leave the student room to change it and improve. Be consistent.
5. POSITIVE LIFE EXPERIENCES. May be cynical and lack a "working philosophy." Personal values may be confused or deficient.	Widening student's world. Discussions, presentations, classroom guests, and trips can help. Teacher can affect student's life with own positive attitude. Let student gain from teacher's own experience (i.e., if teacher has special interests, likes travel, playing an instrument, etc., share it!).

LEARNING DISABLED

Dysfunction in the student's ability to process information, which affects basic learning skills. The student may be very successful in one academic area but very deficient in another.

Learning disabled students should have normal or above-normal intelligence.

May lack:	May Require:
1. NORMAL PERCEPTION. Can't seem to "make sense" out of information and directions. Has difficulty interpreting material. Because of difficulties with thought processes, ability to organize and plan may be affected.	Clear explanations. This doesn't mean "talking down"; it means using simple and straightforward language. Make sure that student understands one step before proceeding to the next. Do not bombard student with information; it tends to be overwhelming. Review requirements and directions whenever necessary.

2. DIRECTIONALITY. May have spatial orientation problems, be poorly coordinated. May confuse left and right, up and down, etc.	A starting point or reference point. This can be a line, a mark, or a physical demonstration. Teacher may need to guide student at certain times, but not at all times. Questions like "Where does it start? What comes first?" can be helpful.
3. BASIC SKILLS. Very common problem is dyslexia—problems with the ability to read. Words appear scrambled or in reverse ("d" for "b", "saw" becomes "was").	Demonstrate steps in lesson or process. Teacher cannot assume that students can read directions from chalkboard or print material.
4. MEMORY (visual, auditory). May lack short- or long-term recall.	Reinforce. Ask students to feed back information. Repeat whenever necessary.

PHYSICALLY HANDICAPPED

Orthopedic or central nervous system impairment that interferes with learning.

When a function is diminished or absent, other more functional physical parts must be engaged to compensate. Adaptive aids can be especially useful to the physically handicapped student.

May Lack:	May Require:
1. MOBILITY AND KINESTHETIC AWARENESS. May not be able to get around without braces, wheelchair, crutches, etc. Movement is restricted.	Activities and materials that are tailored to student's needs. For example, if activity asks for gross movement and student is wheelchair bound, activity will need modification. Engage the kinesthetic sense whenever feasible (see pages 35, 133, 142, 148).
2. POSITIVE SELF-IMAGE. If the disability is "new" (accident, trauma), there may be more emotional difficulty in accepting it. Orthopedically handicapped student with congenital difficulties may or may not be self-accepting—depending on attitudes of family, friends, school, etc.	Offer activities through which student can acquire a sense of accomplishment. Projects should be adapted so that student can function as independently as possible. Provide opportunities for achievement and success.
3. STAMINA, PHYSICAL STRENGTH. Many physical disabilities are energy draining. Student's condition may often weaken him or her, leaving student low on physical drive.	Assistance from teacher—but student should avoid becoming overly reliant. Teacher should be sensitive to signs of strain, yet motivate and encourage whenever possible. Frequently offer activities that student can manage alone, to build independence.
4. CONTROL OF BODY. Student may lack full use of hands, arms, legs, upper or lower torso, etc. May not have normal head movement. May be spastic, athethoid, or contracted. May have partial or complete paralysis of body.	Activities that engage and exercise the body. Many art activities do this: manipulative skills (tearing paper, pounding clay), kinesthetics (large drawing movement), etc. If hand/arm movement is absent, head movement can be substituted. Adaptive aids are very useful (see page 227).

SENSORY LOSSES

Hearing Impaired

Partial to complete deafness. Communication, speech, and language disorders may be involved. Hearing aids may or may not assist condition.

The hearing impaired student is physically and intellectually capable of having positive experiences through art, but must be aware of what is being communicated and the requirements.

Art is an important avenue of self-expression. It is a visual language for those who may have limited skills in the spoken language; a form of pictorial or dimensional communication for those who otherwise have difficulty communicating.

May Lack:	May Require:
1. LANGUAGE SKILLS. May have difficulty in communicating—cannot always understand others or express self clearly. Lacks vocabulary.	Greater teacher awareness that student has real communications problems. More movement should be tolerated in the classroom so that student can get proper attention and can "read" facial expressions, etc.
2. ABILITY TO FOCUS ATTENTION. Not always sure of what is expected. Does not always understand what is happening.	Make sure student sees teacher's face and can read teacher's lips. Light should be on teacher's face. Do not exaggerate or shout. Flick lights on and off to get student's attention. Turn student's face toward speaker. Eye contact is important. Avoid gesturing—it can confuse student. Use concrete examples when giving explanations.
3. SELF-ASSURANCE. Diminished confidence in self and own decisions.	More freedom in making own choices. Hearing impaired students are constantly being "directed" because of their lack of communication skill. Accept the physical nature of the hearing impaired, i.e., touching, moving around, etc. That is how they can get their messages across.
4. A SENSE OF BELONGING. There is a feeling of isolation attached to hearing loss.	Offer opportunities for positive interplay. Group and "buddy" projects are recommended.

Visually Handicapped/Blind

A partial to complete sight loss that interferes with learning. Visual deficiencies may involve varying degrees of acuity and/or field loss.

The visually handicapped student will often respond to bright and highly contrasted colors, illuminated and fluorescent materials with great enthusiasm. The visually handicapped can create dynamic artworks of all kinds—not just three-dimensional art. Severely visually impaired or blind students can develop visual images, although development is slower and adaptive aids are often required (see screenboards, page 241). Visually handicapped students enjoy *all* art materials, regardless of their sight losses.

May Lack:	May Require:
1. CONCEPTS. Real-world objects and ideas may not be understood. May have poor comprehension of "parts-to-whole" relationship, particularly when student is unable to see the complete "picture."	Basic information. Simple pointers, like where facial features are located, may need to be taught. Provide 3-D models and tactual reference material whenever possible, particularly for blind students.
2. ABILITY TO UNDERSTAND VISUAL CUES. May not be able to read regular print, see from a distance or from all angles. If blind, cannot see facial expressions or body language.	Be "extra" verbal with student. Describe what you are doing to blind student. If you want his or her attention, rap on desk (this is helpful for seating student). Use touch (i.e., a hand on student's shoulder) to communicate your presence. Visually handicapped student with some vision requires adjustment of visual material—bringing it closer to student, allowing student to find the right position. Feel free to ask if student needs to change seats, can see material OK, etc.

NOTE: Art activities can engage *other senses;* smell, touch, etc. can be both stimulating and informative for the visually handicapped student (see pages 243-248 for suggestions). |
| 3. AWARENESS OF SELF IN THE PHYSICAL ENVIRONMENT. Unsure of placement of objects and spatial boundaries. May be awkard, physically weak and exhibit poor body postures. Blind students often lack a sense of mobility. Some students may be tactilely defensive towards art materials (clay, paste, etc.) and display "blindisms" (rocking, flicking fingers, etc.) | Guidance. Help student to become more self-aware through activities that emphasize self (see pages 73, 93, 129, 157). Provide concrete experiences for student, using tactual references. Allow student to become familiar with classroom; do not surprise him or her by moving the furniture and not telling him or her. For tactually defensive student, use desensitization techniques. Discourage "blindisms"—they only separate the student more from his or her peers—substitute with positive activities.

To help student better understand where materials are located and to recognize the perimeters of working space, guide student's hand. Student uses free hand as a "marker" to establish where work is taking place. |

GIFTED

Level of intellectual functioning that exceeds the norm.

The gifted student has the ability to understand complex and abstract problems. The gifted have deductive reasoning powers and can hypothesize. Gifted students often display the empirical, scientific approach to problem solving.

May Lack:	May Require:
1. SOCIAL SKILLS. May be set apart from peers by his or her exceptional knowledge or intelligence. May not be well accepted by the group.	Group activities. Opportunities created for positive exchange between students help socialization process.

13

2. CONCENTRATION. Might be "distracted" by mental preoccupations. Daydreaming and fantasizing are recognized characteristics of creative thinkers.	Bringing attention back to task. Remind student to focus. Whenever possible, provide lessons that utilize imagination.
3. INTEREST. Straightforward or predictable assignments may be boring for the gifted student.	Challenges. Present activities that have the problem-solving element built into them. (Adaptations throughout the book under "Gifted" illustrate this point.)

Sign Language in the Art Classroom

The following words are important in any art classroom, but for students who cannot hear these spoken words, the visual signs are essential.

Colors
Color
Red
Orange
Yellow
Green
Blue
Purple
Brown
Black
White
Pink

Directions
Now
Later
And
Begin
Stop
Over
Under
Mix
Cut
Practice
Use
Rub
Help
Clean

Descriptive Words
Bottom
Top
Soft
Hard
Dark
Light
Smooth (a and b)
Rough
Big
Small
More
Less

Materials and Other Art Classroom Terms
Clay
Chalk
Crayon
Paint
Paste (a and b)
Mess
Draw
Water
Paper
Space
Line
Decorate
Picture
Face
Easel
Museum

COLOR—Flutter fingers.

RED—Brush chin down twice.

ORANGE—Squeeze!

YELLOW—Shake twice.

GREEN—Rock hand back and forth.

BLUE—Shake hand a little.

PURPLE—Shake back and forth.

BROWN—Move down.

BLACK—Draw finger across forehead.

WHITE—Draw fingers together away from chest.

PINK—Brush chin down once.

NOW—Lower both hands slightly.

LATER—Rotate right hand forward.

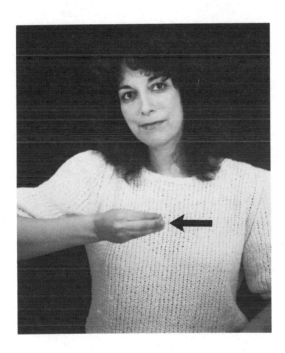

AND—Move hand from left to right.

BEGIN—Make half-turn with index finger of right hand.

STOP—Chop right hand into left hand.

OVER—Pass right hand over left hand.

UNDER—Pass right hand thumb
under left palm.

MIX—Stir right hand over left hand.

CUT—Scissors motion!

PRACTICE—Brush fist over index finger.

USE—Move in circular motion.

RUB—Rub back and forth.

HELP—Raise hands together.

CLEAN—Brush right fingers across left palm.

BOTTOM—Lower the left hand twice.

TOP—Form the letter "T."

SOFT—Close and lower hands.

HARD—Strike the fist with knuckles of other hand.

DARK—Open both hands, palms in, cross in front of face.

LIGHT—Both hands, fingers back-to-back and palms up. Bring hands up, spread wide.

SMOOTH (a)—Cup hands.

SMOOTH (b)—Move hands forward and close.

ROUGH—Push claw hand out.

BIG—Move palms away from each other.

SMALL—Draw palms close together.

MORE—Tap fingertips together twice.

LESS—Lower top hand slightly.

CLAY—Cup hands, move slightly.

CHALK—"Mime" writing.

CRAYON—Move "C" shape of hand
across fingers.

PAINT—Sweep fingers of right hand
up and down on left palm.

PASTE (a)—Place middle finger on palm, draw back.

PASTE (b)—Turn over middle finger, move in opposite direction.

MESS—Stir claw-shaped right hand over left hand.

DRAW—Draw little finger down opposite palm in wavy motion.

WATER—Tap lips twice.

PAPER—Slap base of right palm across base of left palm twice.

SPACE—Circle fists around to touch each other.

LINE—Draw little fingers apart in straight line.

DECORATE—Touch fingertips, turn hands, touch tips again.

PICTURE—Make "C" shape with hand against eye, move down to opposite open palm.

FACE—Circle face with index finger.

EASEL—Place fingertips of one hand on other palm, draw away and down on angle.

MUSEUM—"M" shaped fingers, both hands, tips touching. Draw apart and down, closing fingers over thumbs.

31

ART ACTIVITIES

"I Love Painting. It's Delicious."

**Abraham, age 8
visually handicapped**

TWO

Apples and Oranges—and Bananas, Too

MATERIALS

- Clay or plasticene
- Tongue depressors or wooden ceramic tools
- Bag of fruit
- Bowl or basket
- Paper to cover desk or work table (optional)

TEACHER PREPARATION

If you are using plasticene (oil-based clay), make sure that it is soft enough to use. Place the plasticene in a sunny spot for at least an hour before students use it. Students can break it down and rub it between their hands to get it into working order. Water-based clay should be moist, neither dry and hard nor too wet. If your clay is in a block, you can slice a good chunk out of it (like slicing a loaf of bread). Bring fruit to class or ask students to bring fruit.

DIRECTIONS

1. Carry the bag of fruit around the class. Ask students to reach in, feel fruit, and identify it *without looking.*

2. Give students clay and ask them to roll and pound it until it feels "right."

3. Set up a still life of the fruit in the bowl.

4. Ask students to create their own still life with the clay, making sure to include fruits that they have handled.

SUGGESTIONS FOR FURTHER DEVELOPMENT

A fun way to make students observe the different qualities of the fruit is to try mixing wax or plastic fruits in with the natural fruit. (See Figure 1.) Ask students to differentiate between the real and the artificial—and make them explain their choices. You can even mix in tennis balls, which usually gets a great reaction. Why wouldn't you confuse a tennis ball with an apple? When lessons are over, to the last group doing the still life goes the spoils—give the fruit to the artists. Nothing brings home the quality of an apple like biting into it!

Figure 1

adaptations

Apples and Oranges—and Bananas, Too

Mentally Retarded

Severely retarded students might be tactually defensive—rejecting the clay entirely. These students need to be "desensitized." Introduce clay in a ball or chunk and run students' hands over it. If students pull away or verbalize objections, wait awhile and try again. This might take some time. When students demonstrate readiness for materials, start with a simple shape that requires *one motion* to create, i.e., rolling a ball. Hand-over-hand method should be used.

Some retarded students might "pick" at clay, creating a pile of tiny clay pieces. Help them to reshape the "parts" into a more meaningful "whole."

Socially and Emotionally Disturbed

Pounding of clay has long been considered a healthy emotional release for students. Give students the freedom to pound, but have some idea as to "how much" is reasonable for the working classroom without total disruption. Ask students to think about a character for their fruit, like "Banana Man" (see Figure 2) or "Apple Face," etc. They can create a fruit "family," using the still life as a model. When all are completed, allow time for them to verbalize about their creations.

Learning Disabled

One area of difficulty for the learning disabled learner is dimensionality. If you ask the group to interpret the still life in front of them, you might see pressed and flattened clay shapes on the working tables. To teach the concept, have students walk

Figure 2

around the still life. Talk about what 3-D means. Make sure they roll their clay around. Spatial placement is another illusive concept. Have students observe still life, thinking about questions like "What fruit is in front of the other? What's closest? What's farthest away?"

Physically Handicapped

Clay and plasticene are excellent materials for physically handicapped learners. Allow plenty of time for the exploration of the materials. Squeezing the clay is valuable for strengthening grip. Rolling the clay can involve the body in large, gross movement. Let the movement carry into the creation of the fruit shapes—go from a big, round movement to the smaller movement needed to create a ball or apple. All movements, including the rolling of clay circularly or in back and forth motions, will add to the development of a kinesthetic sense.

Remember, a learned movement can be carried forward, i.e., rolling motions can become the stirring motions needed in other activities.

Sensory Losses

Hearing impaired—Give students a 3-by-5-inch card with a picture of a fruit on it. Pass a bag of fruit around. Have students reach in to see if they can find the fruit without looking. Hold up the fruit and see if they were right. Proceed with clay still life.

Visually handicapped—Talk about shapes and textures of fruit. What do their skins feel like? (Smooth, fuzzy, bumpy, etc.) Give them ample opportunity to examine and compare the fruits as they go along.

While clay is regarded as "the" material for the blind, don't be shocked if some of your blind students don't like it. They are probably displaying tactual defensiveness—and you will need to let them ease into the medium.

Try the scented clays on p. 243.

Gifted

The gifted learner is challenged by problem solving and enjoys abstract thinking. Hold up a fruit and ask about the many ways that a fruit can change its shape. Using a paring knife, alter some fruit shapes by peeling and removing slices. Place in a still life.

Bags Beautiful

MATERIALS

- Unbleached muslin
- Acrylic paints
- Brushes
- Felt
- Manila paper
- Sewing supplies—thread, needles, pins, safety pins

TEACHER PREPARATION

Precut lengths of fabric for bags and felt strips for the straps, for students lacking in scissors skills.

Stiff fabric brushes or oil painting brushes work best for painting on fabric.

DIRECTIONS

1. Use a practice paper to create the design. If you are making belts (see "Belts Beautiful") consider using the same design motif for all items.

2. Cut fabric to twice the size you want for your bag.

3. Paint. Let dry. Fold, wrong side out.

4. Turn top down about 1 to 2 inches to create a channel for bag strap. For a finished look, turn *edge* of fold under ¼ inch, then pin the channel down under. Stitch, leaving an opening to insert strap (see Figure 3).

5. Sew sides closed. Turn right side out.

6. Cut felt strap to fit into channel, making it about ¼ inch smaller than the channel size. (Ribbon or macramé cord may also be used for the strap.)

7. To push through, secure safety pin to one end of the strap and attach straight pin sideways to other end (to prevent the strap from "getting lost" in channel).

Figure 3

Ease through, straightening the fabric out as you go.

8. Even up ends and tie. (See Figure 3 for examples of finished bags.)

SUGGESTIONS FOR FURTHER DEVELOPMENT

The drawstring pouch presented here is but one bag shape that you can make. Other simple bag designs include clutch bags made with wooden dowels, and "envelope" purses. (See Figure 4.)

clutch bag

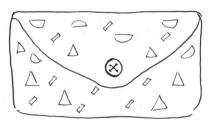

envelope purse

Figure 4

adaptations

Bags Beautiful

Mentally Retarded

For the severely retarded, you will need to familiarize students with the *purpose* of a bag. You might want to start by guiding students' hands into a sample bag, allowing them to explore the inside of it. Appropriate objects, such as combs, keys, brushes, can be put in and out of bags by students for a better understanding of the bag's utilitarian function.

If you do fabric bags with the severely retarded you will have to spend time by preparing the sewn bag in advance for the students to paint. If the construction of bags is too time-consuming or impractical, consider the cigar box. Cigar boxes can be easily made into carryalls. They can be painted by students. Yarn can be knotted into perforated holes in the box to create the straps and ties.

Mildly retarded will need some teacher assistance, such as hand-over-hand methodss, in sewing. You may want to use the Adaptive Aid for acquiring better sewing skills.

Socially and Emotionally Disturbed

Some male students may object to making "girls' stuff." Remind them that many designers are men, that they can give the bags as gifts, and that football stars have been known to carry bags (and who dares to ask *them* why?). However, an alternative to the purse is the bookbag, which is the same basic style as the purse, only many times larger. Football and other sports insignias can be used as design motifs.

Learning Disabled

Create a "sewing line" for the learning disabled students with a marker. They will sew along the edge in a basting stitch, following the marks as indicated. Eye-hand coordination is exercised with this activity.

Physically Handicapped

You might want to use burlap to make the sewing of the bags easier for the less physically able. Burlap is loosely woven and is therefore simple to penetrate with a large needle. Once the bag has been finished, it can be painted for decoration.

Sensory Losses

Hearing impaired—Show a finished bag. If there are other bags available to show to students, point them out.

To personalize students' work—as well as help with language development—ask students to design their names into bag's decoration, e.g., Danny's Bag, Barbara's Bag.

Visually handicapped—Masking tape can be used as a guide for the stitching of the bag. Needles with large eyes (embroidery or tapestry type) and yarn should be used for sewing the bag together. Glue a variety of fabrics for the decoration, such as fake fur, corduroy, lace, etc.

Gifted

Students might want to create their own "designer labels." Many students are aware of designer brands and will find this approach intriguing. They can look through fashion magazines and department store catalogues for ideas.

Belts Beautiful

MATERIALS

- Unbleached muslin
- Acrylic paints
- Brushes
- Felt
- Brown butcher wrap paper
- Crayons
- Belt backing (optional)
- Sewing supplies—thread, needles, pins

TEACHER PREPARATION

You may want to precut the paper belt patterns, the fabric belts, or both. Belt backing is available in fabric stores. It gives the belts a neat, finished look. Stiff brushes (oil painting or fabric brushes) will give better control of paint flow. For belt B, ribbon or macramé cord can be substituted for felt straps.

DIRECTIONS

1. Measure a section of brown paper to the size of the belt that you want to make. Cut out selected shape of either sash belt (A) or cummerbund (B) shown in Figure 5.

2. Create design on paper with crayons.

3. Fold fabric. For belt A, pin paper pattern and cut. For belt B, pin and cut only the *center part* of the pattern (snip away paper straps). Cut felt in strips for belt straps.

4. Sew the sides of the belt together, wrong side out, leaving ends open.

5. Turn right side out. Insert measured belt backing if desired.

6. On belt A, sew sash ends closed. On belt B, attach straps.

7. Paint on the designs. Let dry and show off!

SUGGESTIONS FOR FURTHER DEVELOPMENT

Fabric painting is a decorative, wearable art. Belts and bags go together, but you might want to add vests to the sets that your students make.

Vests can be made from simple, store-bought patterns, or you can measure your own out of brown paper. Often one commercial pattern with a simple design can be adjusted to fit many students.

You can add many exciting materials to your belts, bags, and vests, including: feathers, leather, shells, trim, braidings, and lace.

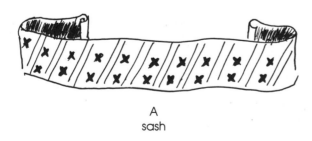

A
sash

B
cummerbund

Figure 5

adaptations

Belts Beautiful

Mentally Retarded

If you wish to eliminate the process of sewing, use felt. Felt doesn't require the finishing of edges. To begin the lesson for the severely retarded, precut the section of felt to accommodate belt. Tape fabric securely to table top. Students trace pattern by holding it in place on the fabric with your assistance. You will probably have to cut the felt. Students can decorate belts by pasting felt shapes on with white glue.

Socially and Emotionally Disturbed

This lesson, believe it or not, can be a nifty group project! You will have to choose belt A to carry it out with several students at once. Here's how: Cut a very long length of fabric. Students work side by side, designing what you might call "The World's Biggest Belt." The full piece is worked on—it will be folded and cut after the students paint it.

After each student contributes his/her painting to each section, belts are cut and sewn individually. This approach allows students to "mix" designs and ideas. Their success is the result of a cooperative effort.

Learning Disabled

After the design is established on the paper pattern, every effort should be exercised by the student to replicate it on fabric. The reproduction of their original pattern will require visual skills that learning disabled students need to develop.

Students should also be encouraged to trace paper belt patterns completely from starting to finishing points. This reinforces awareness of the whole shape.

Physically Handicapped

For students with limited dexterity, substitute felt for muslin. Keep designs simple—they will be painted onto the belts

Figure 6

in acrylic paint. If you want to keep some sewing in the lesson, the belt border can be decoratively stitched for easy stitches.

Belts may need to be stabilized on working surface with tape.

Sensory Losses

Hearing impaired—Show students a finished example of the belt. Who else has a belt on today? Indicate the real belts that students are wearing.

Show each part of this lesson, like the brown paper pattern, as you begin it.

Visually handicapped—For greater sensory enrichment, blind students may want to glue various bits of material to a felt sash. (See Figure 6.) You may want to precut shapes of fake fur, satin, lace, velvet, etc. Students can rip pieces of sandpaper and add. The belt becomes a "wearable collage."

Gifted

Encourage your gifted students to regard their belts as "shaped canvases" and compose a picture for them. For example, belt A might lend itself to a landscape of a broad, horizontal proportion. Belt B suggests a cameo shape that could feature just about any subject—animals, people, still lifes—whatever the imagination yields!

The Brown Bag

MATERIALS

- Textural objects collected by students at home or on a nature walk (shells, buttons, postcards, clips—any assortment)
- White glue
- Lightweight paperboards
- Brown lunch bags
- Scissors

TEACHER PREPARATION

Students will need to know what they should bring to class in their brown bag (which you may want to provide). Another way to get material collected is to take the group on a nature walk—and you can add in other textural details.

DIRECTIONS

1. Students gather textural materials in a brown bag. Roll tops of bags closed.

2. Each student takes turns shaking the filled bag for the rest of the group (or a partner) who will guess its contents.

3. Students then open bags and allow others to reach into bag with eyes closed and further identify objects within. (See Figure 7.)

Figure 8

Figure 9

4. After all the guessing takes place, distribute the paperboards.

5. Students empty the bags onto their desks and reveal their secrets. (See Figure 8.) Glue and scissors are distributed.

6. Students then compose their *collage* by arranging the contents in composition that makes sense to them. (See Figure 9.)

NOTE: This lesson has both mystery and the element of surprise—but the best part is that almost any arrangement of the elements is pleasing to the student and the viewer!

Figure 7

adaptations

The Brown Bag

Mentally Retarded

Have two bags available for the severely mentally retarded to reach into, with teacher assistance. One bag will contain rough objects, such as pine cones, stones, wood bark, etc. The other bag will contain smooth objects, such as leaves, grass, and flower petals. If you are consistent with nature objects, then the students will get a fuller understanding of the immediate environment. An alternative to the nature concept is *man-made objects*. Combs, sandpaper, keys, clips, string, etc., can be provided. If students display tactual defensiveness toward any materials, use desensitization techniques. Arrange chosen objects on paper and glue down. For the mildly retarded, follow core lesson. Be sure to engage students in discussion about the objects: Where are they from? What do we use them for? Talk about the concepts of hard, soft, rough, smooth, etc.

Socially and Emotionally Disturbed

Have students put their names on their bags in a decorative way to personalize them—or you can do it. Ask them to put at least one special or personally meaningful item into their bags, i.e., photo, letter, souvenir. The collage can be built around their personal experiences—a trip, a birthday, etc. Students should be encouraged to share the meaning of their collages with the rest of the group.

Learning Disabled

Students should be made aware of the size of the page and think about how they will compose their space. Questions such as "Does this area look empty? What can be put over here?" helps get the student to make spatial decisions.

Physically Handicapped

Students should have the experience of gathering materials from the environment for their collage themselves. Go on a "hunt," either on school grounds or in the neighborhood, for collage objects. Let students identify objects that they want—you can help with obtaining them for physically limited students. Encourage students to make independent decisions and later to explain their choices.

Follow directions of the core lesson for sharing bags. When collages are worked on by students, secure boards to desks with tape if needed.

Sensory Losses

Hearing impaired—Make sure that students understand the brown-bag lesson in its entirety. Demonstrate the steps if necessary. Show sample of finished product at the outset of lesson.

As a supplement to the core lesson, hearing impaired students would enjoy an old-fashioned "nature walk." Observing and exploring the environment creates greater general awareness and will add to the sensory experience of the brown-bag activity.

Visually handicapped—Textural aspects of the activity are important. Discuss similarities and differences between materials. Make sure students verbally identify the materials as they pull them out of the brown bag. Help make students aware of the perimeters of the page on which they

44

are mounting their collages by leading their hands around the edge of the paper. Also, make sure when pasting elements that the "glue side" goes down on the paper.

Gifted

The focus of this lesson could be the creation of a "theme" collage. Ask students to gather a collection of objects, in advance of the activity, that add up to a specific subject. Some suggestions are: "About Me" (photos, souvenirs, postcards, etc.), "Tools of the Trade" (objects that represent an occupation, such as nails, screws, sandpaper, ruler for carpenter), or "The Seasons" (pick one).

After students have gathered their "theme kit" in a brown bag, they will close them at the top and *switch* with fellow classmates—without revealing the theme or contents.

The fun and challenge will be to construct the unknown theme into a collage reflecting the intended meaning!

Chalk It Up!

MATERIALS

- 11-by-18-inch sheets of construction paper
- Colored chalks
- Cups or containers for water
- Paper towels

TEACHER PREPARATION

Fill water cups in advance and have them ready for distribution.

DIRECTIONS

1. Demonstrate technique. Dip the working end of the chalk into water. Remind students not to "float" the chalk in the water.
2. Dispense materials. Tell students to roll up their sleeves and to try to keep

Figure 11

their arms away from their papers. (See Figure 10.)

3. Draw. Encourage students to use chalk to build up areas of color. (See Figure 11.) HINT: Avoid rubbing chalk-covered papers against each other when you collect work (to keep work from smearing).

SUGGESTIONS FOR FURTHER DEVELOPMENT

Wet chalk has the advantage of eliminating the unhealthy dust that dry chalk produces. The results of wet chalk resemble paintings in their rich surfaces.

Black paper used with colored chalk creates dramatic contrast. Designs have a strong impact, but here are some subject ideas: the city at night, stormy seas, fireworks, snowscapes, the sunset, and winter wonderlands.

Figure 10

adaptations

Chalk It Up!

Mentally Retarded

Severely retarded students might enjoy using jumbo colored chalk—the type often used for the chalkboard. They should also like dipping the chalk in water, which represents a kind of water play activity in itself. Of course, hand-over-hand assistance may be required, and water containers should be stabilized. A bit of rolled masking tape under the watercolor cup will help to keep it in place.

Mildly retarded students could try a *fold-over print* of their names. Fold paper lengthwise and open. Have students write their names on top of the folded line, then fold paper over and *rub* the back. Open—the students have a design made of their names. Printed side will be faint, so tell them to go over it with chalk. When designs are held in various positions, they begin to resemble different entities—trees, monsters, insects, etc. Students might want to develop the suggested image. NOTE: If students can't write, they should print their names. If they can't do either, you can help them. Using students' names should not be overlooked for its impact on self-esteem. Personalizing the lesson involves the student, while recognizing him or her as a special and important person.

Responding to your name may appear simplistic, but it is an integral part of social and individual development.

Socially and Emotionally Disturbed

Seat students so that they are close to each other's papers. You should explain how important it is that they work as a team, because they will be "passing" a line from one to another. They will need the line to do their own drawing, yet the line will connect everybody together. Here's how it works: The student at the end of the table (or desk cluster) draws a curvy line over her paper and ends it on the edge of her paper next to her neighbor's paper. The end of her line becomes the starting point for her neighbor's line. The neighbor then draws a line and repeats process. Lines will need to end where neighbors' papers begin—which might mean at different edges, depending on location of the next student.

Once all students have "the line," they create a picture based on what the line suggests to them—anything from a mountain scene to a "dream"-scape. When all work is completed, match it and discuss individual interpretations. Display with corresponding elements intact, if possible.

Learning Disabled

Learning disabled students could also benefit from the folded paper print method (as suggested for the mildly retarded student). However, students may want to try a design motif. Fold blank paper in half (horizontally or vertically). On *one* side only of the paper, draw a geometrical design with a bold outline. Fold paper and rub the back with fist. Open—a perfectly symmetrical design will appear. The printed side will have a weak replication of the drawn side. Students will need to refer to the original drawing when they chalk in the printed half. This bilateral exercise encourages concentration and makes students aware of relationships of parts, as in the balance of two halves.

Physically Handicapped

Physically handicapped students may want to use a single chalkholder (see Adaptive Aids) in order to adjust their grasp on the chalk. Surface should be at a comfortable angle so that the students can build chalked surface on paper with ease.

If students have real problems dipping the chalk into the water, you can predip the chalk—it should hold water for hours.

Sensory Losses

Hearing impaired—Chalk murals are an exciting form for this activity to take. To add interest to the presentation of the chalk mural lesson, try this: peruse magazines in search of possible mural themes, i.e., towns, resorts, outdoor expanses, crowds of people. Remove from magazine, and for additional language development, *print* the name of the theme on the picture. Place all pictures in a hat (box or bag will substitute). Divide students into groups of three or four. One student, who represents the small group, will pick from the hat. This is the theme that group will carry out.

Be certain that students understand the "game" and its relationship to the activity. Demonstrate all phases of project to avoid confusion.

Visually handicapped—Visually handicapped students might want to use fluorescent chalk with black paper. The effect is visually powerful.

Fine sandpaper works nicely with chalk, and it is a surface that sight impaired and blind students will appreciate. It is tactually interesting and has "tooth" for receiving chalk application.

Blind students will need to build up the surface considerably to feel their work. Decisions on composition will be made with students' fingers, so remind them to wash their hands when finished! Students might also need to be shown where the water cups are—a little rolled tap on the bottom should keep them from toppling over.

Gifted

Gifted students may be interested to see reproductions of work done by the masters of pastel, such as Degas and Redon, and the effects that they achieved. Students should experiment with techniques of rubbing and blending chalk with gum eraser and chamois cloth (tissue or flannel will substitute). Work should represent a variety of suggested textures, from dappled to satin smooth.

Clay Pots: Pinch and Coil

MATERIALS

- Wet clay
- Containers for water
- Jar lids
- Tongue depressors
- Rolling pin

  Optional:
  Clay tools
  Forks
  Revolving clay stands (lazy susan can work)
  Toothbrushes
  Wire—length of approximately 12 to 16 inches
  Small natural sponges
  Old shirts (smocks)
  Manicure sticks
  Old pens

TEACHER PREPARATION

Wet, red clay that comes ready to use in plastic bags is recommended. Clay should be moist and malleable.

Slice clay into individual portions using a wire or an old wooden ruler. You may want water cups to be filled in advance. Have water, sponges, paper towels, etc. available for cleanup. Plastic tablecloths can be used to cover surfaces, but wooden tables and wooden boards work even better.

If students want to continue working on the same clay pieces in the near future (say, next week's art period), they can store them. Wrap moist paper towels around clay and tie plastic over it so that no air leaks in.

Extra clay can be kept in airtight, plastic or rubber containers, or sealed plastic bags. For larger quantities, rubber garbage pails with tight fitting lids are perfect. You can "cyle" dried-out clay by breaking it up, placing in rubber can, and adding water. Put the lid on it (check for consistency from time to time, adding water if necessary). Clay should be ready for future use.

DIRECTIONS

Pinch Pots

1. Push, pound, and manipulate clay to get used to it and to make it workable.

2. Roll clay into a ball. (See Figure 12.) A snowball size is suggested.

3. Press the thumb of your working hand into the center of the ball of clay. (See Figure 13.)

4. Ease into bowl shape by pressing outside edge between thumb and fingers of one hand, and turning pot with the other hand.

Figure 12

Figure 13

Figure 14

Figure 15

5. Make walls of the pot as even in thickness as you can by smoothing and pressing. If you have a revolving stand and clay tools, you can refine the shape.

6. Smooth outside wall with wet fingers (and little sponges if you have them). Remember, not too much water—it weakens the pot! (See Figures 14 and 15.)

7. Let pots dry thoroughly.

8. You may wish to create a "foot" for your pot, which is a lip around the base that helps pots to stand. (See Figure 16.)

Simply turn pot over and attach a coil (see next part of directions for coil method) to the bottom.

Figure 16

Coil Pots

1. Divide your wedge of clay into strips with side of the tongue depressor (or other proper tool), leaving a section of clay for the base of the pot.

2. Roll out strips until they become coils, feeling for evenness. (See Figure 17.)

Figure 17

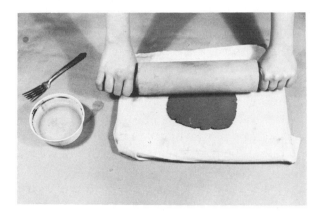

Figure 18

Figure 19

Figure 20

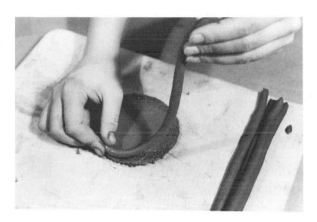

Figure 21

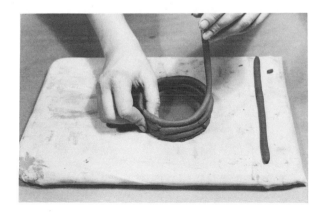

Figure 22

Figure 23

51

3. Use a rolling pin to create a slab. (See Figure 18.) Use jar lid either to stamp out or to trace the pot's bottom. (See Figure 19.)

4. With either a toothbrush, fork, or tongue depressor, create grooves (or rough surface) around inside perimeter of base and around the first coil that you will place on bottom. (See Figure 20.) This is called "scoring." Repeat this process on coils until you have built your pot to desired height. (See Figure 21.) Press coils together gently as you build the pot. (See Figure 22.) NOTE: A mixture of clay and water can be stored in a plastic container until it becomes swampy in consistency. This mixture is called "slip" and can be applied between coils as they are joined. Slip acts as a binder in clay construction and helps strengthen clay joints. (See Figure 23.)

SUGGESTIONS FOR FURTHER DEVELOPMENT

Pinch, coil, and slab are the basic methods for making hand-built pottery. Varieties and combinations of these techniques account for limitless possibilities in clay. Here's one suggestion for changing the modest pinch pot into a completely different object. By turning it upside down, you will have a *clay bell!* While clay is wet, pierce a hole through the center. Using a leather shoestring or cord, attach a clapper. Clappers can be made from "jingle" bells or cut from thin metal. Knot the cord where it will meet the hole in the bell's dome, leaving enough string below for the clapper and enough above for hanging the bell. Bells will be fragile, but can be hung where gentle breezes blow.

You may also want to experiment with *wind chimes,* which can be made from coils drawn through circular shape with cord.

A few final words about success with clay: Squishy, juicy clay is a joy. But when clay is too wet, it is frustrating because it sticks to hands and to work surfaces. Clay will firm as you work with it, but if that doesn't happen soon enough to your satisfaction, you may need to expose it to the air until it hardens up a little.

HINT: Plant sprayers that mist the air are ideal for anytime you want to wet down clay.

Another problem occurs when clay becomes too dry. As you work with clay, some small surface cracks may appear. That's OK—but your clay may be getting "thirsty." Remember, *too much water will weaken the clay.* Water must be *flicked* onto clay with your fingers to keep it moist (or use the plant sprayer).

adaptations

Clay Pots

Mentally Retarded

Severely retarded students can benefit greatly from clay manipulation. It is both a rich sensory experience and an exercise in kinesthetics. However, students might respond to clay adversely at first, displaying tactual defensiveness (see "Apples and Oranges," under Mentally Retarded, for suggestions). Once this has been worked through, assist students in a hand-over-hand manner with making a ball for the pinch pot and squeezing out the shape.

Students will also need physical and verbal prompting in rolling out clay "snakes," which require the motion of an open hand to create. You will need to provide the round clay base and guide the students in joining the coils to make the walls of the pot. A few coils should do it (don't worry too much about "scoring"). Although these pots will probably be produced during separate sessions, you can make one "snake" for your pinch pot and turn it into a *cup*. Attach the coil as a cup handle to the side of the pot and inscribe the student's name prominently on the side. Cups should not be used for liquids, of course, but should be displayed where students can see them.

Mildly retarded students should delight in working with clay. Remember, the pinch and coil techniques are two different methods and should be presented separately. The pinch pot should be a snap for students. Pots can easily be used later as containers for sorting. You might even want students to label pots by inscribing names of items that pots can hold (i.e., beads, clips, pins, etc., into the wet clay pot). You may need to help with the spelling and printing. Also, be prepared to assist with construction of coil pots until students get the basic idea.

Socially and Emotionally Disturbed

Pinch pots are simple to make, offering immediate success to the students. Since the technical part of it is quite easy to manage for most students, it is an ideal lesson to build upon. Ask your students to give their pots another "purpose." How can they change them or add to them that will make the pots into other objects? Have students *pair up* to solve the problem to work on them. Two possible answers: candlestick holders and planters. Planters can be designed to have other smaller pinch pot forms attached to them, or they can have several pinch pots joined together. Coil pots can be treated in a similar way. Coil *baskets*, which can hold dry arrangements, are also a suggestion for expanding on the coil pot.

Students should be encouraged to plan their ideas with their partners and to carry them out to the fullest extent. Seeing their own cooperative efforts turn a lump of clay into a usable finished product teaches students interactive social skills and how to follow through creatively on their projects.

Learning Disabled

Pinch and coil pots are great for demonstrating how things are made, because they "happen" right before your eyes. The dimensional nature of clay work also makes objects more concrete and imparts knowledge on how they arrived at that state. Understanding the process is important for learning disabled students. If you want to add further to the experience, ask students to inscribe patterns on the surface of their pots. Patterns should be continuous, going from end to end. Use a clay tool, manicure stick, or old pen to create designs. This decorative element adds an exercise in closure and in eye-hand coordination.

Physically Handicapped

Pinching a pot involves some pincer grasp. If a student is limited in this area, you may want to get the pot "started" for him or her with your thumb—or experiment with some of your clay tools in creating the center hole. Rotating trays will generally be helpful. Also, check that the level of the work surface allows the student proper leverage. Remember, clay manipulation is a great exercise for the hands and fingers. NOTE: If you take your ceramics seriously, and your art classroom is set up for it, you might consider a pottery wheel. Inquire about wheels from art equipment suppliers that are adapted to be used with the wheelchair bound.

Sensory Losses

Hearing impaired—The strong quality of clay usually make it a hit among students with sensory losses. Clay is not a demanding medium. You can direct it easily, and new ideas occur to you magically as you work. Directions for its use are wonderfully uncomplicated.

After a simple demonstration, let your hearing impaired students develop their own individual ideas for clay works. Put materials forward that will help them—clay tools, objects that create textures (i.e., old kitchen tools, nuts and bolts, twine, etc.). Some freedom of choice is not only a pleasure in itself but helps with decision-making skills. Deaf students are so often given directions from others because of their lack of communicative understanding. It is important that students have opportunities to develop their own ideas in an unrestricted manner. Clay is a perfect arena for this kind of expression.

Visually handicapped—Students with less severe sight loss should be able to follow the core as directed. However, as mentioned previously (see "Mentally Re-tarded" section, on page 36) blind students are sometimes tactilely defensive toward clay. Once you have resolved that through recommended techniques, your blind students should indeed enjoy the medium. Pinch pots should be no problem once demonstrated with physical and verbal cueing. Coil pots need a little more control to get coils "even"—sometimes they get so skinny at the middle and the ends that they break apart. Students should practice making snakes until they get them into shape; you will assist with coil pot's base. Be sure students know how to "score" coils. Show them with your hand over their working hand where the container of water is. You might want to secure it with rolled tape on the bottom. Leave plenty of time for cleanup.

Gifted

Gifted students should be challenged by being asked to build multileveled pots after basic methods have been presented to them. Pinch pots can be given slab bases and can be built in pinch pot multiples (i.e., shapes coming out of the sides, spouts, bottle necks, etc.). Students may also want to create lids for their pots.

In building coils, students should incorporate open space as well as curled and curvilinear coils. This becomes a design problem—the trick is using the right number of clay coil bands so that the pot walls do not collapse as you are balancing decorative elements.

Gifted students may also want to study the period of art history in Greece that produced black figureware pots. Students could actually draw similar figures on the dry pinch pot (try out your black markers and ink), taking the continuous round surface of the pot into their design consideration. Scenes like people chasing animals, balls being thrown, and people dancing are all suitable subjects for the pot. If geometric designs are preferred, American Indian and Pueblo pottery should be researched.

Cowboy's Christmas Stocking

MATERIALS

- Paper
- String
- Staples
- Markers
- Crayons

TEACHER PREPARATION

Precut boots (front and back if necessary) for students lacking scissors skills. You may want to cut string lengths for hanging boots in advance of lesson.

DIRECTIONS

1. Talk about the shape and curvy stitching of cowboy boots. (Some students may be wearing reasonable facsimiles, which work well for observation and discussion.)

2. Give students paper that is large enough to fold and will provide a good sized stocking. Otherwise, give two sheets of paper (the same size) to each student.

3. Offer drawing tools. Some students may want to incorporate Christmas motifs into their designs. (See Figures 24–28.)

4. Cut boots and staple together front to back. Insert string at the top for hanging.

Figure 24

Figure 25

Figure 26

Figure 27

Figure 28

SUGGESTIONS FOR FURTHER DEVELOPMENT

A cowboy's or cowgirl's Christmas stocking is just one other-than-ordinary Christmas stocking that you can make. Consider these: ballet slipper/tights; tap-shoe/mesh stockings; saddle shoes/bobby socks and, of course, jogging shoes—to name a few. You can probably come up with a dozen more interpretations that will liven up the holiday mantel. NOTE: Although "Cowboy's Christmas Stocking" is presented here in paper, the lesson clearly lends itself to *felt* stockings. This is, of course, a sewing project, but the design aspects are almost interchangeable between the paper and felt stockings.

adaptations

Cowboy's Christmas Stocking

Mentally Retarded

Severely retarded students will do well to stick with a traditional Christmas stocking shape. To reinforce the stocking contour and create a boundary, cut yarn to go around the edge. Help students to glue entire outside shape of stocking. When yarn is dry, student will decorate within the shape with crayon and make curvy patterns. You will assist students in carrying out the motion required to make the design. Put students' names on stockings, add fluffy cotton on top, and display where students can see them.

Mildly retarded students should be able to handle the precut cowboy boots and enjoy designing them. You can offer a starting point of reference by illustrating the first curvy line. Students can repeat the linear pattern and develop into a design.

Socially and Emotionally Disturbed

"If you could design a cowboy boot that would be made into a *real* boot, what would you put into it? Zippers, bold patterns, buttons, different textures and fabrics?" Try this as an opener. When students have succeeded with their boot designs, have them use a "Western" design element to incorporate their names into their boots. Some design suggestions are rope, stars, studs, stitches.

A related class project is a mock fireplace that can be made by cutting a cardboard carton and painting "bricks" on it (you can also paint bricks on mural paper and mount to resemble a fireplace front). Students' stockings can be hung on the fireplace, with their names prominently displayed.

Learning Disabled

Remind students that they are designing two sides of the boot—*front* and *back*. Make sure that when students are working, they are decorating the *matching* sides. Students may be capable of tracing a precut boot on paper and cutting it out, but they still need to coordinate the pieces.

To reinforce closure of the shape while adding an appealing touch, have students draw a stitch (saddle or straight) all along the edge, starting at one end and bringing it around to the starting point.

Physically Handicapped

It may be that your physically handicapped students are capable only of decorating the boot, and do not have the motor control to cut it out. Encourage students to do whatever they can manage. If they are able to outline the boot pattern, assist with the cutting. If they cannot decorate the boot with markers or crayons, offer sponges (or corks) to apply patterns in paint. These materials do not require a fine grasp.

Sensory Losses

Hearing impaired—Show students a precut, completed cowboy stocking, a *real* cowboy boot, or both. It would be useful to have some "Western" reference material on hand (i.e., cowboy styles). Make sure that students understand activity. Follow core lesson.

Visually handicapped—Did you ever think about the *sound* of cowboy boots? If you or a student could introduce the lesson with a series of resounding "clacks" of boot heels walking across the floor, blind students could better understand the "character" of the boot. This is a way to give the lesson more meaning. Of course, allowing students to *tactually explore* boots will provide sensory enrichment and "visual" information. Follow up introduction with precut cowboy boots, crayons, and screenboards. Remember, work with *one* side of the stocking at a time on the screenboard. If you want to give the stocking textural dimension, glue yarn in curvy lines.

Gifted

Cowboy boots are the arena for brilliant, contrasting colors and swirling patterns. Stars, snakes, cacti—whatever suitable motifs students choose—have a delightful "handmade boot" quality on these stockings. Students can produce studded effects with paper fasteners.

Gifted students might try "wraparound" designs, to include design ideas that lend themselves to a continuous visual flow. Some suggestions are chase scenes, towering staircases—and boa constrictors.

The Dancing Paintbrush

MATERIALS

- Watercolors
- Brushes
- White paper
- Containers
- Paper towels

TEACHER PREPARATION

You will need a record player and records with different rhythms: fast, slow, soft, strong, etc. Some suggestions: flute music (Jean Pierre Rampal); blues—guitar, vocal; Irish jigs; country and western; rock; classical.

Before you begin painting, make sure that students know how to use watercolors properly (see p. 212).

DIRECTIONS

1. You can either give students several 9 by 12-inch papers to start a new paper with each change of tune, or give one large paper for students to paint all their responses on one page.

2. Tell students to let their paintbrushes "dance" in time to the records. (See Figure 29.)

Figure 29

3. Switch records as required.

4. When work is completed, display. (See Figures 30 and 31.) Have students comment on each other's work, identifying paintings with the music they heard.

Figure 30

Figure 31

SUGGESTIONS FOR FURTHER DEVELOPMENT

Music, as we all know, has the power to set a "mood." Music can either stimulate or soothe—in both direct and indirect ways. "The Dancing Paintbrush" is a direct use for music, as is a lesson in which students illustrate a song that has been sung to them. Indirect influences include the playing of music while students are working—often a very effective tool for controlling behavior.

Records that relate to a given theme, such as Christmas carols, Halloween music, and cowboy ballads (for western themes), can really bring a lesson to life!

adaptations

The Dancing Paintbrush

Mentally Retarded

Severely mentally retarded students respond to music. Start them moving—get behind them and move them around in time to the music, if possible. After students are "loosened up," in a hand-over-hand manner, transfer the body movement into the arm and let it come out through the brush on paper.

Mildly retarded students can "practice" with arm movements in the air before they register their marks on paper.

Use verbal cueing with all retarded students when doing warm-up activities and lessons, such as "slow, slower, fast, faster, etc." This helps with their understanding of concepts.

Socially and Emotionally Disturbed

Be cautious about your musical selections for your students. Music can easily set students "off," particularly very intense, fast numbers. Watch for reactions—if students don't respond in a suitable manner, change the record.

You may want students to use *pictorial imagery*, drawn from the imagination while listening to music. Movie theme music works well for this (e.g., *Fantasia*), also instrumental pieces, such as "Rhapsody in Blue," "Night on Bald Mountain." (Avoid vocal records for this approach.) Students can paint to music with whatever visual responses they are experiencing.

Learning Disabled

What is the shape of a sound? Before you let paintbrushes loose, play some music (preferably instrumental) that suggests a variety of musical sounds. Be "conductors" and let the arms describe the sounds, i.e., up, down, and around; overall zigzag; ladder steps from bottom to top (low to high), etc.

There are no "correct" answers; this activity helps students to translate what they hear into visual terms. It is an exercise of listening and corresponding movement.

Physically Handicapped

This is a great activity for the physically handicapped because it draws on, and exercises, body movement. Students should be encouraged to respond to the music in any way that they are physically able. Use Adaptive Aids to help with painting.

Sensory Losses

Hearing impaired—Deaf students are quite capable of enjoying music—and of dancing. Hearing losses may vary from student to student, but an all-around good bet is to select music that utilizes percussion instruments (drums, piano). Students can pick up the vibrations. If your room has a hardwood floor, it will help to carry the sound. Make sure that students understand the directions.

Visually handicapped—Music has a strong place in the education of visually handicapped and blind students. It is perceived through an unimpaired sense—hearing—and is therefore an important channel for artistic communication. Many lessons can be accompanied by music without considering this to be an overuse of method. In fact, music can be played almost constantly during art to the delight of the blind student who may be grappling with visual concepts. Naturally "The Dancing Paintbrush" should be a hit, but consider also "dancing crayons" (on screenboard) or any other medium that lends itself to making art with musical accompaniment.

Gifted

Here's a group activity for gifted students: ask students for terms that describe music and list them on the board. Some terms are low, high, soft, loud, etc. If students know musical terminology (like forte, staccato, scherzo, etc.) use them, but make sure that students explain them to those who don't know the terms. Students get into a circle. Each student is assigned a musical term.

Taking turns, students "sing" their word according to the word's meaning. For example, "loud" would be sung loudly in a strong voice, "soft" in a quiet voice, etc. After all students have participated, they go back to their seats and do a painting based on the musical word using patterns and colors that they feel best correspond.

When all work is complete, put paintings out for all to see. Ask the class to try to "sing" all the work before them as you point to one painting, then another, and so on. The class is a chorus and uses one common word, say, "paint." Now students *hear* what their art sounds like and see how well they interpret the music into paint.

Go from this activity into The Dancing Paintbrush as presented earlier.

Designs in Wood

MATERIALS

- Wood scraps of various sizes and textures
- White glue
- Sandpaper
- Braided picture wire (optional)
- Picture mounts (optional)

TEACHER PREPARATION

Scraps can be collected from woodshops and lumberyards, or hobbyists. You will need some squares, at least 4-inch or more, on which to mount the smaller pieces. If your scraps are very rough, sand them first. Students can do light sanding.

DIRECTIONS

1. Offer wood to students. Ask them to observe the various textures, colors, and wood tones.
2. Ask students to select the wood they would like for their assemblages.
3. Experiment; move the parts around until a pleasing arrangement is decided upon. (See Figure 32.)
4. Glue; let dry.
5. If you wish your assemblage to be a wall piece, affix the picture mount.

Figure 32

SUGGESTIONS FOR FURTHER DEVELOPMENT

"Designs in Wood" is a construction that can be built up, or can be created as a lower relief (bas relief) sculpture. If the relief piece is designed for wall mounting (see Figure 33), the project can be built to expand laterally, rather than vertically.

Figure 33

adaptations

Designs in Wood

Mentally Retarded

Guide severely retarded student's hand in sanding wood. With student's free hand, "test" smoothness of surface. Repeat "wood is smooth." Place wood shapes into a container within student's reach. Direct student to pick up wood from container and to glue wood to base. For those capable of stacking shapes, practice placing one shape on top of another before gluing.

Lightly sanding wood is a good workshop activity for the mildly retarded student. It is a "job" that represents accomplishment. If wood is splinter-free, have students tactually examine the pieces to relative sizes (big, smaller, smallest). Create assemblage, glue, and display.

Socially and Emotionally Disturbed

Show students a finished sample of the lesson. Ask what it reminds them of: a city, a parking lot, a space station on the moon? Encourage students to think about an imaginary (or real) place when they design their assemblages. This gives students a chance to create their own little worlds in wood.

Learning Disabled

"Designs in Wood" is a "lesson without walls" students can fully use imagination. To add a challenge, you could include a concept in the activity. Ask students to place some pieces *vertically* and some *horizontally*. Explain these terms clearly, giving examples of both. This approach makes good design sense because it will create a more harmonious balance of parts.

Physically Handicapped

This is a good activity for the physically handicapped student because it is not exacting in nature. Students can also benefit from practicing the back and forth motion that sanding wood requires. Attach a sanding block to table top, or tape sandpaper to desk. Have container of wood pieces within reach; students will sand wood until smooth. They will then build assemblages as they like.

Because students are able to complete most phases of the project independently, the results should be very gratifying.

Sensory Losses

Hearing impaired—Make sure that students understand the process before they begin their work. When all individual work has been accomplished, gather all pieces together. Treat assemblages like tiles and create a *group wall*. If parts are protruding, place arrangement out of way of traffic. Students will help decide how to arrange the tiles, which encourages positive interaction.

Visually handicapped—Provide a completed sample lesson that students can touch and discuss. Concentrate on shape, size, and textural differences and similarities. Make sure that students use one hand to position the base, while working hand builds assemblage.

Gifted

Gifted students can create an architectural fantasy of many levels and juxtapositions. Ask students to *connect* the parts to give the overall design a continuity and to give students a building problem to solve. You might discuss the principles of the cantilevered structure and ask students to include this concept in their wood design. (NOTE: *Cantilevered* is a rigid part of a structure that projects far beyond the vertical support on which it is built. It appears almost to defy gravity.) They may also want to include bridges, walkways, terraces, etc.

Face It!

MATERIALS

- White paper
- Construction paper
- Scissors
- Paper fasteners
- Raffia (or yarn)
- Oil pastels, markers
- Paper hole puncher

TEACHER PREPARATION

Gathering examples of African masks, either through illustrations or replicas, is strongly recommended. African masks use straightforward patterns and details, with powerful symmetry. Providing material on masks of other cultures as well would enhance the activity.

You may want to precut a basic mask shape and slit the appropriate notches for 3-D paper features with mat knife or scissors.

DIRECTIONS

1. Introduce lesson with discussion on masks: What makes masks different from real faces? Masks usually distort or exaggerate features. (See Figure 34.)

2. Present your reference material to class. Demonstrate cutting methods. (See Figures 35A and B.)

3. Cut masks. Create desired features. Draw decorative patterns. (See Figures 36, 37, and 38.)

4. Add raffia and paper fasteners. Use paper punch to make "accents" around shapes and features. Also use holes to pull strands of raffia through and knot.

5. Masks may be displayed or worn. If you want students to wear them, openings for eyes and nose should be aligned with students' faces. Attach string to sides and tie in the back.

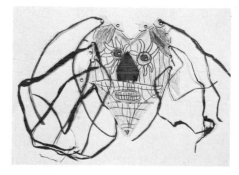

Figure 34

Figure 35A

Figure 35B

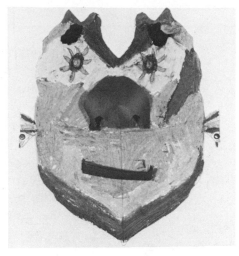

Figure 36

Figure 37

Figure 38

SUGGESTIONS FOR FURTHER DEVELOPMENT

Do masks hide or reveal? The study of masks captivates the imagination. Their uses are manifold. In primitive societies they are often regarded as having magical powers to heal the sick and to ward off evil spirits. In Western culture, masks date back to the beginning of history. They were an intrinsic element of classical Greek theater, where they were used to represent our strongest human emotions. Yet masks are a form of art in their own right—decorative and powerful, with their own special kind of appeal.

Masks can be made from just about any material you can name. Clay, papier-mâ-

ché, cloth, plaster, metal, and wood are but some of the choices. This lesson deals with the paper fold masks, but you may want to go into some other dimensional areas. While any of the materials listed would make exciting masks, papier mâché is a good place to start. By using the recipe on page 246, you can easily build a mask face over a simple cardboard mask shape. Wrap your newspaper strips around the shape. Build features by manipulating wet newspaper (squeezing, shaping) and covering it with flat, wet strips. When dry, paint—you might want to use gesso or white acrylic paint to prime the surface first. After paint is dry, seal with acrylic mat or gloss varnish. Add wall mount inside and the mask is ready for hanging.

adaptations

Face It!

Mentally Retarded

Precut mask shapes for your severely retarded students, cutting out shapes in masks to represent the features. Prepare soap paint (recipe, page 245). Students will apply paint directly to the masks with their hands, so you will need to assist. Use verbal and physical prompting as you work, i.e., "We're painting the eyes now, we're painting the nose, etc." You can add simple expression to the mouth with an upward or downward movement of the paint. Again, explain that "The face is smiling" or "The face is sad." You can add sensory materials (raffia, feathers, fabric) by squeezing white glue onto the mask and pressing the materials on. Students will need to wash hands of the soap paint before adding the textural materials.

Before you begin the mask lesson with your mildly retarded students, say "Show me an angry face!" If students do not respond, tell them to think about something that makes them angry. Do the same for other emotions (happy, sad, surprised). Then ask students what happens to their faces as they change their feelings: Happy, mouths turn up to smile; angry, eyebrows and mouths go down; surprised, eyes and mouth open wide; and so on. After all the play acting, ask students to choose one of the faces that they "made" for their paper masks. Give students materials. If they have problems with notched parts, help them or let them cut and paste directly. Add in any materials that you think will enhance the mask's expression.

Socially and Emotionally Disturbed

There are fairy tale characters—as well as characters in literature—that represent the Villainous, the Pure, the Courageous, and so on. Some examples are the Wicked Witch, the Good Fairy, the Brave Prince. These characters fascinate younger students. Older students may be more interested in heroes (current movies and television series are always replete with them). Masks based on these themes provide an acceptable format for the personification of strong emotions. Socially and emotionally disturbed students are often struggling to control their emotions. Masks vent them safely.

If you want to take this a little farther, you might ask students to write a script for the cast of characters that the group has created. Add string to masks and act out the parts.

Learning Disabled

The mask, because of its symmetry, is the perfect vehicle to help learning disabled students with replication skills. Try this: Precut simple mask shape, then cut in half. Do this for all the students, counting one-half only for each student. Give students the single mask half to design with markers. Then, give out uncut paper. Students glue mask half on right or left side of the paper. Challenge: Reproduce the missing half, using the acquired side as a model. After the design has been symmetrically replicated, cut out the entire mask. Add notched parts and students' details.

Physically Handicapped

Students with restricted dexterity might have some real difficulty with slots and notches. You may want students to use tactual materials—fabric scraps can be used for features. Crushed tissue can be glued on mask to represent crowns, beards, etc. Crushing tissue into balls is a good hand movement exercise.

A subject for masks that physically handicapped can easily create is animal faces. Fake fur scraps can be precut, then glued by students. Wire (any type that you could use for wire sculpture) or pipe cleaners make animal whiskers that are easy to manipulate and add to masks.

Physically handicapped students might also want to paint masks of animal skin patterns. The leopard's spots might be painted by making a simple movement with the brush. Stripes (zebra and tiger kind) are also easy to produce with adaptive tools.

Sensory Losses

Hearing impaired—While the core lesson is most suitable for the hearing impaired once it is clearly demonstrated, you can also try *demi-masks* (which leave the mouth exposed). By using a flamboyant approach, elaborate butterflies, insects with antennas, or oriental fan shapes can make impressive demi-masks. The demi-masks can be secured with string or elastic. Students can wear the masks and communicate with each other since lips are revealed and can be read. This is an ideal opportunity to develop a classroom skit incorporating the masks.

Visually handicapped—Students will give their masks a dazzling effect if they create parts of foil, and use fluorescent paints (or crayons) and glitter. All these materials will make the masks more visually stimulating.

Blind students will appreciate precut mask shapes. Students will need some assistance with location of facial features on mask and with notching of parts. Students might enjoy paper curling—using one side of scissors to curl fringed paper. This makes good "hair" and clothing details. Students may need some teacher assistance learning this technique.

Gifted

Gifted students might want to reach into history and mythology for inspiration. Minotaurs and dragons, gargoyles and Greek gods/goddesses are some of the possibilities. Masks of other cultures—Japan, India, North America—are also great subjects.

Not too far from masks is an activity for your students that we'll call "zany glasses." Not unlike demi-masks, zany glasses impart a "look" without covering the whole face. Zany glasses, made of oaktag, can be constructed in a variety of shapes and sizes.

There are *so* many ways to do them. For example, students can design glasses for famous people: Pablo Picasso's glasses could be decorated in paint dabs and drips, Luciano Pavarotti's glasses should have musical notes all over them, Mohammed Ali's glasses deserve band-aids. Students can also make "working" glasses—goggles and scuba masks, which will look terrific in "metal" frames (use metallic acrylic paint) or in "camouflage" patterns.

A few more to tickle the imagination: gardener glasses, decorated in paper ferns and leaves; ballerina glasses, adorned with satin ribbons (and tutu net?); and magician glasses (add the rabbit ears and magic wand.)

Colored acetate can be fixed with glue inside paper glasses frames to complete the whole act. Take it away!

Faces and Traces

MATERIALS

- Brown butcher paper
- Scissors
- Markers
- Poster paints
- Brushes—regular to ½-inch flat
- White glue
- Optional—costume jewelry (junk jewelry), fabric scraps, doilies

TEACHER PREPARATION

This activity is a good excuse to begin a "costume trunk" to keep in the art room. Suggestions for some costumes you can gather are: kimonos, robes, uniforms, long dresses, men's suits, and Halloween "leftovers." Details such as hats, gloves, scarves, and fans are terrific.

You may want to precut lengths of brown paper.

Figure 39

DIRECTIONS

1. Students select a costume and slip it over their street clothes. Decide on what the "character" of the clothes suggests and take an appropriate pose, such as a cowboy holding a lasso. (See Figure 39.)

2. Students lie down on length of brown paper, retaining a suitable pose for the costume. (See Figure 40.) If costume is fragile, remove it before beginning the tracing, and pose in street clothes.

Figure 40

3. Paint, deciding on what areas need the most coverage. Think about facial expression. (See Figure 41.)

4. Apply fabric, jewelry, and costume details.

5. Display. (See Figures 42, 43, and 44.)

SUGGESTIONS FOR FURTHER DEVELOPMENT

"Faces and Traces" is a kind of full-scale self-portrait in costume. Students definitely get involved. The activity has a theatrical quality and can enter many magic worlds of make-believe. But the tracing format can be used to teach the more "serious" subjects, such as anatomy, as well as increasing awareness of body proportions. "Faces and Traces" can even be turned into seasonal themes. Body contours can yield Santas, scarecrows, and the queen of hearts for Valentine's Day!

Figure 41

Figure 42

Figure 43

Figure 44

adaptations

Faces and Traces

Mentally Retarded

Severely retarded students would need to be somewhat mobile and have physical flexibility in order to partake in the activity outlined in the core. You may or may not want to use costumes, depending on your students' capacity for movement. If students can position themselves fairly straight on paper, either lying down or standing against the wall, trace them. Cut out whole figure. Assist students with facial features (in crayon or paint) using physical and verbal prompting. Print students' names in big bold letters across the front of their tracing. The whole figure might be too much to cover, so you might want students to paint hands and feet (and face). Help students to glue some fabric scraps around body. Display where students can see and touch their work. You can use the completed pieces to teach body parts and awareness of self.

Mildly retarded students should be able to do the core lesson, but make sure that they understand what comes after the beginning (costume workshop). Clearly outlining the steps will help them to understand the logical sequence of the activity. It would be great if students could trace each other. They could practice before the lesson by outlining progressively larger shapes.

Socially and Emotionally Disturbed

The "acting out" part of this lesson is excellent for withdrawn students, as well as providing assertive students with an acceptable forum for their energies. Caution: If the group enters the lesson "charged up," it might be better to re-schedule for next time. Otherwise, proceed with care.

Learning Disabled

"Faces and Traces" is particularly useful for instruction of body parts and parts-to-whole relationships. Questions such as "What is your arm attached to? How far down do your fingers reach when you stand straight?" will help with this concept. Body tracing will increase awareness of closure—completing a whole outline, going all around the shape, and coming back to the beginning.

Physically Handicapped

Costumes may be difficult to get in and out of, so you might not want students to dress in "full regalia." Costume details—hats, scarves, and so on—can carry the spirit of this activity very well also. If a student has a severe impairment, you may want to trace the outline according to the pupil's verbal direction. Taping the paper to the wall may be helpful in tracing the wheelchair bound student.

Sensory Losses

Hearing impaired—Students will enjoy carrying out the core activity, but there is another approach to the body tracing lesson that you might want to try: the Dance "Freeze." Tape two full-sized papers side by side onto an accessible wall. You will need a record player (or tape) and a record of percussion music (see "Dancing Paintbrush"). Students will pair up as partners and dance in front of the paper. When you stop the music, students freeze against paper. You or another student outlines the couple. Partners paint their "pas de deux" together (black paint makes dynamic silhouettes). Repeat the activity until every student has danced and been traced. When all work has been completed, hang works collectively on your walls or halls—you'll have a display starring a lively dance troupe!

NOTE: If you do not want to use music, students can still pair up and move freely (instead of to a beat). Indicate to students when to freeze motion, then trace. Be sure all directions and activities are clearly demonstrated.

Visually impaired—If you are ambitious you can trace the body outline by squeezing a line of white glue. Cotton yarn or string may be applied, which will define student body contour. Let dry, then paint (or glue fabric) within yarn outline. For a more direct method, trace student's shape, then cut the whole shape out for the student. You might want to tape it down to make it more manageable. Fabric application may be the preferred way to deal with the surface for tactual stimulation.

Gifted

Students can research the design origins of costumes. They can then add more authentic details to their tracings, based on the information gathered. Compatible environments may be created for figures. The costume should logically fit into the exterior or interior scene that the student develops around it.

Feat of Clay

MATERIALS

- Colored modeling clay (substitute plasticine)
- Tongue depressors
- Manicure sticks (or dull pencils)
- Garlic press (optional but recommended!)

TEACHER PREPARATION

Try to provide colored clay, or try the recipe on page 244.

Cover work surfaces with paper or plastic cloth. Cleanser will be needed for cleanup. The fluid cleanser that comes in a squeeze bottle is suggested. If you have only powder, you use it (not the students).

DIRECTIONS

1. Students decide on making clay animals or people, or both. (See Figures 45 and 46.)

2. Many students find that the whole piece is best made by the sum of its parts. Students will roll out arms, legs, bodies, heads, in any order that suits them. (See Figure 47.)

Figure 46

Figure 45

Figure 47

3. Assemble. Hair, fur can be made by placing a wad of clay into the garlic press. (See Figure 48.)

4. Add details. (See Figure 49.) Display.

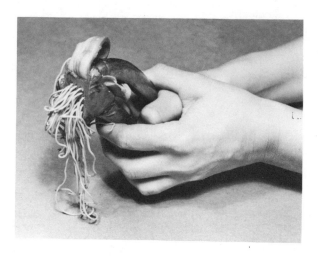

Figure 48

Figure 49

SUGGESTIONS FOR FURTHER DEVELOPMENT

The "feat" of clay is to get clay to stand on its own two—or four—feet! Figures must be built so that they do not fall over. Rule number one is to build figures with a solid bottom and avoid top heaviness. You can incorporate "props" into clay sculpture, such as umbrellas, tree trunks, rocks and furniture, to add support.

adaptations

Feat of Clay

Mentally Retarded

A recommended choice of clay modeling material for the severely retarded student is fluorescent clay. It is available through art supply centers. The stimulating color is ideal. The next choice is colored clay. Severely retarded students may be somewhat limited in producing recognizable people or animals; clay snakes are just fine to make. They provide a good movement exercise and offer practice in making coils for pot construction (see "Clay Pots"). You may need to help students get started. Whenever possible, fade away once students seem to understand the required motion. You can display snakes in their natural habitat with rocks and stones. If feasible, students can gather the rocks and stones in a nature walk.

Mildly retarded students can do a little drama exercise to warm up for making clay animals. But first, you will select some pictures of animals from magazines and print the animal's name on the picture. Fold and place in a bag. When students arrive, shake the bag and have students select a paper. Whatever animal name they withdraw from the bag will be their subject for clay. Now, move back the desks. Each student will "become" the particular animal—move like the animal and make the animal's noise. For example, if Johnny got *elephant*, questions like "How do you think an elephant walks? Slow or fast? Why?" will help play out the animal better. This is a lot of fun for students and makes them think about specifics like weight distribution, size, shape, and movement. Animals are also a good choice for students who have trouble getting clay figures to stand; four-legged animals are the best solution for that problem.

Socially and Emotionally Disturbed

Fantasy environments easily grow around clay figures. When you introduce the lesson, tell students to think about a place that they would like to be—their own "wonderland." They can start with the figures or with environment, whatever comes first. Figures such as elves, kings, queens, heros, and magicians are more likely to fire up imaginations. Dragons and other mythical beasts will complete the scene. Make sure students have the chance to talk about the clay worlds they created.

Unlikely, and lovable, are *mixed-up creatures*. Students will become "buddies" for this activity and work in pairs, with each student creating his or her own animal (or figure). When work is complete, divide each clay animal with a tongue depressor. Buddies will switch halves and join to make a brand-new creation, a sum of both their efforts. Results might resemble minotaurs, flying giraffes, or bears with kangaroo bottoms (pouches included). You might want to display them with name tags created by the students to identify their species. How about a lionoceros or a hippoplatypus?

Learning Disabled

The flexibility of clay people can teach your learning disabled more about the body's movement. Introduce the lesson (see "You're a Doll" for suggestions) and give out materials as directed. Tell students to create figures that are doing something (*besides* standing up straight): bending, leaning over, sitting. Students can also make clay furniture to support the figures.

Encourage students to assume some poses themselves. Posing and constructing figures will make students more aware of the body's movement in space and the balance to support it. Just as getting hit on the top of your head with a ripe apple falling from a tree can teach gravity (a la Sir Isaac Newton), toppling clay figures instruct students on weight distribution and the body's axis.

Phyically Handicapped

Again, clay manipulation is an excellent isometric exercise (see "Apples and Oranges"). Students who are able to follow the core lesson should do so; other students may want to make very simple forms, such as turtles. Tools may help students with controlling the clay better. Tools can also be made more accessible to the students while working by placing the tools in a rotating tray—the kind often used to hold pens, scissors, etc., on office desk tops.

If movement is severely restricted but present to some extent, you may want to abandon clay animals and people for a more simple theme. One suggestion is "pancakes," which is extremely uncomplicated. Another, "spaghetti," can be made with the garlic press—and is that fun to make! Using the garlic press is also good for hand movement. Meatballs and dishes may be added.

Sensory Losses

Hearing impaired—After presenting hearing impaired students with the steps of *Feat of Clay*, emphasize the theme *"two."* "Two" stands for two people (or two animals) doing something that "takes two to do." Some examples are dancing, playing, shaking hands. Students will pair up for this lesson so that they can make figures interrelate properly. It might be advisable to look over examples of figure groups in sculpture in art history books to observe their relationships. When all work is complete, the entire class should place all the pairs into a group display.

Visually handicapped—Visually handicapped students can increase their awareness of body parts with the creation of clay people. Making a person can be divided into six units: the head—a ball, the arms and legs—coils divided into four parts; the body—a cylinder. Other parts (hands, feet, details) get added later.

Blind students will likely need assistance in assembling the parts. Verbal and physical prompting, and a 3-D model (doll or sculptural reproduction) would be of value. The parts-to-whole relationship is a concept that blind students can use some help with, and this activity does concern location and placement of parts.

Gifted

Gifted students might want to design period costumes out of clay while they are creating their figures. Research on costumes would include observing styles and textures. Often peasant and ethnic costumes (i.e., Russian folk costumes, Mexican dress) are challenging to replicate. Perhaps some students have dolls of other nations that they could bring to class as examples.

You might want students to study illustrations of classic Greek sculpture to see how folds and drapes can suggest the structure underneath the clothing. To help students with expressing the costumes and their effects in clay, clay tools of various sizes (particularly fine wooden sticks) will help.

Flying Colors

MATERIALS

- Felt
- Crayon
- Markers
- Scissors
- White glue
- Wooden dowels
- Manila paper
- Rulers
- Yardstick
- String

TEACHER PREPARATION

You will need good lengths of felt to carry out this activity with flair. For easier handling, you might want to have felt pieces precut to manageable sizes. For students with limited skills, you may even want to precut design elements (such as hearts, stars, circles, etc.).

If you want to use actual flag motifs, encyclopedias and dictionaries usually offer full pictorial reference material.

DIRECTIONS

1. Flags are one way to present this lesson, but the banner theme offers a "broader" approach. Banners can be held, hung, or waved. (See Figure 50.)

2. Students work their ideas out on paper before beginning fabric design.

3. Cut felt pieces according to plan. Glue pieces onto the banner section. (See Figure 51.) Leave room at the top (and bottom if desired) for wooden dowels.

4. Sew or staple the channels closed and insert the dowels through them.

SUGGESTIONS FOR FURTHER DEVELOPMENT

If you decide on flags, plan to fly or mount them so they can hang indoors. Banners lend themselves to big, open space, but they can hang beautifully against a big wall.

Should you decide that you like working big and bold, a novel lesson you might want to try is "The Window Shade." You can create a roll-up shade by purchasing the wooden bar and parts and designing the shade itself. The design should be painted (or sewn very flatly) so that the shade retains the roll-up action. This project is decorative, useful, and fun.

Have a banner lesson!

Figure 50

Figure 51

adaptations

Flying Colors

Mentally Retarded

Precut 1- by 2-inch banner felt pieces for the severely retarded student. In a hand-over-hand manner, you can help student cut a simple basic shape of contrasting color (see Adaptive Aids). This is a good opportunity to teach color. Repeat the name of the color(s) as you present the activity.

Glue the one basic shape on the banner. When dry, cut banner vertically to create wide streamers. Hang near students, particularly the less mobile ones. You will be providing an ongoing, student-made source of sensory stimulation as air currents move the fabric.

For the mildly retarded, this lesson can be a tool for teaching colors. Try to find white felt. Cut into small, individual banners. Each student will be assigned a color from the color spectrum. the student will cut simple shape(s) out of his or her color and glue the shape(s) on the felt. When banners are completed, they should be strung together on a clothesline (red-yellow-orange-green-blue-violet). This colorful display can be used as a reference when discussing color usage in the classroom.

Socially and Emotionally Disturbed

When the students design the banner on paper, they should be expected to transfer their ideas from paper to fabric. This procedure will help them understand the consequential relationship between planning and final product. It will also encourage concentration and involvement with task.

Consider doing the banner as a class project or in several small groups.

Learning Disabled

The flag motif will provide a very good visual exercise for learning disabled students. Students should select flag pictures or use real models as references. Duplicate the spatial design of the flag on paper first, using rulers if desired. Students will change the flag's colors to make it their own color arrangement and can integrate their own "initials" as part of the design. The lesson done in this manner will aid visual perception, concentration, and eye-hand coordination. Students may enjoy considering the flag as their *own* flag by personalizing it with their monogram.

Physically Handicapped

Group the students according to a "balance" of skills. For example, students that have scissors skills can do cutting for those without fine motor grasp or use of hands.

To make gluing easier, pour glue into styrofoam tray. Use a cardboard card to dip into the glue and spread it on the banner (before placing down the pieces). This simplifies the whole process.

Sensory Losses

Hearing impaired—Show students pictures of banners or real models. Once students have selected a subject, suggest including the "sign" for that subject, if available. The "sign" will be cut out of felt in the shape of the hand's gesture. This slant to the activity adds a "communications" dimension.

Visually handicapped—For the blind, why not create a multisensory banner that

78

incorporates both textural materials and sound effects? Mount textural materials such as scraps of fake fur, sandpaper, velvet, steel wool, cotton balls. Add small pie plates, shells, old spoons and pot lids, and bells, if available. String up the noisy objects in such a way that they will clang together when banner is placed in a breeze. For students with some vision, you may want to follow the core lesson using yellow or orange felt, which are considered the most highly visible colors for the visually impaired. Fluorescent papers will also increase the visual interest with sight impaired students.

Gifted

Don't overlook other subject areas as motivation for "Flying Colors." For example, science provides weather, nature, plants, and the solar system. Even the common carrot can be a smashing banner. Some periods of history, such as the Middle Ages and Renaissance, are excellent for banners. Think about the Crusades for banner shapes and sizes.

"Banners of the Future World" could be very exciting, drawing on a space age or technological theme.

Guitars

MATERIALS

- Oaktag
- String
- Paper fasteners
- Scissors
- Crayons
- Markers

TEACHER PREPARATION

The best introduction to this activity is a sing-along with a real guitar. If you don't play the guitar, chances are that you know someone at school or outside of school that does. However, to supplement or substitute the real article, tape recordings or records of guitar music (country, folk, blues, etc.) should be played.

For the technical part, precut guitar shapes for students who need that level of assistance. You might also precut "guitar string" lengths out of the string (there are six strings on regular guitars).

Naturally, this is all a perfect reason to talk to the music department about a cooperative lesson unit.

DIRECTIONS

1. Talk about the guitar and its distinctive appearance—the curvy shape, the wooden frame, the number of strings. Try to have a real guitar on hand that can be examined and plucked by students. (See Figure 52.)

2. Students cut guitar shapes out of oaktag and design the surface. (See Figure 53.) Attach three paper fasteners to each side of the top of the neck. Draw a "bridge" across the bottom. (See Figures 54 and 55.) Wrap string around top of paper fasteners and punch through the bridge. You have just "strung" your guitar.

SUGGESTIONS FOR FURTHER DEVELOPMENT

The purpose of this activity is not to produce a real musical instrument that plays. It emphasizes artistic interpretation of the instrument's basic appearance and characteristic qualities.

Guitars can, of course, lead into other instruments of the band and orchestra. This is an exciting way to familiarize students with the distinctive shapes—and personalities—of musical instruments.

Figure 52

Figure 53

Figure 54

Figure 55

adaptations

Guitars

Mentally Retarded

For the severely to the mildly retarded student, lesson can be presented as follows: Play guitar music during activity. Try to get a real guitar that can be traced onto paper. Show students how guitars are held, guiding their hands in a simple up and down strum. Using a paper of proper size and stiffness, help students to outline the shape of the real object with a crayon. Aid with cutting. Decorate by painting (or using crayons freely) while listening to the music.

To string, follow Step 2 of the directions, but make holes approximately ¼-inch round for yarn you will use. Place student's free hand next to hole as a point of reference to indicate where hole is located. This is a good exercise for improving bilateral hand coordination and will help to improve focusing on a task.

Socially and Emotionally Disturbed

You might consider designing a class "band." Some students will design guitars, others can make drums, trombones, banjos, and so on. Be sure to have reference pictures on hand if the real articles are not available. This approach to "Guitars" makes for a unified group project. Display instruments together in the classroom.

Learning Disabled

Having students trace a real guitar will increase awareness of the object's shape and dimensionality. After guitars are traced and cut, have students "pinstripe" along the perimeter of the guitar (thin line drawn along edge). This will reinforce awareness of closure.

Help students who have difficulty in "stringing" guitars; they might have trouble with the end-to-end parallel positions of strings.

Physically Handicapped

Students will learn about the shape and function of the guitar by strumming it, holding it, and exploring it. To translate their sensory experience into 2-D, students will draw the guitar shape with teacher assistance. Students' manual ability will determine amount of teacher assistance needed in all phases of activity (particularly stringing).

You might want students to paint guitars in rhythm with the guitar music that you play for them.

Sensory Losses

Hearing impaired—Try to get a real guitar! When playing the guitar, let students touch the wooden part. Deaf students learn music through vibration. If you play a record, let students place their hands on the side of the record player; this can help with understanding the guitar music.

Otherwise, proceed with the core lesson.

Visually handicapped—It might be of interest to your students to learn that there are many accomplished and famous blind musicians. Guitarists such as Doc Watson and José Feliciano might be mentioned and their records played for the activity.

The sensory experience is very important for visually handicapped students, so try to make sure that a guitar is on hand for their examination.

You may want to help the student by tracing the guitar shape on paper in fluorescent marker for cutting purposes. Blind students who are using screenboards to design the guitars will require a paper that is of a lighter weight than the oaktag. Many will need assistance in stringing their guitars.

Gifted

Using pencils, let students draw the contour, using the real guitar as a model. Students will have the challenge of reproducing guitars symmetrically. When they have arrived at a "pleasing shape," cut out. (It is wise to practice sketch first.)

It would be worthwhile to provide visual reference material on the decorative styles of guitars. Elaborate and ornate designs could be developed on guitars. Replicating various wood grains in a *trompe l'oeil* manner might be fun for the gifted student. NOTE: *trompe l'oeil* means "trick of the eye"—creating an illusion with paint (or pencil, etc.) that is so realistic that it could be mistaken for the real object.

Gumball Machines

MATERIALS

- White paper
- Black paper
- Markers (scented, if available)
- Paper circles
- Glue/paste
- Colored paper squares
- Scrap wallpaper

TEACHER PREPARATION

Precut the gumball machine shapes. A circle can represent the glass bowl that holds the gumballs. The stand can be a truncated triangle (or any other shape you think is appropriate). You also have the option of precutting a one-piece machine by combining both parts (circle and base) and tracing them.

DIRECTIONS

1. Gumball machines are fun to operate and great to look at for their shapes and colors, which are the emphasis of this activity.

2. Cut out gumball machines. Select preferred materials for gumballs and other details.

3. Mount completed gumball machines against black paper. Add a "countertop" using scrap wallpaper. (See Figures 56 and 57.)

SUGGESTIONS FOR FURTHER DEVELOPMENT

You can create a candy counter by displaying gumball machines side by side on the wall. This has an exciting visual impact. Of course, other kinds of vending machines can be added in, such as peanut vending machines, machines that dispense toy rings and whistles, etc. Gumball machines can be made to stand up if they are constructed from lightweight oaktag, and given a tabbed back.

Students often come up with a distinctive variety of "gumballs"—dabs, spots, circles, confetti-like marks, and so on. This gives their work individuality and shows that there are many ways to interpret subjects, even when they may *appear* to have a predictable outcome.

NOTE: Gumball machines are used in this activity strictly for their decorative quality—*not* their nutritional value. You should make it clear to students that this is your aim, and that you do not want to promote tooth decay!

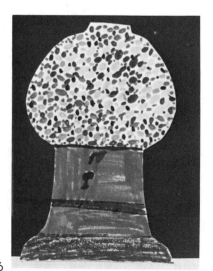
Figure 56

Figure 57

adaptations

Gumball Machines

Mentally Retarded

Precut gumball machine shape. Use tiddlywinks or paper circles for gumballs. Arrange by color in a sectioned tray. Students choose colors (with prompting), going from left to right, one color at a time. They arrange circles inside gumball machine shape and glue with your assistance.

Some students will be more capable of independence in this activity than others. The tray arrangement is particularly helpful to the mildly retarded for its similarity to the techniques used in prevocational skills (i.e., sorting, sequencing, assembling).

Socially and Emotionally Disturbed

When students draw the gumball machines, ask that they put a "prize" into their bowls (like those you often see in vending machines). Suggest that the prize be an object that they would really like to have. When the class's work is completed, ask them to discuss their choices.

Learning Disabled

Discuss the operation of gumball machines. Where does the money go in? Where does the gumball come out? Give your students the precut paper shape of the glass bowl; they can cut a base for it (or you can supply a precut base).

Learning disabled would benefit from outlining *coins* with fine-tip markers or pencils to create their gumballs. Apply color within coin shapes. This will require concentration on task as well as eye-hand skills. It is also fun and challenging.

Physically Handicapped

You may want to present gumball machines as a printmaking activity. Fill shallow cups with different colored paints. Using *corks* in each color, student will print gumballs on paper machine.

Another method is dabbing the paint with a paintbrush. NOTE: This is an excellent activity for adaptive head gear.

Sensory Losses

Hearing impaired—The best introduction to the lesson is taking your hearing impaired students to see the gumball machine at the corner store, if it's possible. You might even consider taking a Polaroid snapshot of a gumball machine if no reference material is available. In addition, demonstrate the lesson.

Visually handicapped—Since it is unlikely that you can bring a real gumball machine to class, have a discussion with students about what a gumball machine is (what it *sounds* like, looks like, what it *does*, etc.) For totally blind, offer tiddlywinks or paper circles to glue onto paper bowl shape.

Visually handicapped can use scented markers to make circles (gumballs). Stationery stores may have fluorescent dot stickers that would be visually stimulating for sight impaired students to use.

Gifted

The challenge for the gifted can be in designing an extraordinary gumball machine. It can be elaborate or have moving parts in the "Rube Goldberg" tradition, that is, a contraption or device that could be done without complexity, but is made decisively complicated; often having moving parts and mechanisms as part of the overall design.

Hanukkah's Tops!

MATERIALS

- White lightweight board (white on *both* sides)
- Colored tissue paper
- Paintbrushes—wide, flat type
- Brightly colored ribbons or string
- Water containers
- White glue
- Paper towels
- Paper (or plastic cloth) to cover work surface
- Scissors
- Dreidels (see Teacher Preparation)

TEACHER PREPARATION

Dreidels are small tops used to play a Hanukkah game. To introduce the lesson, it would be ideal to demonstrate with a real dreidel. If you don't have a dreidel on hand, provide pictures of a dreidel, which you should find in the library. Precut the dreidel shapes for students lacking scissors skills. Cover work surfaces before you distribute supplies. *Dilute* white glue with water in about equal parts.

DIRECTIONS

1. Discuss dreidels and significance of Hanukkah, based on reference materials. Pass around dreidels, letting students explore and spin them. (See Figures 58 and 59.)

2. Give students white boards to cut dreidel shapes from, or offer precut dreidels.

3. Give colored tissues to students for cutting or tearing into irregular shapes.

Figure 58

Figure 59

(See Figure 60.) Lay torn pieces of tissue, one at a time, on dreidel shapes, and "paint" with white glue. (Do not be concerned by tissues that bunch up, tear, or overlap; this will create interesting color blends and textures.)

4. Students should decorate both sides. (See Figure 61.) Glue dries fast, so you may want to allow a short time for drying between working on each side.

5. When dreidels dry, punch hole at top. Twist two or three ribbons together and string through the opening and hang.

Figure 60

Figure 61

SUGGESTIONS FOR FURTHER DEVELOPMENT

You can make a mobile out of several dreidels, hanging them together. You may want to add other elements of Hanukkah, such as Stars of David and menorahs, and cover them with colored tissues also. If you wish to make a three-dimensional dreidel, follow the pattern in Figure 62.

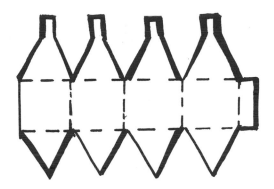

Paper dreidels may be constructed by cutting out the basic pattern as shown. Fold along dotted lines to create the top and bottom, close at tab, and paste or tape together. May be used as a hanging ornament.

Figure 62

adaptations

Hanukkah's Tops!

Mentally Retarded

Tape the precut dreidel shape to the table before beginning the lesson with your severely retarded students. Tearing is, in itself, a good activity for these students, so don't limit the amount of tissue they tear to what they really need to decorate dreidels. Use the hand-over-hand technique for gluing, and for tearing too, if necessary.

Your mildly retarded students should be able to complete the lesson as directed with clear, explicit instructions from the teacher. You might want to spend some time with the last step of the activity—twisting and threading ribbons. This is a good opportunity to work on tying skills.

Socially and Emotionally Disturbed

Students can work in pairs and collaborate on designs. Each student can decorate one side of his or her own shape and then *switch* with a partner. Decorating other side of partner's dreidel represents a cooperative effort between students. Hang dreidels together as one or several mobiles.

Learning Disabled

By using a wide point felt-tipped marker, in bright colors, students can add a decorative border to dreidels after they have dried. This will help closure skills and eye-hand coordination, while creating additional visual interest.

Physically Handicapped

Attach the precut dreidel shapes to the table before beginning. If tearing is a problem, secure one end of the tissue to the table with a heavy book—or clip sheets of tissue to a clipboard. The student can then tear off pieces with greater ease. For help with other steps, you can try adaptive headgear, or paintbrush handles (see p. 233).

Sensory Losses

Hearing impaired—It is important to present reference materials to your hearing impaired students, particularly those who are unfamiliar with Hanukkah and dreidels. If an actual dreidel or top is not available, you can indicate the spinning motion of a top in conjunction with pictures and reference materials. Be sure that directions are clearly presented and well understood before proceeding with activity.

Visually handicapped—Visually handicapped students would benefit from examining a real dreidel in order to better understand its shape and form. If a dreidel is not accessible, try to provide an ordinary top for your students and explain that a dreidel is a special top used for a Hanukkah game.

Because tissues are brightly colored, they are particularly suitable for visually impaired students. Blind students will enjoy the textural surface interest of the finished product. Hang completed dreidels where your visually handicapped students can freely touch them; this provides repeated tactual enrichment experiences.

Gifted

Gifted students who are presented with a real dreidel (or a good illustration of one) should notice that there are Hebrew symbols on each side. What is the meaning of these symbols? The answer to that question is a good opener for further research. Students could find out more about the Hanukkah tradition as well as the ancient language of Hebrew. You might want to carry the study of written symbols and calligraphic signs over to other areas such as researching Egyptian hieroglyphics, Chinese calligraphy, Sanskrit, and the cuneiform alphabet of the Sumerians. Gifted students should be fascinated by the possibilities for interpretations that these topics offer.

How Does Your Flower Pot Grow?

MATERIALS

- Lightweight boards or Manila tag
- Wooden sticks (tongue depressors or popsicle sticks)
- Green-colored tissue
- Markers, crayons
- Paints (acrylic)
- Brushes
- White glue
- Green construction paper
- Scissors
- Sand or plasticene (florist's clay)
- Commercial clay flower pots (see Teacher Preparation)
- Optional—glitter

TEACHER PREPARATION

If each student brings a clay flower pot to class, you're in business! If not, well, you can either provide them or have students make them. Four- to 6-inch squares will serve students well for cutting flower; other students will require precut shapes.

DIRECTIONS

1. Students draw basic floral shapes (tulip, daisy, etc.) onto paper squares.

2. Paint or sprinkle glitter into wet paint if desired. Let dry.

3. Paint sticks green; let dry. Staple or glue flower to stick "stem."

4. Paint simple patterns onto flower pot next, turning pot as it is decorated.

5. Place plasticene or sand into pot. "Plant" flowers. (See Figure 63.)

6. Stuff green tissue into pot. Add construction paper leaves cut from simple shapes.

SUGGESTIONS FOR FURTHER DEVELOPMENT

You can create a "window box garden" by placing the flowers in a decorated shoebox. Or, place the flower pots on a table and draw a window scene. (See Figure 64.) Flowers can also be made of felt (stuffed) and petals can be layered.

Figure 63

Figure 64

adaptations

How Does Your Flower Pot Grow?

Mentally Retarded

Explore the materials that you will be using with your severely retarded students—paper, plasticine, tissue, etc. Students may be tactually defensive, so investigating materials is helpful. Use pre-cut floral shapes. Students may use fluorescent crayons or fluorescent paints for decoration.

Mildly retarded students may benefit by having materials laid out from left to right in order of sequence. For example, set up paper first, then scissors, paint, etc.

Making the clay pot is recommended for the mildly retarded student (see "Clay Pots"). That should be presented as a separate lesson.

Socially and Emotionally Disturbed

One way to use this lesson to improve students' social relationships is to have students design flower pots for someone special. Some choices are secretary, principal, friend, and teacher. It doesn't have to be an occasion; this is an expression of the students' caring.

Students can design a note that goes with the plant. A "John-a-gram" or "Mary-gram" can be created to get the personal message across.

Learning Disabled

Cut paper in sizes to wrap around flower pot. This paper will decorate the pot by illustrating the stages of a flower's growth starting with a seed. Students will create a sequential "comic strip" of five blocks. The first block—planting the seed, second—watering the seed, third—the sprout, fourth—the young plant and bud, finally—the flower!

Physically Handicapped

Students who are less physically able can create a "newspaper plant." Tear sheet out of newspaper and paint it. Crush painted newspaper into a ball, and you have a newspaper flower! Attach to tongue depressor stems.

Another good source for "printed" flowers is an old telephone directory—simply tear out the pages.

Sensory Losses

Hearing impaired—Show students a real plant in a pot. If you have illustrations of a plant growth sequence, also offer to students. Next, get students to imitate the growth of a flower in pantomime body movement (you should demonstrate movement first). Present the precut flowers and other materials. Students go ahead with lesson.

Visually handicapped—Bring in flowers for your students to examine. Discuss the texture of petals as well as the anatomy of the flower. Cut petal shapes out of construction paper. Using the center of the flower as a focal point, paste petals in radiating pattern. Mount on stem, place in pot.

Gifted

Combine flowers and fantasy—have students create their own "species" of flowers. Present illustrated examples of a variety of flowers and plants. Point out some interesting Latin botanical names to students, such as Collinia Elegans (palm family). Students will invent names for their flowers incorporating their subject ideas. For example, if a student wants a flower to represent a sport, it could be a "daisy basketballi"; for a musical instrument, "cat o'harmonicus." You get the idea!

I Can See Right Through You!

MATERIALS

- Pencils
- White paper—9 by 12 inches and 11 by 18 inches
- X-rays (see Teacher Preparation)

TEACHER PREPARATION

Get your hands on X-rays! Resources are your doctor, the local hospital or clinic, or anyone you know in the medical community. Old X-rays, your own X-rays, your family's X-rays—gather heads, backs, legs, arms, whatever you can to make a complete skeleton.

Also try to have some illustrated (or dimensional) reference material on the human skeleton available. Halloween skeletons may be used if they are generally anatomically correct.

DIRECTIONS

1. Hold X-rays up to the window. Have students guess what part of the body they are looking at, such as head, back, knee, etc. Ask students to defend their choice (i.e., how do you know that's an arm and not a leg? (See Figures 65 and 66.)

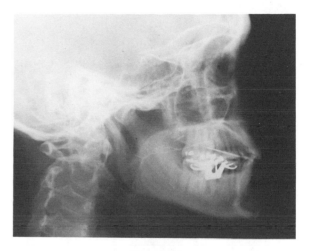

Figure 66

2. Give students X-rays to use as references (students should hold them up to the light). Students then draw the bones that the X-ray reveals. This represents a "study" of a body part. (See Figure 67.)

3. Show students visual (or 3-D) reference material. If you have a 3-D model that moves, bend it and observe where joints are working. Have class get into various positions using bending, reaching, stretching actions.

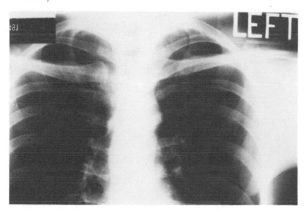

Figure 65

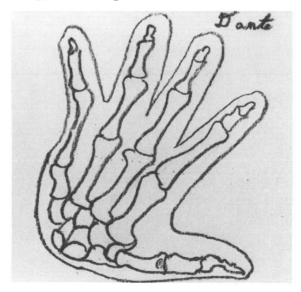

Figure 67

4. One student volunteers to pose for the group. You announce that everyone is going to put on imaginary glasses: *These glasses have the power to see right through to the model's bones!*

5. Draw the model in action poses with "glasses on." (See Figure 68.)

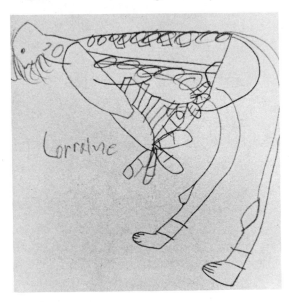

Figure 68

SUGGESTIONS FOR FURTHER DEVELOPMENT

Bones and anatomy are fascinating for children and adults to study. Although there is a definite connection between this art lesson and other subject areas (science, biology, health, etc.), the purpose here is to teach how the body is structured and proportioned—and how we move. It is related to drawing and studio skills. Remember, drawing with anatomical perfection is not a requirement, and this is not a pre-med course.

Also, the bones of mammals and other creatures are quite interesting in their own right. Many artists have shown their appreciation for their unique qualities—artists such as Picasso, O'Keefe, Miro, and Paul Klee. Art activities can explore this area with emphasis on shapes, texture, and structure of bones. Fish bones on a plate are wonderful as subjects for line drawings; the interlocking junctions of the bones will give the class ideas for bold designs. Experiment with your own ideas.

adaptations

I Can See Right Through You!

Mentally Retarded

The retarded student is in need of body awareness. Do you know the lines of that standard children's song, "You put your right foot in, you put your right foot out ..."? That is a perfect movement activity for reinforcing location of body parts, and it leads into the art activity. You will need to guide students with physical and verbal prompting so that they move the correct arm, leg, etc. This introduction should be useful to both the severely and mildly retarded student; the mildly retarded student can move into the core activity from there.

The activity recommended for the severely retarded student is body tracing (see "Faces and Traces"). After tracing student's body, cut it out. Assist student in painting the full-sized shape and name body parts as you work (i.e., leg, arm, body, etc.) You might even want to print the names of body parts in big bold letters on the appropriate area when the paint is dry. Display with student's name prominently printed on body tracing.

Socially and Emotionally Disturbed

This lesson should go over very well with your socially and emotionally disturbed students because of its dramatic flair and high interest content. When students are about to begin the bone "studies," follow the core lesson and try to have the class draw all the essential skeletal *parts*, (i.e., two ribs, hands/arms/shoulders, leg/foot, pelvis, head and neck). When all parts are complete, *assemble* on a large length of butcher wrap or tape together. The class has created a full skeleton composed of everyone's efforts.

Learning Disabled

Understanding how things work is often hard for learning disabled students. Try this game to make a point about body movement. First, have students stand. Then, tell students that a magic spell has been cast over them and they cannot move their joints. Now ask them to imagine that there is a basket filled with a million dollars on the floor. Could someone please pick it up?

This should make the reality of body movement less abstract. Proceed with core lesson.

Physically Handicapped

If you are fortunate enough to have some available windows, *tape* X-rays to them and move your physically limited students (desks) to them. In order to do a "study," materials should be accessible for close observation.

There is no reason why students cannot model for each other, but be sensitive to how students seem to feel about their disabilities. For example, a student with a newly acquired physical handicap may not appreciate a drawing that reminds him or her of the loss. However, if a wheelchair-bound student (or any other disabled student) is comfortable with himself and appears reasonably self-accepting, there is no reason why he cannot model.

Sensory Losses

Hearing impaired—Your hearing impaired students can play a "connecting" game that will "move" them right into the activity, while encouraging positive social interplay. Students stand together. You touch student on a "movable" part, such as an elbow, knee, wrist, or neck. Student moves that part and taps next student on a movable part. Repeat until all students have been "activated." The results are reminiscent of a gigantic robot or a big human machine.

If students can find an X-ray of their moving "part" (the place where they were tapped), do the study of it. Otherwise, follow the core. You will, of course, need to demonstrate the overall activity in physical and visual terms.

Visually handicapped—It is recommended that visually handicapped students use a white pencil on black paper for their studies and their see-through figures. This reversed combination is generally more visible because of its contrast (see "Reflections"). Besides, it also looks more like the X-rays!

Blind students should firmly feel their arms and legs, ribs, back, etc. for the bone and cartilage; have the students describe what they are experiencing. It is helpful to get some kind of three-dimensional model (they are available in toy stores and some school science departments) or, at the very least, get a doll. A lot of clear discussion about where bones are and what shape they are will help understanding too.

Blind students may want to make skeletons by gluing straws or toothpicks (or popsicle sticks) to paper. Help guide student in parts placement; in fact, consider precutting a human body shape to create the proper format.

Gifted

As you know, bones are an important component of anatomy. How about muscles? After your gifted students have followed the core lesson, let them research human musculature. Using an overlay of tracing paper on their skeleton drawings, students will draw muscle tissue. NOTE: Acetate is the ideal material for overlays, but it is more expensive than tracing paper and not as readily available.

(See "You're a Doll" for yet other suggestions about anatomy for gifted students.)

I'm Stuffed!

MATERIALS

- Unbleached muslin
- Fabric (assorted pieces)
- Stuffing (polyester fill or shredded foam)
- Straight pins, needles
- Thread
- Acrylic paints, brushes
- Yarn
- Manila paper
- Tape
- White glue
- Cardboard
- Scissors
- Stapler
- Crayons (fabric crayons optional)
- Gloves

Recommended: Miscellaneous costume and cosmetic details—false eyelashes and false fingernails, scarves, hats, wigs, socks, sunglasses, plastic doll eyes, small sized shirts and tops—whatever you can collect.

TEACHER PREPARATION

Take up a collection of grand junk (see "Recommended" under *Materials*). You can ask your students to bring in old gloves for the hands. White gloves (particularly child sized) are desirable because they can be painted to match the face. False fingernails may be an expense, although they lend realism (you can substitute with oaktag nails). You may want to cut the fabric either in preproportioned pieces or as precut head/shoulders shapes. Fabric scraps and pieces, all sorts of yarn, buttons, and fake furs should be available for student use.

DIRECTIONS

1. Discuss portraits. A portrait is simply a picture of someone's face, often including hands and upper body. But is it more? Can it tell us something about the personality of the person inside? Explain that these will be portraits in fabric, and will have both fronts and backs. (See Figure 69.)

Figure 69

2. Give students paper to sketch out the contour of their portraits. This will serve as the paper pattern for cutting fabric; keep it big, bold, and *simple*. (See Figure 70.)

3. Measure the amount of muslin needed to accommodate the portrait. Pin down the cutout paper portrait to the folded fabric. Cut fabric to yield front and back.

Figure 70

paper patterns
Figure 71-A

pin paper patterns to fabric
Figure 71-B

4. If using crayons to create face, tape the cloth portrait shapes to a flat surface and draw. If student plans to paint the face, proceed to step 5.

5. Baste stitch the front and back cloth pieces together, wrong side out. Reinforce stitching on sewing machine. If there is no sewing machine, go over the stitching with smaller, tighter stitches.

6. Turn fabric right side out.

7. Cut out a section of cardboard (posterboard will do) to create a bottom on which portrait will stand. Stretch and pull fabric over cardboard. Staple closed. (See Figures 71-A, B, and C.)

8. You now have a faceless, unclothed soft sculpture. Dress with whatever costume parts you've collected. Paint the portrait. (See Figures 72 and 73.)

9. To make the hands, stuff the gloves. Use a dull pencil to push stuffing into fingers *before* you stuff the palm area. (Hands can also be made from the mus-

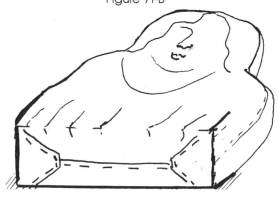

staple over cardboard and fabric
(after sewing and stuffing)
Figure 71-C

Figure 72

Figure 73

lin by tracing students' hands, sewing, and then stuffing.) Add false fingernails and use white glue to attach them to gloves. NOTE: Cut up gloves for 3-D facial features. The fingers make great noses, ears, and lips! (See Figure 74.)

SUGGESTIONS FOR FURTHER DEVELOPMENT

"I'm Stuffed!" is the stuff that dreams are made of. Students can portray themselves in any way that they fancy. If self-portraits do not appeal to you, here are some other suggestions:

- Magicians
- Movie and rock stars
- World leaders
- Literary or historical features
- Monsters

Figure 74

- Superheroes, comic book characters
- Famous painters and paintings

Portraits can be executed simply with crayons or can be elaborate productions. When they are completed by a group, display them all—they look like they belong together, no matter how diverse the characters.

adaptations

I'm Stuffed!

Mentally Retarded

Mildly retarded students can do beautifully with this lesson (the proof is that some of the art in the photos was produced by visually impaired M.R. students). Of course, some help was needed with organization, but the willingness to carry out the project was there.

Now, the big question is, how much of this activity should be attempted with your more severely retarded students? The answer depends on how much assistance you are prepared to offer and how much time you want to allot to the total project. Some teachers who have able-bodied helpers can prepare the soft sculptures for their severely impaired students to paint and decorate, which means that they begin lesson at step 8. For other teachers, who may want to know how to break down the whole activity, here are some suggestions:

1. *The portrait on practice paper* is a precut shape that students can use to identify the placement of the features.

2. Students can *baste stitch* the fabric halves together with you in a hand-over-hand method. You will need to reinforce stitches.

3. *Stuffing* the sculpture can be done in cooperation with the teacher. Help the student reach into a "stuffing bag," get a handful of stuffing (you may need to cup your hands with the student's), and push the stuffing securely into the fabric form. You will staple the bottom.

4. When 3-D muslin shape is stuffed and ready for painting, bring out the paper portrait for a frame of reference. Use the same technique for feature placements.

5. Help with the adding of fabric details. Hat and wigs make things easier. Glue (instead of sew) whenever you can.

When "I'm Stuffed!" is presented to the severely retarded in its entirety, it often becomes a full-term project. But you are teaching concepts and skills: portrait reinforces body parts; sewing and stuffing eye-to-hand coordination; and sensory awareness through use of diverse materials. REMEMBER: Each step is an activity for the profoundly retarded and will need constant repetition.

Socially and Emotionally Disturbed

This activity has tremendous potential because it draws upon fantasy and imagination. It is almost like creating another "self" in the same sense that actors create characters when playing a role.

Choices of subject are often heroic, powerful figures—and they should not be discouraged. However, if students get a little too "charged up," don't sacrifice reasonable classroom order to pandemonium for the sake of art. This is the kind of lesson that can be picked up easily and worked on at varying intervals—so, "stop the works" if necessary.

When work has been successfully carried out and projects are ready to display, try to place them in a prominent area in the school where they will receive positive recognition.

Learning Disabled

The learning disabled students need guidance on sequencing, and this activity is an activity of "steps." To help students with directions, try to show them the project as it will appear at different stages, i.e., the paper pattern, the partially sewn shape, etc.

There are some basic concepts that might escape your students, such as where the hands go on the sculpture (body parts). Sewing will need some attention, mostly remembering to start at one end and go around, leaving room for stuffing.

Physically Handicapped

The manner in which your physically handicapped student is impaired will dictate the type of assistance that will have to be provided. For instance, if movement is severely limited, sewing might be a problem. You might want to get another student to be an assistant to the less able one to "fill in" what the other cannot physically do. Students with different strengths could help each other through various requirements of the activity. Of course, your assistance and support helps too—but so does a sense of independence. See the Adaptive Aid section for some suggestions.

Sensory Losses

Hearing impaired—"I'm Stuffed!" may easily be converted to animated activity. Those otherwise quiet, soft sculptures can be turned into "talking heads" through creating movements in the arms and hands. This can be accomplished by leaving enough room so that the student can insert his/her arm. The glove, loosely attached, is filled by the student's hand (therefore, you skip stuffing the gloves).

When students complete their work, they might want to get into groups of three or four to hold a little play. A script can be developed by the students or through your suggestions, or it can be improvisational. Simple little situations like "Mary Lou is unhappy, and the Magician wants to help" can set students up for interesting interplay. Of course, make sure your students understand what is expected; write it out if necessary.

Visually handicapped—Precut the fabric and the practice paper to the contour of a portrait so that students have perimeters within which to place features. Students who are able to create "3-D parts," noses, ears, and lips, should be encouraged to do so. This makes the dimensionality of portraits more concrete. Teacher assistance may be required for assembling of parts. This activity is a real enrichment for visually handicapped students, from sensory awareness to the logical placement of body parts. Remember, visually impaired students did the soft sculpture on these pages!

Gifted

Use reproductions of famous portraits to point out how artists observed their subjects' faces. The slant of an eye, a heavy eyelid, a droopy mouth—all helped give expression and life to the work. For the student with sewing skill, these details in fabric are achievable. Satin makes great lips but the muslin itself can be used successfully for features. Encourage students to try to create meaningful objects for the sculpture's hands: for example, a rabbit for a magician, an instrument for a musician, a book for a teacher. This approach creates a greater challenge.

It's a Print!

MATERIALS

- Linoleum blocks or wood blocks
- Brayers (printmaker's rollers)
- Manila paper
- Paper—newsprint, colored construction paper
- Wooden spoon
- Printmaking tools, V gouge and U gouge
- Printing ink *(water based)* in desired colors
- Sheets of plexiglass (or cardboards)
- Paper towels
- Felt-tipped markers
- White or black crayon
- Newspapers
- Rice paper (optional)

TEACHER PREPARATION

All materials for printing should be on hand for a demonstration before you begin the activity. Tools are sharp, so it is absolutely imperative that you show students their proper use! Linoleum or wood blocks should be the kind that are intended for printmaking. Consider the sizes of the blocks in relationship to the time frame for the activity. Larger blocks usually take longer to finish. HINT: Linoleum blocks can be made easier to cut by placing in a warm spot (like a radiator) prior to use. Heat softens linoleum.

DIRECTIONS

1. Introduce lesson by asking students if they can think of anything that is printed. You can show them a dollar bill to get them started. Some good examples are books and newspapers.

2. Explain to students that they will be printing by carving wood (or linoleum) away from the block. Ink will stay on the raised areas.

3. Students should first plan out their printing designs on paper using thick markers (this discourages fine details, which are inappropriate for the activity).

4. Once ideas have been established, begin demonstration.

5. Cover work surfaces with newspaper. Have all material at hand.

6. Draw the image on the block with a crayon (black or white) that contrasts with the wood (or linoleum). (See Figure 75.) This helps students to visualize the reversed look of the print. You might also mention that the printed image will appear as a mirror image of the block design.

Figure 75

7. Show cutting method. Place non-working hand *behind* the working hand. All cutting movement must be done away from the body. (See Figure 76.) Supervise students during the activity to make sure that this method is being strictly followed. (A bench hook, or holding jig, may be used to secure the linoleum block in place. See "Adaptive Aids" for further information.)

Figure 76

Figure 77

Figure 78

Figure 79

8. Demonstrate inking the block. Plexiglass (or cardboard) is the surface on which you will roll out the ink. Squeeze ink across the top of the cardboard. (See Figure 77.) Use the brayer (roller) to "pull" ink over the board's surface until it becomes tacky. (See Figure 78.) Notice that the brayer will stand when rested on one of its sides. Roll ink over the block. (See Figure 79.)

9. Place your paper on top of the block, leaving a border. Use the back of the wooden spoon to rub the back of the paper. (See Figure 80.) You can make a fist and rub with the blade of your hand, too. (If you are using rice paper or other thin paper, the print will begin to appear through the back.)

Figure 80

10. When you think you have it evenly rubbed, grasp two corners on one and gently pull the paper away from the block. (See Figure 81.) You have just

Figure 81

Figure 83

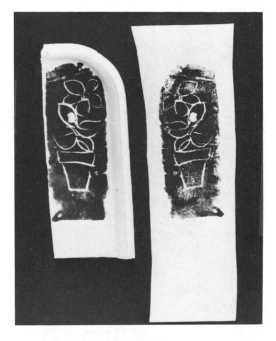

Figure 82

Figure 84

printed your first "proof"! (See Figures 82, 83, and 84.) Repeat the process (steps 8-10) for as often as prints are desired. NOTE: It may take some practice to get the ink "right" on your proofs. You will notice you have too much ink on the block when it pools in the incised areas; too little when the print is weak. If print is uneven, try to rub the back of the paper more evenly. HINT: A suggestion for drying prints is to use a clothesline and clips strung up temporarily in class.

About Printmaking

There is a real thrill in the moment when the print is pulled from the block. What will it look like? Excitement builds as the paper is peeled away to reveal the image that so much energy went into preparing. Then, magically, it appears!

The world of printmaking is indeed vast. It encompasses everything from the tire tracks made in the mud to the sophisticated graphics produced through state-of-

104

the-art technology. We can define a print as the transfer of an image from one surface to another, whether it is a single print (monoprint) or in multiples of thousands.

The ways in which prints are made are boundless. They can be carved, stamped, rubbed, engraved, rolled, and pressed. They are produced by silkscreens, metal plates, blocks or stone tablets—and can be run by hand or by printing press. Even photographic processes are often regarded as "printed."

But printmaking is more than mastering techniques—it can become a way of seeing. Objects and textures to ink, rub, and print are everywhere. One student made a remark that summed it all up. After leaving a particularly stimulating printmaking activity, she paused outside the classroom door and surveyed the familiar surroundings of brick walls, pavements, signs, and buildings. "Boy, look at this place," she exclaimed. "Let's print it!"

adaptations

It's a Print!

Mentally Retarded

Using sharp printer's tools with severely retarded students is NOT recommended. Yet printmaking is an excellent activity for severely retarded students. Here's what to do: Save Styrofoam trays, the kind that meat comes wrapped in (you can always ask the friendly neighborhood butcher for some trays on behalf of your students). These will become your "printing blocks." Ballpoint pens become your "cutting tools." Students will draw their designs and pictures directly into the Styrofoam. Lines should be deeply incised, but be careful not to poke the pen through the tray. Water-soluble printer's ink is fine, but you might need to water it down a little to pick up the print. Students will use the brayer and perform other parts of the process, with your assisting in a hand-over-hand manner. Let the prints dry. Display samples of students' work on the clothesline or elsewhere in the classroom.

Your mildly retarded students should be able to follow the core lesson. You will need to be *very* clear about the steps of the activity. Also, supervise the block cutting very closely. Smaller blocks produce more immediate results and will work well using a theme such as calendar prints.

Using the months and seasons is a recommended activity for mildly retarded because it increases awareness of the world and its sequence of seasons. Students should be asked to first draw pictures of the four seasons (step 3, Directions). If students are more limited in their concepts, simple images of weather (i.e., snow, rain, sun, etc.) should be within their understanding. More comprehensive pictures can include people dressed in sweaters, bathing suits, with umbrellas, and so on, or depict seasonal changes in nature (i.e., trees and flowers).

Teacher preparation should include having commercial calendars (or copies) to which prints can be affixed. With your students, decide on whose print matches what month(s). Divide the decisions within the group so that every month is covered and every student has an appropriate season (to cut from block). Proceed with the core. When all work is completed, students should have prints to keep as well as one for the class calendar. You might want to make extra calendars for others in the school—you can always make more. Make sure that students sign their prints at the bottom border. Keep your class calendar in a prominent place so that your students have a daily reinforcement of their ability all year long!

Socially and Emotionally Disturbed

This approach ought to suit your students to a tee: T-shirt prints. Using the theme of a face or a place, ask students to design self-portraits (or portraits of friends, celebrities, famous portraits), or a symbol of a favorite place. Symbols or abbreviated scenes would be much easier to cut than entire landscapes. Some suggestions are the Empire State Building, palm tree, boardwalk, or a ferris wheel. Students will need white or pastel cotton T-shirts. Painting will be done with fabric paint, available at art supply stores and hobby shops. It is sometimes easier to brush the paint onto the blocks instead of rolling it on. (Acrylic paint and printer's inks do not hold up in the wash.) Place a clean board into the shirt to keep the print from bleeding through to the back. Turn the block over and carefully press onto the shirt in the desired location. You might want students to initial or sign their names by cutting them into the block. Remember that all printing comes out *backwards* so you have to cut it backwards for it to appear normal. Students can use the block for other prints with paper and printer's ink.

WORD OF CAUTION: Printing tools are sharp and can be a real hazard. If your students are showing aggressiveness or are not following directions for cutting properly, DO NOT proceed with lesson. An alternative are Styrofoam block prints (see Mentally Retarded). Also, it is a good idea to monitor behavior closely and to make sure, by counting, that all tools are returned. Guidelines should be clear at the outset.

Learning Disabled

What's so funny about money? It is when it has students' faces printed on it and their own original borders. Use real dollars as samples and talk about money as the product of a printed process. (Of course, this lesson would be even better if coordinated with a trip to the Mint!) Review the activity as presented in the core, going over the steps clearly, particularly the cutting instructions. Linoleum or wood blocks should be presented in the rectangular shapes that resemble oversized paper currency. Students will decide on an appropriate motif for the border and put their portraits in the middle. If they want to show monetary value, numbers will need to be inscribed backwards (remember, block prints are always reversed). It would be eye-catching to display the finished products against background created by students, such as a teller's window, a treasure chest, or a giant piggy bank. This lesson is not only fun, but it also exercises closure (border), helps with replication skills (using real money as a reference), and teaches about a process (printing money).

Physically Handicapped

Physically handicapped students with limited hand-and-arm movement could have some real problems with the core lesson. Manipulating printing tools requires good grasp, some hand strength, and fine control. For students who are unable to use gouges, use the pen and Styrofoam method suggested under Mentally Retarded. Also, see Adaptive Aids for improving grip.

Another printing experience for the physically handicapped is the Texture Collage Print. Gather fabric scraps, lace doilies, sandpaper, corrugated paper, etc., and adhere these with white glue to a piece of cardboard. Let dry and print as you would a linoleum or wood block. Using the brayer and rubbing the printed paper are both good arm-and-hand exercises.

One more suggestion. You can adapt sanded wooden block scraps of various shapes and sizes for press-on prints. Simply glue on or screw in wooden furniture drawer handles. Set up shallow trays for dabs of paint for students to dip into and then press assorted designs onto paper.

Sensory Losses

Hearing impaired—Presenting the lesson as it is outlined in the core should give your hearing impaired students a good idea of what printing from blocks entails. But, be sure they understand all the details, particularly how to handle the tools.

A very nice direction for this lesson to take would be in the production of notecards. Students must use paper that is twice the size of their blocks and think about where their prints will come out on the paper with respect to the folded card. Holiday greeting cards, especially Valentines, are always a good bet. But creating notecards to be used for all occasions is just as good. The whole idea is to use the art to encourage communication via the written card, so whatever fits that bill will do. Personalized cards (remember, names and words backward!) are also worth considering.

Visually handicapped—Visually handicapped students can use printing tools. The more severely sight-limited student will require hand-over-hand assistance and should stick with very simple designs.

Something that is very exciting for your students to try is to take the cut block (when printing is done) and wash it off. Roll out some clay tiles (see page 148) cut to the block's size. Press your cut block into the clay. The raised image will appear to provide a tactual "picture" of the print. Poke a hole through the top of the clay tile, and let dry. You have an embossed wall plaque of your printing block.

More printmaking suggestions for the visually impaired can be made with yarn and white glue. Yarn can be glued to the board in a pattern, and when dry, it can be printed. Did you know that the white glue itself can be squeezed to create a linear drawing or design, and when it has thoroughly dried, can be printed? Try it. NOTE: Again, watch hands and tools closely to avoid mishaps!

Gifted

The gifted student may become very involved with printmaking as an expressive means because it has so many technical facets and is so challenging. It would be interesting to bring in reproductions of a variety of different printed images in art (engraving, lithograph, silkscreen, etc.) and see if students could guess the technique by looking at the finished product. Students might even want to set up a lab where they can bring in and experiment with techniques and materials (appropriate to the particular classroom setting). You might set up a collection for "printables" (i.e., ribbons, small flattened boxes, natural objects, souvenirs, etc.). Keep some printmaking tools on hand with a nearby clothesline as a kind of print activity center.

When students do the core activity, they should use their technical ability to the fullest, cutting the block with a variety of textures and using all available cutting tools. Prints should be pulled at various stages of the print's development so that students can decide on what "goes" and what "stays."

The printed image works beautifully with poetry and prose. Students may want to create a book as a class (a great group project), illustrating their favorite poem or making up poems of their own. If students want to do a whole book individually (and you *don't* want an extended project), students can do a monoprint for each page. Monoprints are simply done by carefully inking a piece of glass or plexiglass and inscribing a drawing with a stylus, pen, or brush handle. Make a single print and wash the glass, ink again, draw again, and print until all page illustrations are completed. Leave room for written prose or poetry.

Macaroni Townhouses

MATERIALS:

- Milk cartons
- Lace doilies
- Construction paper
- Glue
- Crayons, markers
- Watercolors
- Scissors
- Uncooked macaroni wheels
- Absorbent cotton or stuffing
- Steel wool (optional)

TEACHER PREPARATION

Collect milk cartons, the small-sized kind that children get at lunch. Rinse them out. Not all stores carry macaroni wheels, so substitute with whatever pasta will make good shingles. You will also want to acquire some lace doilies for "curtains." Provide precut paper to cover the milk carton house's sides to eliminate the students' having to measure them.

DIRECTIONS

1. With the milk cartons in front of them, ask students to imagine they are looking at houses in a neighborhood.

2. Cut out the necessary house parts—windows, doors, walls—from paper.

3. Cut the milk cartons to the desired size. Measure walls, decorate, apply.

4. Glue the macaroni to the flat roof, leaving room for a smoke stack. First, cut slits in a 3-by-4-inch piece of paper as shown in Figure 85. Then roll the paper into a cylinder, fold up the bottom slits, and glue the smoke stack together and onto the roof. (See Figure 86.)

5. Add "smoke" out of a mixture of steel wool and cotton. (See Figure 87.)

6. Houses are now ready for immediate occupancy! (See Figure 88.)

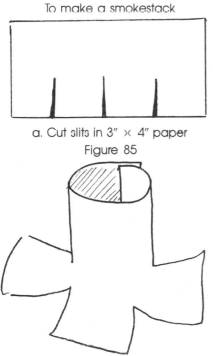

To make a smokestack

a. Cut slits in 3" × 4" paper
Figure 85

b. Roll into cylinder, pull out the slits. Glue together; attach to roof
Figure 86

Figure 87

Figure 88

SUGGESTIONS FOR FURTHER DEVELOPMENT

While "Macaroni Townhouses" appears to be an activity for younger students, there is potential for more advanced projects. Elaborate structures can be built by placing several milk cartons on each other, creating architectural interpretations of Greek temples, skyscrapers, etc. The macaroni wheels when painted white have a dazzling effect.

adaptations

Macaroni Townhouses

Mentally Retarded

Most severely retarded students will not understand the abstract concept of a house that has been made from a milk carton. The lesson should concentrate on the cube as a shape, rather than making it represent something else. However, the cube will have meaning as a solid shape and as a tactual experience if fabric is applied to it. Corduroy, velvet, burlap, etc., can be pre-cut to fit the milk carton sides. Students will paste these on with your assistance. Result: a sensory cube. This can be used repeatedly after it is made to teach simple discrimination between textural differences.

The mildly mentally retarded should be able to understand the meaning of making a house from a milk carton. Direct discussion of "Where do you live?" and "Who knows what a house looks like?" generally will bring the house concept into focus. Proceed with the core lesson, giving assistance when indicated.

Socially and Emotionally Disturbed

Open with some discussion about students' own neighborhoods. What kind of stores are near you? Are houses close together? Far apart? Ask students to think about houses or stores in their community when they create their houses. It is good if one student can create a shoe store, another a grocery store, etc. When all projects are completed, the group will display houses together as a community.

Learning Disabled

The basic shape of a house and its square dimensionality may not be understood clearly by students. It may help to demonstrate how the box shape is formed by dissecting a sample milk carton. Students can help reassemble it. The concept becomes more concrete through this "discovery" method.

Let students decorate milk carton walls, but be sure to discuss the placement of windows and doors. Why are they located where they are? Follow the core lesson for decoration.

Physically Handicapped

Materials should be laid out in an organized manner. (See "Adaptive Aids.") Small and loose items, such as cotton balls and macaroni, can be placed in shallow cups. This can make the lesson generally more accessible for physically handicapped students. The empty milk cartons are so lightweight that students may have trouble applying decorations to surfaces, so stabilize them by temporarily placing a heavy object inside, such as a paperweight, rock, etc.

Some students lacking fine motor control may require teacher assistance when applying the smaller parts, such as macaroni and cotton.

Sensory Losses

Hearing impaired—Show pictures of houses or, better yet, take students on a neighborhood walk. Observe and touch various wall surfaces, such as brick, stone, and stucco. Bring some paper to make simple sketches of different surfaces. Students will apply this information to their macaroni townhouse walls.

Be sure that students understand the steps of the lesson before you begin. Presenting a sample finished product would be helpful.

Visually handicapped—Blind students can use the screenboard for making textures on the paper that will go on the carton as walls. Other materials, such as sandpaper and aluminum foil, can be added to enhance tactual experience. These materials are close to real building materials (sandpaper feels like stucco and foil resembles aluminum siding).

Students with some sight will be able to draw brick and stone patterns. This is generally a very tangible project for the visually handicapped student.

Gifted

Ask each student to save several milk cartons. They will be asked to create a neighborhood using as much architectural variety as possible. Encourage students to make observations concerning their neighborhoods—the stores, buildings, schools, etc. In a city, students should look up because often architectural detail is above the storefronts.

Posterboard or panels of cardboard boxes are recommended for the base of these milk carton neighborhoods.

Mirror, Mirror on the Wall

MATERIALS

- Mirror squares, 8-by-10-inch, 9-by-12-inch or smaller
- Paper, 12-by-15-inch
- Cardboard that can be cut with scissors
- Sharp scissors
- Masking tape
- White glue
- Acrylic or poster paints
- Yarn
- Gesso (or substitute white paint)
- Braided picture wire for hanging
- Papier-mâché ingredients (see page 246)

TEACHER PREPARATION

When presenting this activity to young children or students with limited technical skills, production of frame parts is going to be *your* assignment. If older and more skilled students are available, enlist their assistance in precutting the frames. Exercise extreme caution with the glass mirrors—they often have sharp edges and are, of course, fragile. The mirrors are available as squares in variety stores, home improvement centers, discount stores, department stores, etc. If you can get wholesale manufacturers to donate mirror scraps, it's great, *but you, not the students, handle the mirrors!* If possible, use metal mirrors. You can substitute tinfoil or foil paper for real mirrors, but it's not the same thing. Go through the steps of this lesson before presenting it, perhaps stopping at the part where decoration will begin.

DIRECTIONS

Day One:

1. Show your students the sample that you prepared for demonstration pur-

poses. If you have not decorated the frame beforehand, do it with the students. (See Figure 89.)

Figure 89

2. Cut the oval pattern to be traced on the cardboard. First, fold the 12-by-15-inch paper in half lengthwise. (See Figure 90.) Then fold again into quarters. (See Figure 91.) Cut a curve along the outer edge and the inner edge as shown in Figure 92. Be sure not to cut the fold! Now open the cut paper to reveal your oval pattern. (See Figure 93.) If you are using lightweight board, you should do parts as *doubles*—two frame backs, two frame fronts. To use heavier boards, you have to be pretty handy with a mat knife, which is not recommended for student use.

3. Punch two holes in back for picture wire. Knot one end and thread through, then knot the other.

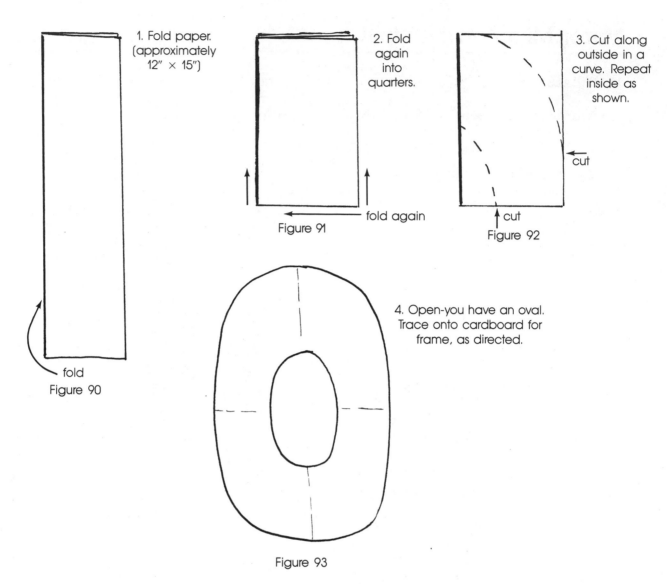

1. Fold paper. (approximately 12" × 15")

fold

Figure 90

2. Fold again into quarters.

fold again

Figure 91

3. Cut along outside in a curve. Repeat inside as shown.

cut

cut

Figure 92

4. Open-you have an oval. Trace onto cardboard for frame, as directed.

Figure 93

4. Glue to second back cardboard. Turn over, glue mirror down.

5. Glue frames to each other, mount with glue on top of each other.

6. Papier-mâché is next. Prepare according to the recipe. You might want to protect the mirror's surface with a piece of paper taped over it temporarily.

7. Begin laying newspaper strips onto frame. Build up; this provides the strength for the frame to support the mirror on the wall.

8. Let dry for at least 24 hours.

Day Two:

1. Gesso is painted on the frame. Allow 20 minutes drying time to each coat (one coat should be good enough).

2. While gesso is drying, students can sketch out design ideas on practice papers. Suggestions: simple patterns, hearts, rainbows, birds. Mirror can serve as the center of a flower; the frame, its petals!

3. Paint the designs on the dry frame. Squeeze out white glue in curvy patterns to add the yarn. Keep paints rich, avoid watery, weak color.

4. Let dry.

adaptations

Mirror, Mirror on the Wall

Mentally Retarded

You may want to begin with papier-mâché. Make sure that the mirror is secure; you should closely supervise students to avoid dropping mirrors.

Break down the steps of papier-mâché—it may take an entire lesson simply to tear the newspaper. Students can assist in mixing ingredients and in applying newspaper to frame. An approach to decorating the frame that carries over from the papier-mâché application is the fabric frame. White glue, thinned with water, is poured into a shallow cup for students to dip fabric scraps into before applying to frame. By building a variety of textures, students will be provided with sensory enrichment and a touchable, lively frame.

NOTE: The severely retarded student will require greater teacher intervention.

Socially and Emotionally Disturbed

Make sure students know how special this activity is and how you know that they will treat materials respectfully. Point out that mirrors are fragile and that you are sure they will be careful. If your students are too hyperactive or aggressive on the day that the lesson is planned, reschedule and let them do the sketches for the frame design instead.

Learning Disabled

Students will have a wonderful time—just make sure they understand the *sequence* of events. Showing the lesson sample and all the parts that led up to the finished product should help with perceiving the logical progression. The oval decoration is a good format for the concept of closure. Measure yarn (with students) that will fit the frame, with extra length for design. Squeeze out glue, starting the pattern at the beginning and bringing it all around the frame back to the beginning.

Physically Handicapped

Students with use of their hands can take this activity all the way through but others will want to start at step 6. Papier-mâché is a playful activity for the physically handicapped student, yet is also excellent for manipulative experiences. Great design ability is not a prerequisite for frame decoration—even simple patterns look fine. You might want to place mirrors onto easels or lean and prop securely against flat surfaces for easier decoration.

Sensory Losses

Hearing impaired—Demonstrate to make sure that students know what is expected of them. The demonstration should include a sample of each major stage of the frame's completion. Papier-mâché is a separate technique that must be clearly shown within its sequences.

Visually handicapped—Some students will be able to cut and prepare frames. Keep in mind that squares are sometimes easier to cut than other shapes. Blind students may be tactually defensive toward the papier-mâché, so ease them into it. For decoration, you can rely on the yarn design, tracing around and curling it. Yarn may be applied to glued surface or dipped in a container of glue and then applied.

Gifted

Your gifted students should be able to accomplish this lesson smoothly because of their ability to handle procedures with many steps. When they design their frames, the students should think in terms of a sculptural relief. For example, they can make a landscape and build up selected parts, such as trees and mountains, with papier-mâché. Art history books can provide inspiration for subject ideas; the early and classical periods should have good examples of relief works.

Mittens, Mufflers, Hats, and Gloves

MATERIALS

- Paper—Manila or white
- Paper—light oaktag
- Crayons
- Yarn
- String
- Scissors
- Spring-type clothespins

TEACHER PREPARATION

You and your students can bring actual winter gloves, mittens, etc. to class to examine patterns. You can precut the hat and scarf.

DIRECTIONS

1. What is a *pattern*? It is a repeated design, as on wallpaper. Ask students, "Who is wearing a pattern? Are there patterns in your house? Where?"

2. Present pattern samples. Talk about varieties of patterns.

3. Make enough paper available to carry out the parts of the lesson you want to tackle. You may want to sequence the lesson into parts such as gloves, hats, mufflers, etc. A "set" looks great.

4. For gloves, trace hands on paper and cut. Scarves can be measured on a straight fold. Scarves can be fringed with scissors. Hats can be drawn freehand (or also on a symmetrical fold).

5. Decorate. Hang "sets" or parts on a yarn clothesline for display. (See Figures 94, 95, and 96.)

Figure 95

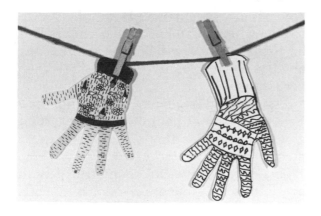

Figure 94

Figure 96

adaptations

Mittens, Mufflers, Hats, and Gloves

Mentally Retarded

Help your severely retarded students to make gloves by tracing their hands onto paper. Cut out. Offer fabric scraps for gluing onto gloves, which provides a sensory experience for students. To make sets, use same method and precut shapes.

For the mildly retarded, talk about change of seasons. These students should try "their hands" at doing their own outlining. Offer assistance in cutting sets.

Be sure to practice zigzag patterns, etc. before students begin their projects.

Mentally retarded students generally should be encouraged to hang their work on a clothesline—*they* should squeeze the clothespins (spring-type). This helps develop the pincer grasp.

Socially and Emotionally Disturbed

For a little fun, while prompting positive class interaction, try this: Each student designs a winter pattern on a 3-by-5-inch card. All finished cards are collected and the deck is shuffled. Each student picks a card (without looking). This becomes the pattern design for their set.

When all sets are displayed, hold a class discussion on how the students feel their original designs were interpreted.

Learning Disabled

Once the student has established a design motif, it will be used on all the clothing accessories (hat, gloves, scarf, etc.). Repeating the same pattern faithfully will require visual concentration. Establish linear pattern outlines and block in colors; this exercises fine motor skill.

Physically Handicapped

Do parts of the set that make sense for the student, that is, a student with severely contracted hands should do mittens, not gloves (since fingers cannot be easily outlined). When decorating, students with good motor control can create "stitchy" geometric patterns. Other students may want to paint instead.

Again, the manipulation of the spring-type clothespin is a good manual exercise.

Sensory Losses

Hearing impaired—To introduce this lesson, be a mime. Pretend to put on your gloves, your hat, and your scarf. Throw in a "br-r-r-r-" shiver for good measure. Present a complete, finished product ("set") before handing out materials.

Visually handicapped—Let your visually handicapped students do their own tracing when possible. Fluorescent crayons or paint creates a visually stimulating quality. Offer precut scarf or hat when necessary.

Assist blind students in tracing their hands on screenboard for gloves. Cut gloves out. Other items may need to be precut.

One way to present geometric pattern possibilities to students is to have students draw zigzags and other linear patterns in the air. This reinforces the pattern in a "moving" way. For blind students, you can further create pattern samples on the screenboard that students can feel. Yarn may also be used to demonstrate linear patterns.

Gifted

The world of woven fabrics and fibers can be examined through illustrations and example. Have students use crayons or markers in their work to reflect the look of "stitches." This gives the project a colorful, intricate appearance. Students can sew actual stitches into their flat work using light oaktag paper, light embroidery thread and sewing needles. Sewing will require good control in order to avoid tearing the paper. The gifted student should have no real problem with the skill and regard it as a challenge.

Mosaic Magic

MATERIALS

- Construction paper (several colors)
- Manila paper, 9-by-12, 11-by-18-inches
- Paste or white glue
- Scissors
- Thick marker
- Ruler
- Crayons
- Ceramic tiles (optional)
- Clay (optional)
- Cardboard or posterboard (optional)

TEACHER PREPARATION

Precut construction paper into strips. (Be sure to have uncut papers of contrasting color on hand for background.) The mosaic technique—the joining of smaller parts to form larger shapes and patterns—can be demonstrated in several ways: with small colored tiles (available from craft catalogues and tile stores), with cut paper squares, or with loose coins from your pockets! Simply move pieces together to create designs.

DIRECTIONS

1. What is a mosaic? Ask students if they have ever seen ashtrays, coffee tables, or floors made out of little colored tiles. Demonstrate mosaics with available materials. (See ''Teacher Preparation''.)

2. Have students pick a simple subject to use for mosaic design. Some suggestions are: boat, fish, fruit, face, animals, house, tree. NOTE: Mosaic technique does not lend itself to very fine details, so keep that in mind when designing subjects.

3. Practice ideas on Manila paper with thick markers; plot out color areas. (See Figure 97.)

4. Cut paper strips into squares as needed. Paste squares on to background paper until surface is complete. (See Figure 98.) NOTE: There is no "right" order to pasting down paper squares. Some students may start with tile outline, while others will start from any point. (See Figures 99 and 100.)

SUGGESTIONS FOR FURTHER DEVELOPMENT

Once a paper mosaic project is completed, *ceramic* mosaics are a cinch. Ceramic tiles may be fixed to wood or heavy board with white glue. Craft possibilities include trays, plaques, decorative boxes (e.g., cover-

Figure 97

Figure 98

Figure 99

Figure 100

ing a cigar box), mirror frames (see "Mirror Mirror on the Wall"), etc.

An alternative to buying tiles is making tiles. Roll out clay with rolling pin, use ruler, and cut out tiles with appropriate knife. Let clay harden and paint with acrylic paints.

Other materials that can be used for a "natural" mosaic are seeds, beans, stones, and shells.

adaptations

Mosaic Magic

Mentally Retarded

You can draw a simple shape with marker on paper for severely retarded students. Students then tear paper squares with hand-over-hand assistance. Use prompting and verbal cues about the shape (i.e., "We are putting our paper into a circle."). Some students may be able to use scissors (see "Adaptive Aids"). Students paste their torn paper "mosaics" into the "target" shape. Remember, paste may cause tactile defensiveness, so use the gradual approach.

Mildly retarded students can create their own mosaic using this plan: You precut (or assist students in cutting out) a simple object, i.e., a ball, a house, a tulip, etc. Cut paper squares of basic colors and place in trays for organization. Paste appropriate colored squares into the precut shape, then paste the precut shape down on the larger paper. Now paste other colored squares on the larger paper (which is blank) and you have a complete mosaic!

Socially and Emotionally Disturbed

It is important that your students carry through ideas from start to completion. "Mosaic Magic" lends itself to this process well. Ideas must be thoroughly thought through to succeed.

Students should try out several ideas before selecting one. Set up a color plan on practice paper, indicating each color group that is needed. Prepare colored squares to the plan and proceed.

Once students are involved with mosaics, it's like popcorn—you can't stop until you finish it all.

Learning Disabled

Learning disabled students could easily become confused by this lesson if it is not presented in the proper sequential order. To prevent confusion, try using graph paper (which is conveniently broken down into squares) for plotting out the mosaic design. It is a good idea to start with a strong outline of the shape, then block in the colored areas with crayons. Use the filled-in practice grid as a reference and pick out corresponding colors, then proceed with core.

Mosaics exercise eye-hand coordination as well as organizational skills and help with closure of contour.

Physically Handicapped

For students with reduced dexterity, mosaics provide an excellent fine-motor exercise. However, cardboard or posterboard mosaics would probably be easier to grasp than paper. This will mean precutting boards into small tiles for students. (Many paper cutters are constructed to handle the cutting of boards and save you time—otherwise mat knives or extra sharp scissors are in order.)

You may want some of your students to practice their scissor skills and cut their own paper squares (see "Adaptive Aids" for adaptive scissors). Once squares are cut, use cups or divided trays to hold colored squares, so that students can reach them and handle them with greater ease. Dividing by color is recommended.

Sensory Losses

Hearing impaired—Once the basics are understood, expand the project into a small group activity. Two or three students should plan a "wall" mosaic, using a length of butcher paper (2 feet to 3 feet). Outline the agreed-upon design (after sketching it first) and block in the tiles. The subject choice is open, but one suggestion is a class portrait, stressing the characteristic features of each student.

It is important to go through *all* the steps of this lesson. Even if it is not to scale, include a sample finished product.

Visually handicapped—Fluorescent or intensely bright paper would be exciting for visually impaired students to use as mosaics. Mix them in with construction paper squares, and offer fluorescent crayons to color white paper (before cutting into paper tiles).

For blind students, tiles can be cut from sandpaper, corrugated paper, oaktag, etc., to create a texture mosaic. These tiles can be cut from strips (you may need to assist with cutting). A shape may be precut on which students can apply tiles, or a yarn outline of a specific shape can be glued down to create boundaries for contour.

Students will need to place their nonworking hands on the last area where they worked for point of reference. This indicates to the students where further work needs to be done. Some guidance may be needed for logical placement of elements within students' design scheme.

Gifted

Mosaics have a rich history dating back to ancient times. Art history textbooks and encyclopedias should illustrate examples of mosaic art. Gifted students may enjoy the challenge of reproducing some early designs (e.g., Byzantine wall mosaics, Islamic tile patterns). Students' work should reflect various characteristics of tile work within specific periods, such as differences in shapes, sizes, and styles.

Nature Weave

MATERIALS

- Yarn (several colors)
- Ruler, pencils
- Scissors
- Cardboard (approximately 9-by-12-inches)
- Twigs or dowels
- Tape
- Feathers and other decorative pieces (optional)

TEACHER PREPARATION

Cardboard looms should be notched vertically about 1 to 1½ inches apart on both ends. You might want to precut yarn in desired lengths. Twigs will need to be collected for the cross bar on which weaving will hang. NOTE: If your students need an introduction to weaving, see "Weave a Turtle."

DIRECTIONS

1. Wrap yarn around *one* side of the cardboard. Start at first notch at top of cardboard (tape yarn to back side of loom); bring yarn down to notch at bottom opposite. Continue wrapping yarn to next notch from bottom to top. Repeat until you finish winding the yarn on all notches. (See Figure 101.) Tape end to back. This is called "warping" the loom.

2. For a closed weave simply follow the left-to-right, under-over—following with right-to-left, over-under technique starting at the bottom and working to the top. Yarn can be continuous from one line to the next. When you want to change colors, finish the yarn you are using by clipping it off through the back of the piece. Overlap new color where

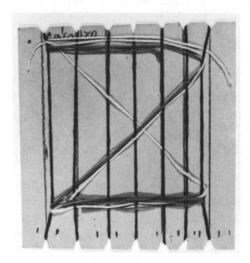

Figure 101

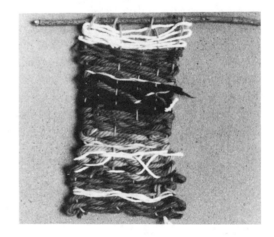

Figure 102

you stopped the last one. (See Figure 102.)

3. For an open weave (see Figure 103), set up the loom as you would for the closed piece. Weave yarn lengths randomly through the front of the loom in various directions, including diagonally. You can work section by section or in any free-form manner. Just make sure that some of the yarn goes all the way across the piece so that it holds it together. To ensure stability, a few straight rows can be woven across the top and the bottom.

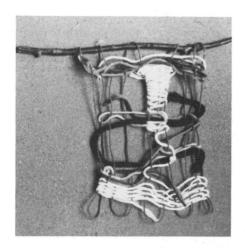

Figure 103

Figure 104

4. To remove piece from the loom, first trim and tie off loose threads. (NOTE: You may want to let yarn endings intentionally hang from front of piece for decorative purposes. They can be tied into tassels and cord, adding beads, shells, feathers, etc.) Next, insert twigs into loops, one by one. Gently lift weaving away from board (board may need some bending).

5. Hang on the wall. (See Figure 104.)

SUGGESTIONS FOR FURTHER DEVELOPMENT

Do you have any idea of how many objects can be converted into looms? Shoeboxes, cartons, wooden crates, twigs, cylinder drum container lids, wheels (without spokes), frames, cut cardboard shapes, upside-down chairs, even plastic soda straws (they can be used for belts). Professional weavers use large, standing looms. But beautiful weavings can be accomplished on just about anything you can string yarn on—there are lots of looms to make and to discover.

As for the fabric of your weaving, the possibilities for creativity are just as varied: gift wrapping ties, hair ribbons, silk cord, fabric scraps, socks, assorted trimmings (braiding, gimp, fringe) and lots of natural items (dry grasses, dried flowers, weeds, bark strips, bamboo shoots, etc.).

adaptations

Nature Weave

Mentally Retarded

In advance preparation for the lesson, you might gather fabric sample books. Look for books that have woven and textural material sample (with paper backings). Some sources for out-of-date sample books are upholstery shops, home decorating centers, furniture departments in stores, some larger fabric stores, and wallpaper stores carrying fabric wall coverings.

Precut strips of paper-backed fabric for your severely retarded students. These strips should be easier for students to grasp. Remove a full page sample for your "loom" (or use oaktag). Cut three or four slits into it. Using a few fabric strips, assist students in the hand-over-hand motion required for weaving (see "Weave a Turtle"). If you prefer to skip actual weaving, students can paste the strips directly onto cardboard. Assist with pasting and with applying strips, going from the bottom to the top (or vice versa). Use physical and verbal prompting about the directions your students are following (i.e., describe what you are doing while you are doing it). The motion that weaving provides is a good movement experience, but both approaches provide sensory enrichment. Feathers are a welcome addition in either case. Display where students can touch them.

Mildly retarded students should be able to follow the core lesson but will need the steps clearly outlined and demonstrated. If a nature walk is possible, it is a good opportunity to gather not only twigs, but possibly pods, bark strips, and other weavable natural things. In the classroom, all textural materials should be sorted into trays or boxes marked SMOOTH and ROUGH, or HARD and SOFT. Students can organize materials themselves, which adds to their learning experience.

Socially and Emotionally Disturbed

As pointed out in the introductory weaving lesson, weaving is a structured and involving activity for socially and emotionally disturbed students. In addition, to make the Nature Weave project more personalized, try this suggestion: the favorite color scheme. Ask students for their favorite colors and what it is about the color that they like. If students are not able to identify a favorite color, other possibilities are school colors, camp colors, even some flag colors. Students will select their yarn so that their weaving will clearly reflect their choices. Proceed with core.

Learning Disabled

Constructing the loom is a recommended way for learning disabled students to begin this activity. Rather than notches, or hammer and nails, try the clothespin loom. (See Figure 105.) Use a sturdy piece of cardboard or a wood board and wooden spring-type clothespins. Students will first measure and draw vertical lines about 1½ inches apart with ruler and pencil, going from left to right. The lines should be fairly even. Clothespins will be clipped on corresponding ends of the loom. Set up yarn by looping it over and around pins (tape ends to the back). Clothespins should fit board snugly so that they do not slip as student weaves the yarn. When work is completed, slip twig into the piece as directed and clip clothespins off the loom. NOTE: You can secure clothespins with tape, wrapping

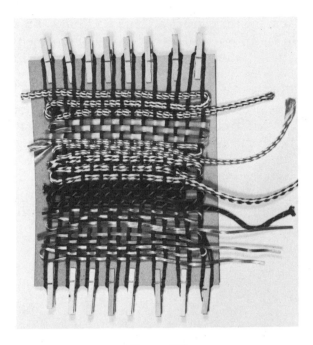

Figure 105

tape around the top and bottom. Loom will then need bending to remove piece.

You may also want your learning disabled students to try weaving a shaped cardboard loom. Create an oaktag template of simple shape—a fish, a flower, a heart, a standard kite shape, etc. Copy template onto cardboard and cut to make the loom. Weaving a specific contour should improve closure skills, while weaving is, in itself, an excellent eye-hand coordination exercise.

Physically Handicapped

The kind of loom that you will want your physically handicapped students to use will depend on their range of motion. Wooden crate looms can be placed in an upright position and may allow for a little more freedom of the "under-over" movement. You might want to experiment with different ideas for looms (see Suggestions for Further Development) but if you want to adapt the cardboard loom to students' needs, consider clamps, vice, and reading stands. Also, try using a shuttle. They are available in hobby stores and through art catalogues. But they can be simply made by notching a tongue depressor at both ends. Yarn will then be securely wrapped around the stick.

Weaving is a highly recommended activity for the physically handicapped. Using a flat loom of cardboard can help with finger dexterity. Larger, open looms also add exercise to the arms and shoulders.

Sensory Losses

Hearing impaired—Here are two ways to implement "Nature Weave" as a group activity with your hearing impaired students, once the steps of the lesson have been demonstrated.

First suggestion: Students will stitch their finished weavings onto a large felt banner. Shaped looms (see Learning Disabled) will yield a more varied visual effect. Skip the individual branches or dowels; instead, you will use a large wooden strip to hang the entire banner. (See "Flying Colors.")

Second suggestion: Make an ongoing group weave. Set up a frame or box loom in the classroom. At a designated time, each student will add their yarn lines to the piece. Each student should have a turn. When the work is done, it will truly have everyone's efforts woven into it!

Visually handicapped—Fluorescent (Day-Glo) and intensely colored yarns are available, often in yarn stores and variety stores. These, along with metallic yarns and trim, make visually stimulating weaving. Fabric strips and yarn can also be painted or dipped in fluorescent paint, but that does tend to make yarn stiff. Visually handicapped students can mix these bright and shiny materials with yarn in contrasting colors for a dazzling effect.

Blind students will need hand-over-hand guidance with their weaving. To help students tactually discriminate between the "over-under" lines, use one distinct texture for "over" (e.g., smooth), another contrasting texture for "under" (e.g., rough). You might want to use fabric strips in combination with yarn.

Gifted

Show your gifted students examples of the range of themes and styles of weaving. Pictures or real samples of tapestries and other woven cloths should stimulate ideas. Weaving magazines are an excellent source for this. Ask students to design a representational subject that would work well in the woven medium. Some suggestions are sunsets, landscapes, seascapes, and sand dunes. Students will want to plan their ideas and color schemes on paper before they begin to "weave a picture." Encourage students to experiment with open spaces and creative knotting techniques in their piece. They could also try threading the yarn through previously woven sections to build textures.

Our Native American Indians

MATERIALS

- Paper, all colors, including white
- Crayons
- Markers
- Paper circles
- Paper strips
- Wire
- Paste
- Scissors
- Thick yarn, brown and black
- Feathers (dyed turkey feathers are best)
- Beads (optional)

Wrap yarn around the top of a chair, and cut one (or both) side(s) to produce cut yarn lengths.

Figure 106

TEACHER PREPARATION

It's handy to precut the paper strips in bunches. You might want to pre-measure yarn by wrapping yarn around a chair and cutting the lengths. (See Figure 106.) Where do you get turkey feathers? Try a hobby shop if you don't live in a big city (where they actually have feather *stores*!). If you have no luck, precut the feather shapes and fringe them; it will be fine. You might want to keep paper waste at a minimum by offering paper that is precut to sizes the lesson requires (e.g., the bodice is about one-third the page).

DIRECTIONS

1. Discuss the unique style of American Indians. How can we recognize an Indian design? The distinctive geometric patterns? How about the artistic way they blend feathers, fringe, beads, etc. into clothing and jewelry?

2. Give out paper for the Indian portraits. Basic head/shoulders shape is cut.

Figure 107

3. Gather materials:
   - Braid yarn for hair.
   - Design paper-strip headband. Staple feathers to band and braided hair.

- Draw face. Paper strips can be used for face decoration.
- Make wire hoop earrings. "Pierce" ears (beads can be looped through wire).
- Create front of clothing from paper. "Fringe" with scissors.
- Add feathers and paper jewelry as discussed.

4. Mount completed Indian portrait on contrasting color paper and display. (See Figure 107.)

SUGGESTIONS FOR FURTHER DEVELOPMENT

This is a perfect companion lesson for "Thanksgiving Feast." You might even want to produce pilgrim portraits to make the scenario complete! NOTE: Parts of this activity can be developed as separate lessons. The headband can certainly be used as a costume effect, particularly at Halloween. The jewelry can lead to actual jewelry design projects, involving earrings and bracelets with feathers and beads.

adaptations

Our Native American Indians

Mentally Retarded

For the severely mentally retarded, provide precut portraits, paper strips, and paper circles. Assist students in pasting facial features (circles for eyes, strips for mouth and nose). Prompt verbally and physically. Color eyes, nose, and mouth to reinforce features.

Some severely retarded students may be able to braid. Gather yarn in a bunch. Student can manipulate yarn by "flipping" or twisting it. End can be secured by pipe cleaners. Decorate headband and staple braids onto it and add to Indian portrait.

Ask your mildly retarded students, "Where are your eyes, nose, mouth?" Have students put their hands on their own facial features as you point them out. Refer to precut paper portrait with same technique, pointing out features. Now, let students draw faces. Decorate as presented in core lesson, according to choice. Use the previous suggestion for braiding.

Socially and Emotionally Disturbed

Introduce the lesson as indicated in core, stressing design. Discourage any "wild Indian" references. In fact, this is a good opportunity for developing respectful attitudes toward Indian contributions to the American heritage. Get students away from the negative Indian stereotyping!

Students can pair up for "Indian Shadow Silhouettes" activity. First, sit students in chairs (about one foot from the wall). Attach paper to wall at each student's head level. Place lamp at head level (high intensity, if possible) on other side of student to create shadow. Light should shine directly on student to give proportional shadow image. Student should sit very still as "buddy" traces. They change places, then cut out the images and decorate. The Indian profile is actually the student's profile. Give Indian names such as Running Stripes and Little White Dots, based on their decorations and imaginations.

Learning Disabled

When you discuss placement of facial features, point out that portraits are flat interpretations of real three-dimensional faces. Students should put their hands to their faces to feel their facial bones.

To help understand the transition from flat to dimensional, make part of the portrait three-dimensional. A paper nose can be made simply from a folded paper triangle. Eyes can be made from folded paper circles; the mouth can be made from a folded oval.

If braiding is hard for your students to follow, yarn can be bunched and tied with pipe cleaners. (See Mentally Retarded section for other suggestions on braiding.)

Physically Handicapped

There are so many different lessons rolled up into this one, that you can pick and choose the parts your physically handicapped can do. For instance, students without much fine-motor control can paste the precut paper (circles, strips, etc.) on the precut portraits.

Braiding aids in fine-motor development. Clamp down bunches of yarn so that students can go through braiding. Stringing beads also fits into Indian portraits, which is an excellent exercise for the physically handicapped student.

Sensory Losses

Hearing impaired—You might want to do a little studying of Indian life. The way that Indians can communicate through smoke signals might be of some special interest.

Completed portraits can "talk" to each other via cartoon-type balloons. For instance, "I'm Princess Waterfall. Do you have any beads to trade?" A student can start with one message in his or her portrait; the next student will respond in his or her balloon—a visual "whispering down the lane."

If you are lucky enough to get hold of some tom-toms, your hearing impaired students will enjoy them! Drums are among the most easily heard musical instruments because of vibrations. NOTE: Make sure your students understand this lesson. Students must have some reading and writing skills to make talking "balloons."

Visually handicapped—A precut portrait will help to teach facial feature placement. Blind students may want to place the strips and circles to represent eyes, nose, and mouth. For fun and sensory enrichment, you could use fake fur for trim, buttons or bottle caps for eyes, folded triangles for noses, even macaroni for lips. Have blind students use their free hands as a guide to where they are working on the paper, particularly for cutting (avoid sharp scissors!).

Gifted

You can use "Our Native American Indians" as one aspect in a larger study of the decorative folk arts. Examples of African, Mexican, Chinese, and European—to name a few—could be discussed for similarities and differences.

One particularly fascinating area of folk art is body (facial) decoration. The Indians did paint their faces, as did many cultures. Children are intrigued by this art. *National Geographic* magazines are generally a good resource if you wish to pursue this exotic approach. You could extend lesson to include portraits of other cultures who use facial decoration, i.e., Japanese (Kabuki), North African (facial tattoos), African (ceremonial face paint), etc.

Over the Rainbow

MATERIALS

- Lightweight board or heavy paper
- Ribbon or string
- Markers, paint, crayons
- Scissors
- Dowels (approximately 12 inches) or coat hangers
- Hole puncher (optional)

TEACHER PREPARATION

You might want to precut the rainbow arch shape. You might also want to have paper squares and rectangles on hand for the clouds, stars, and so on.

DIRECTIONS

1. A discussion on rainbows should precede lesson. Just what are rainbows: When do they appear and why are they considered so special, so magical? What other elements can we use with them—e.g., stars, clouds, lightning?

2. Distribute materials.

3. Decorate *both* sides of all elements.

4. Punch holes at the tops of all parts. Attach string to elements and to dowel. You will need to experiment with placement to achieve the right balance. (See Figures 108 and 109.)

5. Ready for hanging? Windows that allow room for some rotation are perfect.

Figure 108

Figure 109

SUGGESTIONS FOR FURTHER DEVELOPMENT

Rainbows will really shine if you mix in foil paper. The best way to mount foil is to cut the desired shape *after* it has been glued to the paper.

You might also want to try creating mobiles out of baker's clay (see page 244) ornaments. Rainbows can be constructed from precolored and scented clay coils. (See Figure 110.) They are easy to make and perfect for mobiles. They can be hung with fish hooks (be careful!), paper clips, or Christmas ornament hangers.

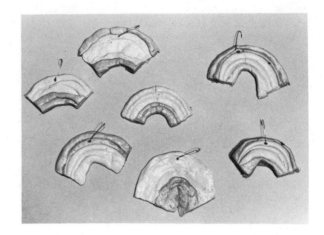

Figure 110

adaptations

Over the Rainbow

Mentally Retarded

Precut the rainbow arches for your severely retarded students. This lesson will involve fingerpainting on one side of the rainbow and crayoning on the other. Students will follow rainbow's arch with crayon; you can prompt student to use several colors. You will put out five cups of fingerpaint, each filled with a different rainbow color. With your help, student will dip each finger into a different color using all five fingers. Guide student's hand in painting the curve of the arch. Let dry and hang either on hanger or hanging freely, within student's view for visual stimulation.

Mildly retarded students can do the core lesson but may need precut rainbows. This is a good opportunity to teach and reinforce color. Provide an example of a rainbow that illustrates the colors and their order (this can be drawn on a black chalkboard in colored chalk, which has good contrast against the blackboard). Make sure, too, that students have some awareness of what a rainbow is.

Socially and Emotionally Disturbed

Your students can create mobiles with "messages," so they should make them a bit oversized. Paint bright bands of color and let dry. Write a personal response to each color on the mobile, following the band of color; e.g., "yellow is warm, it makes me feel good," etc. Messages can be different on both sides of the mobile. When mobiles are hung, students should have a chance to read and react to each other's remarks.

Learning Disabled

Make a demonstration rainbow, with colors in a given order. Ask your students to replicate the successive order of the colors on at least one side of their mobile.

The problem of the mobile's balance might be shown by giving students a heavy object (like books) to hold in one hand, then asking what the "other hand" feels like it needs. Follow core lesson for the rest of the activity.

Physically Handicapped

If you can get a chalkholder that is used for making fine lines on a classroom chalkboard, your physically limited students will have extra fun with their rainbows. Bright colored markers will replace blackboard chalks. Cut a rainbow surface, large enough for the span of the chalkholder. Students will control *all* colors at once with one movement, which should give them a sense of mastering the materials. NOTE: If a chalkholder is not available, experiment with punching holes (for markers or crayons) in a piece of cardboard to create the same effect.

Sensory Losses

Hearing impaired—Show illustration of rainbow or sample of finished lesson; verbally point out colors. The Sign Language Chart has colors listed; why not try signing them as well? Take students through the steps of the mobile's assemblage before attempting it.

Visually handicapped—You might use the rainbow to teach color concepts. Scented markers or flavored paints (see "Adaptive Aids") will help explain color to your blind students. If you choose to use the screenboard, give students the precut rainbows and have them follow the rainbow's curve in their designs.

Gifted

Rainbows can be multileveled mobiles. Students would benefit by studying the physical principles of more complex mobiles in order to construct them correctly. They should experiment with balance before launching into their final projects.

As an added attraction, students can visually "catch" a rainbow by using a plant mister near the window light. Rainbows will appear in the mist in a certain angle. This is as close as you are likely to get to a real model—unless a rainbow happens outside your window on cue with the activity!

Personality Plus Puppets

MATERIALS

- Pantyhose or nylon stockings (optional: acrylic or cotton socks)
- Fiberfill (or cotton stuffing)
- Sewing needles
- Thread (in colors to match stockings)
- Scissors
- Watercolor (or acrylic) paints
- Small brushes
- Fabric squares
- Yarn
- Miscellaneous decorations (sequins, feathers, buttons, etc.)
- White glue

TEACHER PREPARATION

Old pantyhose are worth saving for this lesson. If stockings have runs in them, position them away from the puppet's face. Cut stocking to high sock length (or use "half stockings"). Collect all sorts of materials for details—artificial flowers, feathers, fake fur, buttons, sequins, etc. Little beads can be sewn into mouth for teeth; wire can make convincing glasses. False eyelashes and plastic dolls' eyes are worth considering. You might also want to precut some fabric scraps for bowties, kerchiefs, and scarves. Also, you can precut cloth for puppet's fabric body shape. (See Figure 111.)

DIRECTIONS

1. Cut and stuff end of stocking. You can make a loose temporary knot at the "neck" to keep fiberfill in place.
2. Thread your needles.
3. Demonstrate technique: Pinch out nose. Sew *through* stocking to shape

Figure 111

nose and nostrils. Folds that look right for eyes and lips will appear as you pull and pinch the stocking. You will be manipulating the stocking as you make your artistic decisions.

4. Measure fabric square to fit hand. Cut.

5. Sew fabric, leaving openings on the sides for puppet's hands (the student's fingers), and top and bottom openings to slip puppet over hand.

6. Add details to puppet's head: hair, (yarn, cotton, or steel wool), jewelry, etc. Use paint to color lips, cheeks, and so on. (See Figure 112.)

7. When puppets are not being manipulated by student's hands, they can be "preserved" in mason jars! (See Figure 113.)

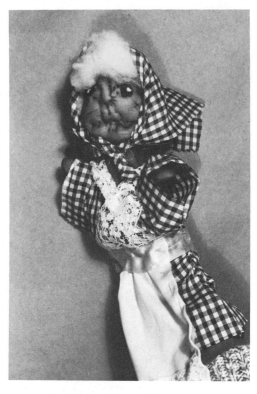

Figure 112

Figure 113

SUGGESTIONS FOR FURTHER DEVELOPMENT

You can use the stocking soft sculpture technique for many other projects in human, vegetable, or animal forms. Tiny soft sculptures can be made into jewelry such as pins and necklaces. Other soft sculpture can be sewn onto clothing as decorative details—they can add punch to belts, bags, and vests. If you want to stuff stockings on a grander scale, you can make oversized dolls. (See Figure 114.) Cut the "hips" part of the pantyhose to use as the head, using the same technique as outlined in directions for features. Head may be planted into a "stuffed shirt" (rags make economical stuffing) using an old T-shirt or blouse, as well as pants or shoes, if you want a whole person. Hands, legs, and feet can be made from stockings, too.

One final note of love for all puppets. Puppets are wonderful, whether they are made of clay, papier-mâché, or pantyhose. Even the modest paper bag puppet (see Figures 115 and 116) should not be overlooked for its potential charm when you combine it with enthusiastic students and lively scrap materials.

Figure 114

138

adaptations

Personality Plus Puppets

Mentally Retarded

You will need to assist severely retarded students in first stuffing the stockings. Help students to reach into stuffing bag in a hand-over-hand manner, gripping a handful of fill to stuff the stocking. Use verbal prompting to explain in simple terms what you are doing. If you wish to sew facial features as outlined in directions, you will need to use an extra large needle. You may want to create oversized puppet heads made out of the "hips" part of the pantyhose. The bigger size is easier to work with for severely retarded students. If you want to stuff stockings and avoid sewing, simply paste on faces and details of fabric scraps. Be sure all parts are secured to the puppet so that they will not detach when students play with them.

Mildly retarded students are capable of following the core lesson, but it will need to be broken down into steps. After stuffing, the sewing of the face is step number one, and students may need some help with threading needles (see "Adaptive Aids"), instruction on the way in which to sew puppets, *through* the stuffing from one feature to another. When puppets are completed, give them names—the students' own names or made-up ones.

Socially and Emotionally Disturbed

Puppets have long been regarded as an important tool in psychodrama—a way to acknowledge feelings without direct confrontation. It is your "character" that is saying he's hurt, angry, or afraid—not you. This is a nonthreatening way to express yourself.

Your socially and emotionally disturbed students should be able to follow the core.

Offer technical assistance at any point when needed to avoid blocks of frustration. Suggest that students give their puppets identities that will later be acted out in a puppet show. An empty large appliance box (check your neighborhood appliance and department stores) easily can be converted into a puppet theater. Painting and decorating the stage becomes a unifying group project around the puppet-making activity.

Learning Disabled

"Personality Plus Puppets" has several aspects that can be beneficial for your learning disabled students. Pinching out the eyes, nose, and mouth from a flat surface clearly demonstrates dimensionality of facial features—an often illusive concept. In fact, the entire project is related to body awareness, i.e., placement of parts and body movement. When puppets are completed and ready for play, you could use puppets to draw students' attention to body image and spatial awareness. For example, puppets can represent the class—you can do a puppet "Simon Says." "Puppets, put your right hand up. Puppets, bow your heads. Simon says jump." This is a pleasant way to use your finished artwork to learn important concepts.

Physically Handicapped

If your physically handicapped students have no pincer grasp for fine-motor skills, sewing puppet faces independently could pose a problem. Again, you can assist, and there are some adaptive aids that may help, but you might want to consider other methods for making your puppet. One good alternative is the sock puppet, which can be manipulated even with severe dexterity losses. Features and details of precut fabric scraps can be glued on sock directly. You may find that slipping the sock over a full plastic jar of poster paint makes gluing the parts on the puppet easier for the student. When sock puppets are completed, playing with them provides an excellent hand exercise.

Sensory Losses

Hearing impaired—If your hearing impaired students can read and can express themselves in writing, students can create a "closed caption" puppet show. You will need to make a puppet stage (see suggestions under Socially and Emotionally Disturbed). After all puppets are completed, students will create a simple written script for them, consisting of one or two lines. Students should probably work in groups of three or four. Using markers, students will write out the line(s) for their puppets on a long narrow strip of paper. Students will decide the order of each character's part within the group. When they present their play, papers with captions will be tacked to the front of the puppet stage as puppets act out their lines. You might want to appoint a "stage hand" to assist with the production. Also, it would be good to have a student stand next to the stage to "sign" the parts.

Consider presenting the play to the rest of the school. It would be a valuable social outreach experience for your hearing impaired students.

NOTE: Make sure students are aware of the technical requirements of the activity. Demonstrate the steps!

Visually handicapped—Visually handicapped students may need some assistance with threading needles (see "Adaptive Aids"), and with some of the finer details. But basically, they should be able to follow the core lesson. They will enjoy both the dimensional and tactual nature of the activity.

Blind students will clearly need help with sewing, but they can manage details well. They too will respond to the tactual qualities of the materials and their manipulation. To add yet another sensory dimension, try this: Bring in samples of shaving lotion, perfume, and suntan oil. These fragrances will help form puppets' identities. Shaving lotion, male; perfume, female; suntan oil, bathing beauty (male or female). Smells form strong associations! Puppets' characterizations will be formed by details that students create. The fragrances they choose will help describe their puppets' identities and make them a little more concrete. Animating the puppets through play will help bring them to life.

Gifted

How about a group project for puppets? The challenge to be met by your gifted students is to create a puppet society or civilization. It can be an ancient, modern, future, or imaginary society. Students will have to decide in a group (or with a few small groups) on what they want to do. Once a society is established, puppets will be created to fill positions within the social structure. For instance, suppose the group decides on Ancient Egypt. You will need Pharoah puppets, king and queen puppets, slave puppets, etc. You might even want specific historical figures represented by puppets, such as Cleopatra or King Tut. You might even want to include "non-people" puppets like animals, idols, or birds.

Selecting or inventing a society in which puppets have their place will take research and discussion. Special materials might be needed (as in the case of Egypt, gold acrylic paint and metallic cloth) for authentic touches. Gifted students should also be expected to design a puppet theater that is compatible with their theme. When all is finished, present a play. A good title around which all themes could fit would be "A Typical Day in (you name it)."

Pieces of the Sky

MATERIALS

- White paper
- Brown butcher paper
- Acrylic or tempera paints
- Brushes, all sizes
- Scissors
- Paper towels
- Cups or containers
- Glue

TEACHER PREPARATION

This is a mural lesson that can be done with several students at once, or just one to a paper. This decision will determine what size you cut the brown paper. For larger surfaces, keep flat paintbrushes on hand. Plastic cups or containers should be available for mixing colors.

DIRECTIONS

1. How does the sky look at different times of day and in different weather conditions? See how many sky "changes" students can name.

2. Students select colors appropriate to their choices. Encourage the mixing of pastel tones for sunsets, clouds, etc.

3. Paint large area with big brushes. (See Figure 117.) For "sky details" such as stars, birds, snowflakes, etc., students can paint them into their work directly or create parts separately on another paper, cut, and apply to mural.

NOTE: This is an excellent subject for studio painting (on canvas with acrylics). It is colorful and "loosens up" the hand.

SUGGESTIONS FOR FURTHER DEVELOPMENT

The sky is blue? Who said so! The sky is also pink, orange, purple, gray, and black—and is often in multicolored combinations. (See Figure 118.) Skies can be painted loosely and freely in the style of "action" painting. They can be treated like Monet's "Waterlilies," a sum of color parts (dots, dabs, etc.). Or they can be graphically designed for clean-cut, dramatic contrast. The sky's the limit!

Figure 117

Figure 118

adaptations

Pieces of the Sky

Mentally Retarded

Painting in a big, loose manner is both a kinesthetic and sensory experience. Your severely retarded students will enjoy painting "Pieces of Sky," using shaving cream brushes. They are easier to handle and require less fine-motor skill. Offer hand-over-hand assistance when necessary. When painting is complete, glue on "cotton clouds" for further tactual enrichment.

Mildly retarded students are capable of understanding the relationship of the subject (sky) to what they are being asked to do (paint the sky). Use the view from your window or go outside, if possible, to make experience more concrete; e.g., what does the sky look like *today*?

If you plan to use pastel (or mixed) colors, you will need to instruct students clearly on *how* to mix them. This is the kind of lesson that lends itself to teaching color blending. Proceed with core.

Socially and Emotionally Disturbed

This is a natural for a multiple group activity. The entire group should decide on one theme, e.g., times of day, seasons, weather conditions. Once that is determined, smaller groups of three or four will carry out the aspects of the bigger theme. For example, if the theme is "weather," one small group does "rain," another does "snowstorm," and so on. Within each group, students decide who wants to do details. This approach teaches cooperation within the larger groups as well as within the closer, interpersonal one.

Learning Disabled

Students should enjoy a lesson that is as open and unstructured as this one—and one that is free from organizational demands. Students still need to think about covering the paper in a logical manner, i.e., composing the space effectively, using the materials to express their ideas successfully.

Physically Handicapped

The big broad movement that painting "Pieces of Sky" affords is a healthy exercise for those with the range of motion to do it. For those with greater restriction of motion, try using a shelf paper roll in a tear-off dispenser. (If it does not come with one, see if you can find a wax paper or foil paper dispenser that will work.) Use double-faced tape to secure dispenser to the left or right side of work surface, leaving enough paper out for student to start work. As student paints (or draws with oil pastels), he or she can pull fresh paper to continue in the mural size panel until complete. NOTE: You may need to assist in pulling paper from roll and in finding the most convenient placement of paper on the desk for the student.

Sensory Losses

Hearing impaired—An intriguing way to do this lesson with your hearing impaired students is to create a giant puzzle! Students will develop, as a group, a big sky mural. Another piece of butcher wrap is cut to the same size as the first. The finished painted sky is cut into large puzzle pieces when dry, then scrambled up. The class must put it back together on top of the other cut butcher paper (rolled masking tape on the back of the puzzle pieces will make puzzle stick to uncut paper). This all needs to be demonstrated, even in a smaller sample size, before the project begins. It is a project that benefits hearing impaired students by combining play with creativity while encouraging positive student interaction.

Visually handicapped—Visually handicapped students will enjoy using fluorescent paints. These can be used in combination with the poster paints to create a dazzling visual effect. Sunsets would be particularly dramatic.

Blind students may have some difficulty with the concept of a sky. It is not a tangible object. You can talk about weather, the smell of the air when it rains, and most importantly, the spatial expanse of the sky, which students can relate to when they stand in a large open space without nearby walls.

Blind students, too, will enjoy the pure sensory enjoyment of painting "big," but you may want to add texture to the paint (e.g., sand) for variety.

Gifted

Your gifted students might be interested to discuss how cloud formations and sky conditions are used to predict the weather. It would be fun to learn about skies—researching what cloud patterns can mean and using that information in painting "Pieces of Sky." When work is complete, the class can become "weather reporters" and "read" each other's work for probable forecasts!

Another direction for this lesson is "celestial bodies." Paintings that include the stars, the planets, and the constellations would definitely be out of this world!

Pizza to Go

MATERIALS

- Paper large enough for at least a 9-inch circle
- Markers
- Crayons
- Scissors

TEACHER PREPARATION

Here's how to make the pizza:

1. Cut a square to the size you want.

2. Fold in quarters, then fold again for "slices."

3. Cut as shown in Figure 119. Open the paper to reveal the "pizza." (See Figure 120.)

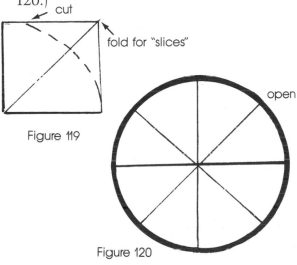

Figure 119

Figure 120

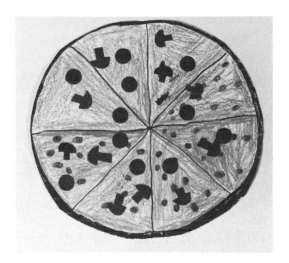

Figure 121

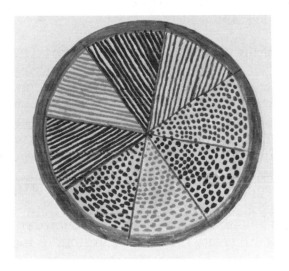

Figure 122

DIRECTIONS

1. Be a waitress or waiter and take orders. After students state their favorites, ask them to name as many pizza toppings as they can: pepperoni, mushrooms, sausages, etc.

2. Cut out pizzas.

3. With a dark marker, delineate *crust* and *slices.*

4. Add "the works." (See Figures 121 and 122.) Serve!

SUGGESTIONS FOR FURTHER DEVELOPMENT

Do you need to be convinced of the overwhelming appeal of this lesson? You might consider turning a corner of your classroom into a temporary "pizza parlor" to display the pizzas. (You could put brown paper up as the "window," and give the pizza parlor its name.) Tomato pies are really loved, but if you want to turn the lesson into apple pie (or blueberry pie) then do it!

adaptations

Pizza to Go

Mentally Retarded

Precut mushroom slices out of brown construction paper. Red paper circles can represent pepperoni; yellow corrugated paper can be your cheese. Help your severely retarded students to paste these parts onto their pizzas, with verbal cueing as you progress.

Mildly retarded students can search magazines for photos of appropriate food for pizza toppings. They can cut out illustrations, with your assistance when needed, and paste.

Socially and Emotionally Disturbed

Because this activity is exciting, don't overdo your presentation! Students will be asked to create a giant pizza, which will contain a combination of everybody's favorite toppings. You can do several oversized pizzas or one enormous pizza, depending on class size and available classroom space.

When pizza is completed, encourage students to create their signatures out of topping, e.g.,

TIMMY

(in pepperoni)! Display finished product in a prominent place in the school.

Learning Disabled

Have students trace the circle that is the pizza shape. Clearly instruct students in method of folding pizza into slices (see Teacher Preparation), and assist when necessary. Draw lines on folds to indicate slices. Students then cut along line to "cut slices" out. They have just made a "pizza

puzzle." If desired, students can paste pizza slices back onto white paper. You might want to help students with their understanding of the parts (slices) to whole (pie) relationship by using the "fraction" approach, i.e., a slice is $\frac{1}{8}$ of the pizza.

Physically Handicapped

Some physically handicapped students have cutting skills but need practice. The pizza is a perfect exercise for staying on the lines of the slices and cutting the slices out. Once slices are cut, students can paste them onto a larger circle that they will cut. That will be the pizza plate. Decorate pizzas as outlined in the core lesson.

For those students with less dexterity, precut pizzas and decorate with finger paint using "pizza colors" such as orange, red, and yellow. For decoration, dip string into white glue and drape around pizza (it resembles cheese). Add paper circles for pepperoni if desired.

Sensory Losses

Hearing impaired—Save a frozen pizza carton to show students that they will be making a pizza. Present the pizza circle, and indicate that the students will decorate it. Provide colored construction paper that students will cut for toppings. You may want to look up sign language color names (see the Sign Language Chart) and "sign" colors with students.

Visually handicapped—Do you know that pizza cutters and tracing wheels are almost the same tool? (See "Adaptive Aids.") Blind students enjoy using tracing wheels, and they are perfect for the imaginary slicing of pizza. Students enjoy the movement of the wheel on the paper. Tracing wheels can be used in combination with crayon on the screenboard to decorate the overall surface. NOTE: A curved line (such as the crust) is hard to do with tracing wheels. The more sighted students may want to cut out toppings and paste them on the pies. They can share their mushrooms, pepperonis, etc., with the blind students.

Gifted

Not only can gifted students create fabulous pizzas but they can also make pizza boxes. Bring in a take-out box as a sample. Supply class with paper of suitable weight and size. Students can look at the sample box, then figure out how to construct their own. Students can design logos for their pizza boxes, which brings in possibilities for a unit on advertising art.

Pocket Planters

MATERIALS

- Wet red clay
- Rolling pin
- Tape
- Containers for water
- Ruler
- Tongue depressors
- Wire or string
- Burlap
- Newspaper
- Optional:
  Clay tools
  Old shirts (smocks)
  Toothbrushes
  Dried flowers (baby's breath, penny plants, etc.)

TEACHER PREPARATION

(See "Clay Pots: Pinch and Coil" for advance preparations.) NOTE: You may want to precut burlap into 8-by-12-inch pieces and tape to work surface in advance.

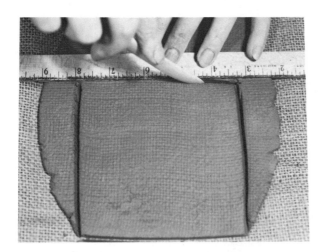

Figure 123

DIRECTIONS

1. Give students a chunk of clay about the size of a grapefruit, and a piece of burlap. Tape burlap to work surface.

2. Students will roll out clay with a rolling pin on top of the burlap. They will need two slabs to form the "pocket." Use tongue depressor (or clay tool) and ruler to cut appropriate matching shapes. (See Figure 123.) Squares are recommended, but other shapes can be used.

3. Wet and score inside edges of the two clay tiles. Fold a wad of newspaper (see Figure 124.), and make a "sandwich"— two "slices" of clay, newspaper in the middle. (See Figure 125.) Pinch along the three sides of the clay tiles to join the two sides. (See Figure 126.)

4. Pierce a hole in tile for later hanging. (See Figure 127.)

5. When thoroughly dry, carefully remove newspaper. Thread wire or string through the hole. Place dry materials inside and hang on the wall. (See Figure 128.)

Figure 124

Figure 125

Figure 126

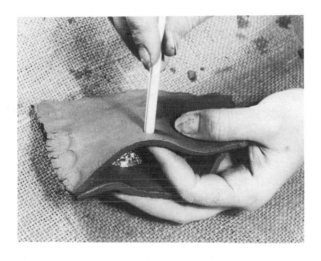

Figure 127

Figure 128

SUGGESTIONS FOR FURTHER DEVELOPMENT

In creating pocket planters, you have learned the slab method. Slab, along with the pinch and coil, is among the most versatile techniques in hand-built ceramics. Slabs readily become tiles and plaques. Slabs can also be wrapped around and over existing bowls, vases, and cardboard molds to create new replications of the object. It is also the slab technique that is best suited for making clay boxes.

Slabs deserve lots of experimentation. They make tall, sturdy vessels and can be combined easily with other hand building methods.

adaptations

Pocket Planters

Mentally Retarded

Severely retarded students will need your assistance in rolling out the clay. Show students how to use the rolling pin in a hand-over-hand manner. Both the severely and mildly retarded students may want to use a one-piece slab to create their pocket planters. Slab should be of a longer shape to accommodate the double-sided fold. Place the newspaper in the middle and fold clay slab over. Student will pinch the sides of the clay together or press one finger against edge to close the pot. Let dry as directed.

Retarded students should enjoy the novelty of pushing the rolling pin, and it is also a good exercise for the hands and arms. Severely retarded students might want to use another kitchen device on their clay slabs—the cookie cutter. Encourage "people" shapes; gingerbread men are perfect. Assist student in stamping out a man; use a dull pencil to create features on the face. Physical and verbal prompting should take place as the cookie man is coming to life (i.e., "Here are the eyes, here's the mouth, etc.") Decorate pot with cookie cutter shape. You may need to help with attaching the forms.

Socially and Emotionally Disturbed

Consider taking your socially and emotionally disturbed students on a fresh-air adventure that will expand their daily experience. Turn your students into makeshift archaeologists, and the nature walk will become a mock "dig." Collect nature items such as stones, leaves, twigs, and pods. See also what artifacts of man-made civilization you can find: bottle caps, empty matchbooks, keys, pens, etc.

(NOTE: Supervise the "found" objects so that they appear reasonably safe and clean. You may even want to "plant" some items along the trail in advance for students to uncover later such as broken clocks, furniture coasters, jar lids, etc.)

Back in the classroom with the collection of items—what happens next? You create *instant fossils*. Roll clay out directly on work surface (skip the burlap). Press objects into the clay and encourage sharing. Follow the core as directed.

Learning Disabled

The pocket planter as presented in the core requires matching and measuring. Learning disabled students often need reinforcement in these areas. It might be a good idea to use a cut oaktag or cardboard template for slab shape. Place on top of clay and cut clay out with tool. Pull clay away from work surface. Follow with core.

You might want students to do other projects based on the slab and pattern principle. Try the hot plate. Students can design a simple shape out of oaktag—apple, fish, house, etc.—and cut out clay as described above. Roll out clay slab and cut. Push away excess clay and pull the paper off the clay. Decorate surface. Let dry. You have a wonderful gift for the right person! (These can easily be converted into wall plaques. Just remember to perforate a hole for hanging while clay is wet.)

Physically Handicapped

If students have the range of motion that is required to operate a rolling pin, it is an excellent exercise. Pressing the object into the clay to create textures is not a physically difficult movement, and it is something that students enjoy doing. Offer clay tools to students who are very limited physically. It is sometimes easier to use a tool to accomplish a task, such as closing the seam between the two sides of the planter. Students who cannot pinch the clay will want to press the seam closed with a tongue depressor (a one-piece foldover slab is suggested, instead of two pieces).

Even students with limited dexterity can make "a dozen long-stemmed colored tissues." Students can crush colored tissues into flower "balls" (another good hand exercise). Stems are made of pipe cleaners poked through tissue to hold in place (you might need some tape inside flower). Plant colorful flowers into pocket planters; it makes a dazzling array!

Sensory Losses

Hearing impaired—It is always a good idea to help the hearing impaired student to develop language skills. Bring in some poetry books that include nature themes. Haiku (short Japanese verse) is perfect. After demonstrating technique (skip burlap), provide students with books to choose poetry from. Demonstrate by picking one line from a poem and inscribing it in the clay with a suitable tool (clay must not be too wet). Draw a compatible motif (flowers, stars, clouds, etc.).

Of course, students have to know how to read to do the activity in this manner. If they don't, follow core as directed. Make sure students understand the lesson in either case.

Visually handicapped—Clay slabs receive textural impressions beautifully. Visually handicapped and blind students particularly can enjoy and learn from this characteristic of clay. Kitchen tools make a

great "impression." Try out utensils: forks, spoons, egg beater, whisk, meat tenderizing hammer (less common but terrific is the Swedish rolling pin).

Both visually handicapped and blind students will enjoy using these objects in the clay to create new textures and patterns. They will also delight in using the rolling pins. Blind students may require some guidance as to the location of the water cups, the objects, and the boundaries of the clay. Direct student's hand when needed.

One more object that is suggested for clay impressions: the alphabet block. Pressing letters into the clay makes a playful and appealing design, but also helps the younger sight-impaired student with identifying the alphabet.

Gifted

The planters themselves can grow and grow, and grow, in the hands of gifted students. Students should be shown the basic lesson, then asked how they could make planters with additional pockets. Smaller slabs attached to wall of clay slab will do it. Pockets can go on top of pockets or students can create a clay "shoe bag." The challenge is to create a greater design complexity out of a simple basic idea. When dry flowers are planted in all the many pockets, the effect is quite charming.

In addition, students should give thought to decorating clay surfaces. They may want to treat slabs like tiles and use a *different* texture for *each* pocket's surface. Some suggestions are shells (nutshells and seashells), rubber bands and clips, lids, string—the choices are endless. Don't forget your own hands, knuckles, or nails. Pictorial rubber stamps, if available, are quite "impressive!"

The Pop-Up Dozen

MATERIALS

- Egg cartons
- Paper
- Paint
- Paintbrushes
- Crayons
- Markers
- Scissors
- White glue
- Cotton (optional)

TEACHER PREPARATION

Each student brings in an empty egg carton or you can start an egg carton drive. They are a snap to collect because just about everyone has them readily available. (If you have a cafeteria, it is a perfect place to start collecting.)

You may want to precut paper rectangles and squares proportioned to the egg cups and the carton's inside lid if your students do not have scissors skills.

DIRECTIONS

1. What are the signs and symbols of Easter? Bunnies, carrots, jelly beans, baskets—and the egg. One or more of these choices will be used as the "pop-ups" for the egg cups.

2. Students choose any of the above, color them, and cut them out. (See Figure 129.) Leave a tab of paper at the bottom for gluing to the egg cups.

3. The greeting of "Happy Easter" or "Happy Spring" can be written decorating on paper and glued to inside of lid.

4. Cotton or cellophane grass can be added inside the cups for a more festive look. (See Figure 130.)

SUGGESTIONS FOR FURTHER DEVELOPMENT

The egg carton is an object that seems to invite craft projects. If you brainstormed, you could probably come up with egg carton activities that range from sculptural constructions to Christmas tree ornaments. Here is one suggestion that can work well with special students: egg carton garlands. Create these by tearing egg cups away from the carton. Pierce a hole in the center of the cups, and thread length of wire through (like stringing beads). This is an excellent eye-hand coordination task—and good sewing orientation.

NOTE: The egg carton can be admired for its own unique design. Egg cartons can be painted or decoupaged to make terrific gifts such as sorting boxes (clips, pins, tacks, etc.) for the home or job.

Figure 129

Figure 130

adaptations

The Pop-Up Dozen

Mentally Retarded

For your severely retarded students, concentrate on decorating the carton itself. Tear colored tissue and assist students in pasting tissue on carton. When cartons have been decorated, it would be gratifying to offer a "treat" in them (such as raisins) to students—in containers they have made themselves.

Socially and Emotionally Disturbed

Students can work as partners on the egg carton, with each responsible for one half dozen. After everyone has been paired up either through mutual consent or teacher assignment, explain how they must take time to discuss how they want to blend their ideas. For example, one student does six rabbits, one does six carrots. When projects are completed, students will get one-half of the carton, which reflects the merging of both their ideas. Since you have emphasized the socialization process in this presentation, give lots of positive reinforcement and praise for appropriate behavior.

Learning Disabled

Try an *assembly line* for the "packaging" of the cartons. Pop-ups will be pasted in egg cartons in sequence as they are passed from student to student. One student may be the "packaging manager" and help to decide how many cartons will be produced. This approach forces students to think in terms of a process. Also, there is the value of working together toward a unified whole.

Physically Handicapped

Some students have poor coordination and cannot work small areas like precut eggs. If that's the case, you can let students paint a broad area and when paper dries *then* cut egg shapes. Help students to assemble eggs in cartons—or substitute cotton puffs (or crushed tissue balls) for eggs.

Sensory Losses

Hearing impaired—Draw some suggestions for pop-up ideas on the chalkboard (rabbits and so on). Give students the paper to draw their own pop-up ideas. Make sure they know how many they will need, the design specifics, and how the project should look. Show example of finished product before you begin.

Visually handicapped—If you can pass around a hard-boiled egg for exploration, students will better understand what the precut paper eggs represent. Using the screenboard, students can create patterns on the eggs. They may want to paste some colored tissue on eggs to add extra decoration. Blind students may want to braille their Easter message for the inside of the egg carton lid.

Gifted

Gifted students can treat this project as a 3-D greeting card. Humor can be brought to the pop-ups in large doses. How about "funny bunnies"? Students can create a dozen rabbits dressed in bonnets and top hats, popping up in a chorus line. If students want a more up-to-date approach, do disco bunnies sound like fun?

Pretzels

MATERIALS

- Manila paper
- Large sheets of brown butcher wrap paper, about 2-by-3 feet
- Markers
- Crayons
- Scissors
- Newspaper
- Stapler

TEACHER PREPARATION

The most solid introduction to this lesson would be a clay activity. Students roll out clay "snakes" and create a pretzel (see "Clay Pots"). This shows how pretzels are formed from one piece. To precut the paper pretzel for students, you need only to cut along the outside contour. Negative space can be cut later.

DIRECTIONS

1. Students can use one large folded sheet of brown paper or two sheets of the same size.

2. Practice drawing a smaller pretzel before attempting the full-sized outline. (See Figure 131.)

3. Draw pretzel shape to edges of paper. Decorate. Cut negative spaces with scissors. (*Negative space* refers to space that is *not* part of the concrete object. It can occur between, within, or around the object.)

4. Staple and stuff with newspaper that has been crushed into small balls. (See Figure 132.) NOTE: You will be stapling and stuffing *portions* of the pretzel until it is all stuffed. Many students will need some assistance with the stapling and stuffing.

SUGGESTIONS FOR FURTHER DEVELOPMENT

In Philadelphia, Pennsylvania, putting mustard on pretzels is a tradition. If your students can think of other possible garnishes, let them decorate the pretzels with their ideas.

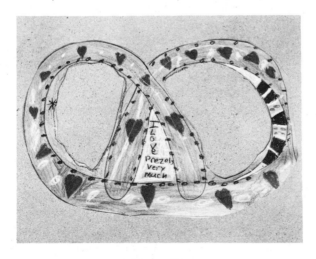

Figure 131

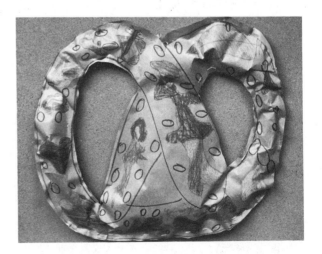

Figure 132

adaptations

Pretzels

Mentally Retarded

Severely retarded students should explore the basic pretzel shape by examining pre-cut pretzel forms. Help students draw on shape, following the pretzel configuration. Make newspapers available so that students independently can locate them. Have students tear and crush newspapers. Offer aid when necessary, especially in stapling and stuffing. Hang completed pretzels within students' view; this creates an interesting visual activity.

For the mildly retarded, use a clay introduction to pretzel shapes. By using clay "snakes" to create clay pretzels, students will become familiar with the unique pretzel shape. In addition, students can physically imitate pretzel curves with their arms and legs! Continue with the regular directions for paper pretzel.

Socially and Emotionally Disturbed

What's your favorite kind of pretzel: crispy or soft? Get students involved, then ask them to "cook up" their own unlikely specialties. Decorations for pretzels could include cherries, stars, whipped cream, etc. Hence, pretzels become students' own creations, i.e., "Bill's star-studded pretzels," "Mary's deluxe pretzel model," and so on.

Learning Disabled

Draw pretzel shape as a model for students' reference. After they draw and cut shape, students can decorate by using a design that basically duplicates the pretzel's configuration. Flowing linear patterns that repeat the pretzel's shape will improve students tracking and closure skills. Staple and stuff to complete.

Physically Handicapped

Try to do the clay introduction (see Teacher Preparation). Have students with arm mobility draw their own pretzels on a stable surface; others may opt for precut pretzels. Tearing the newspaper and crushing are good movement exercises for the physically handicapped students.

Sensory Losses

Hearing impaired—Students can "pair up" for this activity. Explain clearly and draw a pretzel on the board. Students will share the designing, cutting, and stuffing of the pretzels. This makes a nice opportunity for communication between students.

Visually handicapped—If you don't do the clay introduction (as appears in Teacher Preparation) then bring some real pretzels to class. Students can feel their shapes (and later devour them!) Precut pretzel shapes with the negative parts cut out will be helpful in better understanding the project. For a 3-D touch, the "salt" could be paper fasteners, Styrofoam packing chips, or even sugar cubes. (Paper fasteners should be inserted before stuffing.)

For body awareness, students could also imitate pretzel shapes with their arms and legs.

Gifted

Why not make a mock pretzel vending business? You could construct a vending cart out of cardboard cartons to display the pretzels.

Another approach that engages abstract thinking is to ask students to identify other "pretzel" configurations that are not food; for example, highway ramps, figure skating on ice ("figure eights"), etc.

Reflections

MATERIALS

- White crayons or white pencils
- Black paper
- Mirrors (portable sizes)

TEACHER PREPARATION

If it is not possible to provide each student with a mirror, students can share mirrors. Remind students to handle mirrors with care! If available, use metal mirrors.

DIRECTIONS

1. Students may study their images in the mirrors. Observe individual characteristics such as hair style and texture, size and shape of features, etc. (See Figure 133.)

2. Draw self-portrait with white crayon or white pencil on black paper. (See Figure 134.)

3. Selectively develop areas that further describe details. (See Figure 135.) Block in details with white crayon as you would with a black pencil on white paper. (See Figure 136.)

Figure 133

SUGGESTIONS FOR FURTHER DEVELOPMENT

This approach to self-portraits allows students to study their own faces. However, self-portraits that are created solely from the mental image that students have of themselves can be just as revealing. Mirrors provide a reference and are fun to use, but should not necessarily dictate a standard for perfect duplication of reflected images on paper.

To develop compositions around self-portraits, ask students to think about a compatible environment—either reflected or imaginary.

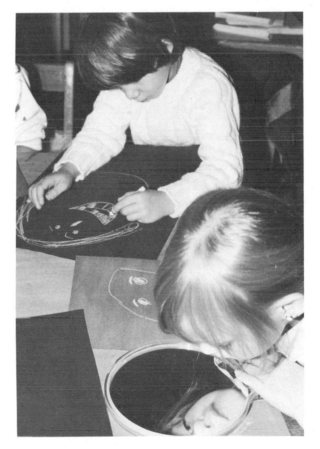

Figure 134

Figure 135

Figure 136

adaptations

Reflections

Mentally Retarded

Severely retarded students will need teacher assistance for reflected self-portraits. Hold mirror so that student can see his or her face. With free hand, engage student's hand and place his hand on facial feature *with verbal prompting*, i.e., "Joey's eyes, Joey's nose, Joey's mouth," etc. Put down mirror and introduce black paper. In a hand-over-hand method, guide student in outlining shape of "portrait" on the paper. Further guide student in drawing simple representations of facial features. Continue verbal cueing. To create a sensory quality and a touch of realism, you can add yarn or fake fur to represent hair.

Mildly retarded students will need reinforcement regarding the placement of facial features when looking in the mirror. Remind students that eyes are in the middle of the face, nose between eyes and mouth, mouth near the bottom, at the top is the forehead, at the bottom is the chin. Follow core as directed.

Socially and Emotionally Disturbed

What is a portrait? Is it merely a visual account of a person's face? A report on the particular order in which hair and facial features are arranged? Portraits can do more than report facts; they can reach into the character and express the personality.

Your socially and emotionally disturbed students should be encouraged to observe their faces in the mirror and try to show many different expressions. To create them, students should think of specific incidents or feelings that make them feel happy, relaxed, or angry. Ask them to describe what happens to their faces when moods change (i.e., cheerfulness—eyes open wide, corners of mouth turn up, posture straightens). Students select the mood they want to capture by "posing" for themselves in the mirror.

Another way to explore moods is to do multiple self-portraits. Using a larger paper, do several "selves"—reflecting many expressions. Have an open class discussion when all work is complete.

Learning Disabled

Ask students to examine the anatomy of their faces with their fingers. Press fingers around the eyes to feel that eyes are set *within* the face, not *on top* of it. Feel the nose from its bridge to the tip to make students aware of the nose's protrusion from the rest of the face. Place tips of fingers firmly against lips to understand that it is the teeth and the jaw that define our mouths.

This exercise should help with understanding volume and dimensionality.

Physically Handicapped

The degree of students' movements should determine where mirrors are placed. It may make sense to hang a mirror on the wall (if it is possible to do so) and to move the student so that he can see himself comfortably. Be sure that drawing surfaces are compatible to mirror level. See "Adaptive Aids" for drawing aids that may help with manual grasp.

Sensory Losses

Hearing impaired—Try this movement activity that is often used in drama workshops. Two students sit opposite each

159

other, face to face. One student begins a motion, such as a circular movement of the hand. The other student "mirrors" (follows) the movement with his or her hand. There is no leader; students take their own "turns" spontaneously within the exercise. The challenge is to anticipate the other person's move—keen concentration and observation are needed. This game is fun for the hearing handicapped student; it requires a form of kinesthetic communication. It will also serve to loosen students up before drawing and activate observational skills. Studying the mirror image ties directly into the lesson, "Reflections."

Of course, you will need to demonstrate clearly the fact that students will follow the game with a self-portrait from mirror's image.

Visually handicapped—To increase awareness through tactual means for all visually handicapped students, use the introduction suggested under "Learning Disabled." The visually handicapped student will enjoy using the mirror as a reference and may need to get very close to see himself. The white on black drawing will increase the visibility of the line work through contrast (in advertising art, this is known as "reversed" and is recognized to have greater visual impact). Blind students may be curious about the object known as a mirror, so let them explore it carefully. You will then become the "talking mirror" and describe to the student what the mirror is reflecting of each student's face. Portraits may be done on screenboard with physical and verbal prompting regarding placement of features. Blind students may want to add sensory materials and real effects such as a tie, a scarf, earrings, yarn hair, etc., to further enhance their experience.

Gifted

The gifted student should also have an opportunity to do the self-portrait as presented in the core activity. However, after that has been accomplished, you could follow up with the "magic mirror." Tell students to imagine that they are holding magic mirrors that can add or subtract years (making you older or younger) or can change your identity (i.e., your face is still your face, but you are a spy, a king, a rock star, etc.). Mirrors can also go back or forward in the history of time, turning you into a caveman or a spaceman!

She Sells Seashells

MATERIALS

- Paper (lightweight, i.e., newsprint, tracing paper)
- Crayons, broken or stubs
- Shells (flat shells work well) (NOTE: If shells are not available, see Teacher Preparation.)

Figure 137

TEACHER PREPARATION

Did you ever wonder what to do with those shells you saved? Bring them into class—encourage students to bring them in, too. (See Figure 137.) Besides the beach, seafood restaurants are a good source for shells. Pet stores selling aquarium supplies should stock seashells. If shells are not available to everyone, shell shapes can be created from corrugated paper. Show students a real shell (or picture of one). Draw shell contour (or trace the real one) on the wrong (flat) side of the corrugated paper. Cut out and use for rubbings as you would use shells. You may want to precut shells from corrugated paper for some students.

DIRECTIONS

1. Give each student at least one shell.

2. Place shell under paper; use broad side of crayon (wrapper removed) until texture emerges. You may need to manipulate paper over shell to rub whole shape. (See Figure 138.)

3. Move shells around under paper to create a multicolored (use many crayons) and varied overall pattern. Students should exchange shells to make their designs more interesting.

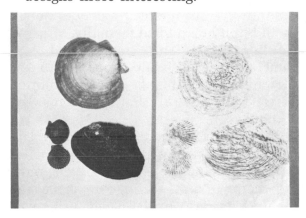

Figure 138

SUGGESTIONS FOR FURTHER DEVELOPMENT

Seashells are one group of natural objects that make good rubbings. Leaves, in the fall, are another. Rubbings can easily have seasonal themes, but there are many kinds of approaches and materials. Simply emptying your pockets can provide many items for rubbing—combs, ticket stubs, paper clips, and especially coins. (See Figure 139.) Remember, pencils can be used, as well as crayons, to create your rubbed images on paper.

Figure 139

adaptations

She Sells Seashells

Mentally Retarded

For the severely retarded student, a shell should first be explored tactually with you guiding the student's hand. Hand-over-hand assistance should be given to the student in learning the drawing motion (with the crayon) that produces the rubbing.

Mildly retarded students should be clear on the steps that will lead to a finished rubbing: placing shells under papers, moving them around; feeling for shells and rubbing crayon over the paper; using side of the crayon. Demonstrate the activity. You might want to talk about the size differences and how you will mix sizes in the rubbings to make designs more interesting.

Socially and Emotionally Disturbed

Memories associated with shells and the seashore should prompt students to "open up" and share pleasant experiences. Vacations, summer camps, etc., evoke good feelings. This is an excellent opportunity for students to have a positive exchange around their art activity.

Learning Disabled

Try to have students rub the whole shell for its entire shape. Students will become more aware of its contour by rubbing the outside edge of the shell. Shape and texture awareness will help with the concept. Ask questions: Where do you find shells? Have you ever pressed them into wet sand? What mark did it leave? Does the shell feel the same on the outside as it does on the inside? Which side is rough, which one is smooth? And so on. A discussion of this kind leads to a broader understanding of the subject.

Physically Handicapped

Students may need teacher assistance with the rubbing motion, which is a good hand and arm movement activity. Another way to do it is to wrap shells with paper tissue (arts and crafts or wrapping type). Rub the wrapped shell, then open. Repeat for other parts of your design. This is fun to do; it has an additional surprise element when results are "unwrapped." Also, wrapping the shells provides another manual dexterity exercise.

Sensory Losses

Hearing impaired—Your hearing impaired students should be able to follow the core after it has been presented in a step-by-step demonstration. After your students have accomplished their rubbings, here's an adventure you could send them on: the *Texture Safari*. Students will pair up. Armed with pencils and lightweight papers, students will go on a hunt for interesting surfaces around the school that they can rub. Brick walls, fences, gratings, doors, etc., are fair game. When students return to the artroom or classroom, see if students can identify the objects (language impaired students may want to write out their guesses). This project not only expands on the seashell lesson, but it also gives hearing impaired students an opportunity for some independence and decision making outside the classroom. The "Buddy" system will help with intersocial relationships.

Visually handicapped—This activity is excellent for visually handicapped students because of its nature. Experiment with fluorescent crayons for rubbings with your students. Blind students will enjoy the experience of the rubbing of the shell texture, but you might want to add to it by sprinkling sand on the paper (use white glue first) when rubbing is completed. Low-vision students might find the combination of sand and glitter visually stimulating. For your absolute finishing touch, bring in some suntan oil. Lightly scatter some drops on the paper to round off the complete sensory picture!

Gifted

Gifted students can use their shell rubbings as part of an undersea composition that they will develop. At the beginning of the activity, students select a particular ocean environment to draw or paint, using a specific example of tropical, or arctic, waters. Based on their choices, students will create appropriate flora and fauna. Students will need to research the project so that their underwaterscapes are correct; i.e., tropical fish belong in a coral reef, not in the North Sea. The one exception will be the rubbed shells, which will not necessarily match in the environmental picture, but will add the textural interest.

Silhouettes of Places Near and Far

MATERIALS

- White paper or brown butcher wrap
- Black construction paper
- Scissors
- White glue
- Pencils
- Watercolor or tempera
- White oil pastels or white pencils

TEACHER PREPARATION

You may want to use "Pieces of Sky" as the backdrop to this lesson. If mural paper is being used, cut to size. Try to provide visual reference material that illustrates appropriate subjects for silhouettes such as skylines or tropical plant life. For dramatic use of silhouettes in art, look for examples of cut paper folk crafts, using sharp contrast silhouettes (e.g., Haitian oil drum art, Pennsylvania Dutch, Polish papercuts, etc.)

DIRECTIONS

1. Paint colorful "backdrops" to silhouettes that will represent the sky.

2. Select a subject for a silhouette. Deserts, tropical islands, cities, and bridges are some possibilities. (See Figures 140, 141, 142, and 143.)

3. Students draw outside contour of silhouette and cut it out.

4. Decide if white outline on drawing adds or detracts from silhouette. Glue silhouette on paper.

SUGGESTIONS FOR FURTHER DEVELOPMENT

There are many ways to create exciting backgrounds for your silhouettes. You can use watercolor (see "Working Wet"), color broad bands with crayons, or apply foil stars on bright blue paper.

You might want to "reverse" the elements of this lesson by creating a colorful foreground (e.g., brightly patterned buildings) against a black sky!

Figure 140

Figure 141

164

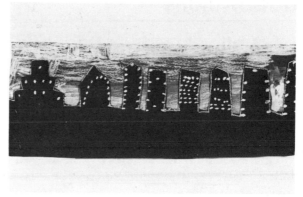

Figure 142.

Figure 143

adaptations

Silhouettes of Places Near and Far

Mentally Retarded

The lesson as presented in the core may be too abstract for your severely retarded students. However, the high contrast of a dark area against a bright area is visually stimulating. So, forego the skyline silhouette; turn the activity into a torn paper collage of dark and light contrast. Black paper will be folded, pieces torn out of center. Repeat—fold, tear—until paper looks like Swiss cheese. Paste perforated black paper against a fluorescent or brightly colored paper. Display within students' view. NOTE: If student does not have tearing skills, hold your hand stationary over student's hand (the hand that is grasping the paper) and pull down with student's other "working" hand. Use verbal and physical prompting. Assist with pasting in hand-over-hand manner.

The mildly retarded student may or may not be able to comprehend the concept of a silhouetted skyline. If you think your students would be perplexed by this concept, it may make better sense to have them work on simple images of a house or a tree. Cut out the objects and mount them on prepared backgrounds. When all of the class's work is complete, they can be shown side by side as silhouettes. At that point, what comprises a silhouette should become more concrete for your mildly retarded students.

Socially and Emotionally Disturbed

Where is your favorite place? The seashore? The city? An amusement park? Or an imaginary place you like to think about? If you don't have an imaginary place (or favorite spot), invent one.

Once the special place is established, your students can draw the details on black paper, cut, and mount it against the colorful backdrop they created. They should be encouraged to title their work (e.g., Fantasy Park, Paradise Mountain, etc.). Class discussion on why their places are unique should follow.

Learning Disabled

It may be worthwhile to remind students that silhouettes are flat representations of three-dimensional volumes; spatial reality may be confusing to your learning disabled student. Students may want to sketch out their ideas before proceeding with core activity.

A corresponding lesson you could try is "Shadows." Have students fold a piece of paper into four blocks that will represent morning, high noon, afternoon, and night. Students pick a single object, such as a cactus in the desert or a cat on a windowsill. In each block, students will show the object, the sky, and its shadow reflecting the time of day. Students may need to observe an object at home or at school at different times to carry out this lesson with confidence. The "night" block will be a silhouette, but what is valuable is that students will better understand the time sequence that led up to the darkened object. Sequencing is also an area that generally needs building in learning disabled students.

Physically Handicapped

Creating a cut silhouette depends on scissors skills. (See "Adaptive Aids" for scissors.) However, if student's hand movement is too severely limited for working with scissors, consider "City Lights." Offer students several sizes of rectangular and square construction paper. Cut a dry sponge into strips (about the size of a pen). Students will dip end of sponge into bright paint (orange, yellow, white) and print "windows" on the paper. You can assist students in mounting the "buildings" against a backdrop to create a lively city. (See "Adaptive Aids" for other tools to use for printing.)

Sensory Losses

Hearing impaired—Skylines can be considered the "autograph" of a city. Much like well-known personalities, many skylines are famous and recognizable—New York, Paris, San Francisco, Athens, Istanbul, and Moscow are good examples. Travel brochures and pamphlets are free and readily available from national tourist bureaus, travel agents, and chambers of commerce. You can also collect "famous city" reference material from travel magazines and often from the travel sections of the newspaper.

Once you have a selection of cities for your hearing impaired students to review, ask students to pick one. Provide posterboards on which students will paint the celebrated skyline. When everyone has finished, tape the boards together to create a panoramic fanfold of international skylines!

By presenting "Silhouettes" in this way, you are widening your students' world and giving them an important role in an exciting group project where their efforts can be displayed with pride. NOTE: Students should do all work either horizontally or vertically so that boards will "match" each other for fanfold. Of course, make sure that students understand all phases of the activity beforehand.

Visually handicapped—The visually handicapped should respond well to the high contrast qualities of this lesson: the black silhouette against the bright background, the white drawing on the black paper. You may want to add a little "extra" by including fluorescent (or brightly colored) paper squares as windows and details on the black silhouette.

Blind students will need to understand what you mean by the term "silhouette." Some students with light perception may be seeing this world in a very similar way.

You may want to precut basic skylines and let blind students explore the outline. Explain to them what they are feeling (i.e., roof, top of skyscraper, etc.). Of course, if you have 3-D models, bring them into the lesson. Students can use screenboards to draw windows into the buildings. Mount against background paper.

Gifted

Observe Figure 140 for a moment or two. Does it begin to remind you of something familiar? If not, here's a hint: "Wish you were here" usually appears on the back. That's right, when scaled down, this activity closely resembles a postcard. Your gifted students would be intrigued by first creating a travel poster of an exotic place (let's say the tropical island with the palm tree). After completing the travel poster students will show *another* view of this island (maybe an aerial view of the village) on a postcard. This will require other materials such as smaller brushes, finer felt tip markers, etc. Leave the backs of the postcards blank for messages, and for step 3 of this activity—which is approximately a ½-by-1-inch painting—the postage stamp.

Students will need to switch materials again to very fine marker or colored pencils. Postage stamps might show the "official" flower, a country's ruler (kings, queens, presidents) or another scene from the island.

Places that your gifted students choose can be real or imaginary—from the land of Oz to a resort in France. Do drop us a line!

The Sketchbook: Observations and Interpretations

MATERIALS

- Pencils
- Fine-tip markers
- Sketchbooks—white drawing paper
- Newsprint or other inexpensive paper (optional)
- Charcoal drawing sticks (optional)

TEACHER PREPARATION

If your budget does not provide for sketchbook purchases, students may want to buy their own sketchbooks. Other alternatives are: clipping papers together (with paper fasteners, staples, or paper clips) and working on a hard board (drawing board), keeping papers in oaktag folders. The idea is to keep work together for reference and to note the continuity and progress of visual expression.

Figure 144

DIRECTIONS

To Do Outdoors

1. Take your students for a neighborhood walk, or simply explore school grounds.

2. Ask students to find an object or area (such as a tree, a bench, a fence) that interests them. (See Figure 144.)

3. Students will do a study of the chosen subject, with attention to texture, shading, and line. Allow an appropriate amount of time.

To Do Indoors

4. Students will model for each other. It is best to "warm up" with short poses before drawing students in longer poses. (See Figure 145.)

5. Students will begin with sketches of student modeling in an "action" pose,

Figure 145

which should last no more than five minutes. Poses include bending, pretending to catch a ball, dancing, etc., all in a "frozen" motion (model does not move while posing).

6. Use charcoal and newsprint. Draw in a big, loose manner. The object is to capture the *direction* of the pose, not the details.

7. After students have "loosened up" with their drawings, use sketchbooks for the longer poses (at least 20 minutes a pose). Student models may pose in seated, standing, or reclining postures. (See Figures 146, 147, and 148.)

Figure 146

Figure 147

Figure 148

SUGGESTIONS FOR FURTHER DEVELOPMENT

Keeping a sketchbook is a stimulating and exciting experience for children as well as for older students. You may want students to have two sketchbooks, one for home and one for school. Students may surprise you with their enthusiasm for their out-of-school sketchbooks; they are often eager to share their world with you in this visual form.

You may want to create a studio-like atmosphere at school around the modeling setting. You and your students can collect "props": hats, empty bottles, used musical instruments, old lamps, scarves, umbrellas, etc. These are welcome additions to the modeling sessions and are worthy of attention for their own qualities and in still lifes. The transition from sketchbook to easel is a natural one. Painting from palettes on canvas epitomizes the studio experience, which is strongly backed up by the drawing skills that keeping sketchbooks helps to develop.

adaptations

The Sketchbook: Observations and Interpretations

Mentally Retarded

The severely retarded student may not be able to respond to an object or subject with a drawing that explains its qualities. However, students can learn about line by keeping sketchbooks. Using a fat crayon, students will be shown various lines in a hand-over-hand manner by you. You might want to start with a straight line, moving into a curvy, wavy line, then circles. Try varying width of line by rubbing the side of the crayon (crayon wrapper removed) and experimenting with different hand pressures. After students have practiced line work with you and can do it with a minimal amount of prompting, draw combinations of these simple lines with color and texture. NOTE: Severely retarded students might also benefit from drawing with some of the "Adaptive Aids." This adds the element of play and exploration of materials into the sketchbook activity.

Mildly retarded students should be given charcoal and large paper before working in sketchbooks. Save the charcoal sketches in large folders or portfolios. Boldly print students' names on them. Sketchbooks may also be slipped inside. On a regular basis, review all the work with students individually and in a group. This will reinforce their learning experiences and give you an opportunity to observe their progress.

Socially and Emotionally Disturbed

Sketching nature and the environment raises awareness and develops appreciation for the world we all share. There is something relaxing and humanizing about spending time with a tree or sitting on a grassy hill. Students should be given a specific time frame for selecting objects, observing and drawing them, and should be encouraged to complete their work within it.

Studio (indoors) modeling is a wholesome vehicle for students to "act out" in a pose or costume. It is closely akin to role playing. Students should have input in taking poses; avoid "directing" the activity completely.

Sketchbooks are in themselves a healthy vehicle for self-expression, personal thoughts, and feelings. They are in many ways like visual diaries.

Learning Disabled

There are often confused perceptions among learning disabled students that can be identified in their artwork. These perceptual distortions often exist in the students' misunderstandings of spatial depth and the placement of objects in space. Remind students of logical perspective by asking "What tree is closest to us? Which is farther away?" etc. This is also useful with studio work, e.g., "What part of that object does the model's head hide? What part of the chair is nearest to you?" etc.

Another approach that helps students to organize their thinking is to provide a reference point immediately. The first thing that goes down on the paper can do it. For example, suppose the student draws a tall tree. Establish its location on the page compared to the rest of the landscape. Is the park bench on the right or left of the tree? What about the little bush in relationship to the tree? And so on.

Drawing from objects and people is indeed an exercise that develops observational skills and helps with ability to respond to the visual world in a cohesive manner. Also, it is a way of improving eye-hand coordination.

Physically Handicapped

Drawing is not merely an act performed by two well-coordinated hands. We don't *really* draw with our hands—they are subservient to our mind's interpretation of what appears before us. Sensitivity, determination, and spirit also have a lot to do with it. Think about the quadraplegic young man who created exquisite drawings of frogs (his favorite theme) by holding the pen between his teeth. There are many others like him. There is more to drawing than learning mechanically correct technique.

Physically handicapped students will need to experiment with adaptive aids and methods until they find the ones that best express their own individual style. Sketchbooks may also need to be adjusted so that the surface of the page is accessible. Reading stands and, of course, drawing tables can be of great help.

Sensory Losses

Hearing impaired—Nature walks and neighborhood trips with sketchbooks will widen the world of your hearing impaired students. Keeping "outside" sketchbooks—where students draw about the events and people in their lives outside of school—is highly recommended. The sketchbook provides students with a way of making visual notes and impressions in the universally understandable language of art.

The modeling experience can offer students a social exercise through group poses. Use two to four students as models together. Try this: Demonstrate to students that they will be having an imaginary tug-of-war. This will create interaction, as well as animate the poses. Indicate to the class that they will all have a chance to pose; and that they should leave room on their drawings for add on figures (this means drawing more than one set of models per page, showing a multifigured group pose). Through this method, visual interest and movement are introduced, and everyone gets into the act! Make sure your students are clear on what the activities require.

Visually handicapped—The visually handicapped student might benefit from using a magnifying glass when doing studies outdoors—particularly when drawing small details. Magnifying glasses are fascinating and may aid visual understanding for some sight losses.

For studio work, a spotlight or photographer's strobe type light is suggested, which is inexpensive and easy to mount. Light on a model or still life can help. NOTE: Albinism (and some other eye conditions) can include extreme sensitivity to bright lights. Even though this is far less common than most visually handicapped students' need for illumination, be aware of it. If a student complains that the light is hurting his eyes, giving him a headache, or making him feel sick, remove him from the brightened area immediately.

Blind students can keep sketchbooks, but the paper must be light enough for screenboard penetration (newsprint sketchpads are good). Screenboards can be slipped under each sketchpad page as students draw. Students will need to explore outdoor objects tactually in order to draw them. Three-dimensional anatomical models are suggested for studio work. Also, blind students might enjoy using yarn or string as their "line." Drawing with yarn provides tactual information for blind students when they touch their work.

Gifted

Gifted students are able to comprehend the effects of light on a figure or object, and can interpret texture, scale, and spatial relationships. Ask students to bring into class some illustrations of master drawings, from the Renaissance to the twentieth century. Examine how the artists handled these elements. Students' work should reflect dimensionality through shading, plastic line (line that varies in expression), and textural richness. Drawings should also suggest students' selectivity; i.e., students should choose *parts* or details of the object or setting, and avoid reporting everything in front of them.

Here's a related activity that gives gifted students a chance to analyze action poses and understand the basics of animation at the same time. Students can use little unlined notepads or precut about 30 small pages (about 3 by 5 inches). A model will select an action pose, such as lifting an imaginary balloon from the floor to above his or her head. Each pose (which lasts about two minutes) will be drawn on a separate page showing *each movement* that comprises the whole action; the first page shows the model with hands at the floor; the last pose shows the model with hands above the head. When all phases of the movement have been sequentially drawn, staple all pages together at the top. Flip pages with thumb for a moving experience!

A Snake in the Grass

MATERIALS

- Paper (construction or plain)
- Scissors
- Crayons, oil pastels, or markers
- Black felt-tip pens (optional)

TEACHER PREPARATION

Be a snake charmer and present your class with a basket full of precut snakes. Have some good reference material around or create sample snakeskin patterns for them.

DIRECTIONS

1. Introduce snakeskin patterns.
2. Either give students paper to cut out snakes or give them the snakes precut.

3. Create designs based on either real snakeskins or whimsical ones. Add forked tongue—don't forget the "snake eyes"! (See Figures 149, 150, and 151.)

SUGGESTIONS FOR FURTHER DEVELOPMENT

Snakes have notorious reputations. They inspire fear and awe, so naturally they are fascinating to children. There are lots of ways to develop this activity. Students can use snakes to "weave" through the tall paper grass in larger theme formats, such as "jungles." Compositions can expand to include lizards and other reptiles that might make some say "yuch." Yet, crawly creatures have a design impact that is perfect for artroom study.

You may also want to turn "A Snake in the Grass" into a rubbing activity.

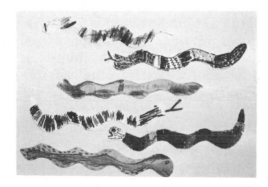

Figure 149

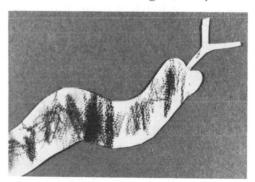

Figure 150

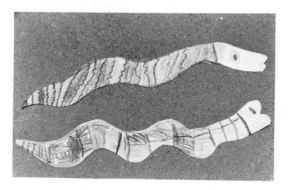

Figure 151

adaptations

A Snake in the Grass

Mentally Retarded

Give your severely retarded students practice paper, and help them to draw curvy lines over and over. Next, present them with the precut snakes. You may need to tape snakes to the work surfaces to keep them from slipping. Give students hand-over-hand assistance in transferring "big movement" used in practice to the smaller movement required for drawing the precut snake. Try fluorescent crayons; they are more visually stimulating.

Completed snakes can be tied on to a coat hanger to create a coat hanger mobile. Display mobiles where children can see them.

Mildly retarded students can practice snake-like motion in the air with their arms. Explain to them that this is how a snake moves; showing pictures of snakes will help them understand more also. Assist children in cutting their own snakes (see "Adaptive Aids"). Decorate in whatever manner is desired.

Socially and Emotionally Disturbed

You can precut a "jumbo" snake large enough to provide each student with a snake "section." Students design their own part. When everyone is finished, reunite the snake. You have an instant group project and a dazzling display of everyone's patterns!

Learning Disabled

"A Snake in the Grass" can be a perfect connect-the-dots lesson. Use a precut snake as a pattern and trace in the dotted line. Students then connect dots, which is great for eye-hand coordination and closure. Decorate snakes as desired; prompt students to cut them out.

You may want to display finished snakes in a group mural, encouraging students to develop an appropriate theme (e.g., jungle, desert, garden).

Physically Handicapped

For wheelchair bound students, place a length of brown wrap paper across the floor. Draw a big wavy line that becomes "a snake's path." Wheelchairs can be navigated by students over the wavy course. To further imitate a snake's journey, chairs could become "trees" that the student will need to go around; this adds a little drama.

If your physically handicapped students have some motor ability (but it is restricted) gently ease into the "snaky" line drawing by practicing S-curves. Then go on to precut snakes.

Sensory Losses

Hearing impaired—See if the science department has a spare snake to lend you. It's the perfect model for drawing snakes. Show students a finished sample snake (and a picture if available), pointing to markings. Proceed if all is understood.

Visually handicapped—Let blind students draw designs on the precut snakes on their screenboards or let them use yarn to decorate the snakes. If you have a toy rubber snake, let your students explore it, but tell them that it's not real and that it might feel funny! If you want to add dimensionality to this lesson, students can fold snakes in an accordion manner, but that does alter the wavy contour of the snake shape.

Gifted

Gifted students can do some fancy snake skin designs—use felt-tip markers. Students can create coiled snakes, cobras, interlocking snakes, etc., in addition to the common garden variety. Their scissors become the drawing tool for executing the contours. You might want to talk about the amazing nature of snakes; specifically, the fact that some snakes are able to swallow animals whole. A snake contour that reveals another shape within it could be amusing and unique!

Something's Fishy!

MATERIALS

- Paper
- Pencils, markers
- Newspapers
- Stapler
- Watercolors (silver and gold watercolors are great)
- Paintbrushes
- Scissors
- Tackle line or invisible thread (string may be used)
- Cellophane tape
- Paper reinforcements
- Glass fishbowls (see "Suggestions" for other alternatives)

TEACHER PREPARATION

If you or your students can get real goldfish bowls, the results are terrific. You might want to precut squares and rectangles that will be folded for cutting of fish shapes.

DIRECTIONS

1. Talk about fish and their undersea environments. Ask students to imagine that they are skin divers going down deep into the ocean; have them describe what they see and hear.

2. Hand out paper. Let students select the sizes they want for their fish.

3. Students design contour of fish shape with pencil or marker. Decorate with paint and/or markers (add glitter if you want).

4. Cut fish out of folded paper.

5. Staple around edges of fish leaving enough room for stuffing.

6. Tear newspaper into strips and crush into balls.

7. "Stuff your fish"; staple closed.

8. Punch a hole at the top of fish, thread tackle line through, and tape to side of bowl. Or, push paper clips through to attach fish to bowl.

9. Add details like "air bubbles" made out of reinforcements. (See Figure 152.)

Figure 152

SUGGESTIONS FOR FURTHER DEVELOPMENT

Shoeboxes can make good aquariums for your fish. Add the blue colored tissue paper and other desired sea world details (starfish, coral, seaweed, etc.). You can also float your fish in air; they make fine hangings. (Haven't you ever heard of flying fish?)

adaptations

Something's Fishy!

Mentally Retarded

Divide severely retarded students into small groups. Precut fish large enough for several students to stuff, then you staple one side. Students take turns in coloring fish. You will help the students tear newspapers and guide students in stuffing the fish as it is passed from one student to another. You staple the fish closed and hang it in a prominent place.

If possible, introduce this activity to your mildly retarded students with a real fish in a fishbowl. Point out the special features of a fish: fins, tail, scales, placement of eyes, and the way fish appears suspended in water. If students are able to sketch the fish, let them—if not, use teacher-made fish patterns or precut fish. Tear newspaper and stuff fish; then staple it and hang it in a bowl or in a window.

Socially and Emotionally Disturbed

Why not use the undersea world as an excuse for a group project? Gather a cardboard box or a real glass aquarium (if you should be so lucky) for all fish to be placed within. A few students could be the designers of the box/aquarium; some could work on other elements besides fish, such as seaweed, coral, and buried treasures.

Learning Disabled

Students should be made aware of the fish's dimensionality. Point out both sides of the fish to add an element of realism; to exercise eye-hand coordination, have students fold and attach fins. With small colored paper squares, use the simple fan fold technique that everyone knows for making a quick fan out of paper on a hot day. Follow core lesson for stuffing.

Physically Handicapped

Crushing newspaper is an excellent activity for manipulative skills. You will assist when needed in the stuffing of fish. Some students will cut the fish themselves while others will require precut ones. All should be able to find a medium for decorating fish that suits their skills; some students will draw scale patterns, some will paint freely, etc.

Sensory Losses

Hearing impaired—Bring in real fish or pictures of fish for observation. Point out scale patterns; you might want to draw some sample pattern possibilities for student to consider. Then introduce basic elements of the lesson so that students can see the lesson's progressive steps.

Visually handicapped—Use watercolor with blind and visually handicapped students. Blind students do enjoy watercolors! Use precut fish for students without cutting skills or with severe vision losses. Point out to students that there is an association between the watery quality of the painting method and the fish's world—this adds some meaning to both the lesson and the painting experience. Other materials to consider using with students are fluorescent crayons and paints. Fluorescent materials are reminiscent of fish's iridescence. NOTE: See "Working with Watercolor," page 215, for suggestions on painting for blind students.

Gifted

There are so many gorgeous tropical fish that the gifted students can study before creating their own fish. Researching scale patterns, intensive fish colorations, and the variety within the different species should provide the stimulation for this lesson.

Spectacular Sandwiches and 12-Layer Cakes

MATERIALS

- Brown butcher wrap paper
- Poster paint, brushes
- Oil pastels
- Scissors

TEACHER PREPARATION

Because the subjects of cakes and sandwiches are so similar in this activity, it is being presented here as a "double choice" lesson. In order to make sandwiches or cakes "spectacular," you will need 3-to-6-foot lengths of brown paper. (See Figure 153.)

DIRECTIONS

1. Talk about wedding cakes; how are they different from everyday cakes? Answer—many, many tiers (layers). How about the decoration? Pastry guns create rosettes and frilly designs.

2. Now, for the sandwiches. Again, *layers* are the key here. If you keep adding layers to your sandwich, you can have a sandwich as tall as a wedding cake.

3. Unroll brown butcher wrap to desired size. Cut.

4. Create the sandwich or cake of your dreams! (See Figures 154 and 155.)

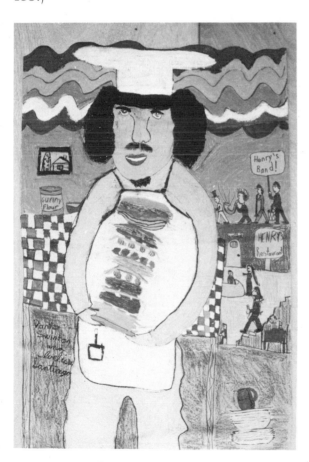

Figure 153

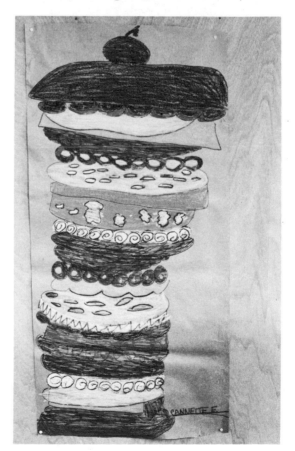

Figure 154

Figure 155

SUGGESTIONS FOR FURTHER DEVELOPMENT

There are other food fantasies besides cake and sandwiches that can be oversized wonders. Take the case of the super fruit bowl; rather than building layers, build up shapes on shapes instead (apples, plums, oranges, etc.). NOTE: Refer to "Recipe File," specifically "Goopi" for cake decorating ideas.

adaptations

Spectacular Sandwiches and 12-Layer Cakes

Mentally Retarded

The subject of multilayered cakes and sandwiches may not have great meaning for the severely retarded. Instead, precut comic strips, fabric widths, colored paper strips, etc. Assist students in pasting various strips, starting at the bottom and working your way up. As students progress in layering, they will be exercising their abilities to reach physically from one point to another.

NOTE: If student cannot reach out, see the "Physically Handicapped" adaptation.

Mildly retarded students should be able to paint layers of the sandwich *or* cake (pick one for presentation to students). Talk about building from the bottom up—you could stack blocks or books to illustrate the principle of layering.

Socially and Emotionally Disturbed

After introducing the lesson, have students decide to make either sandwich or cake. Pair students with each other on the basis of their choices, as well as their potential for working together. They should decide on materials, designs, etc., together. When work is completed, have a group discussion. Allow partners to explain how they reached their mutual decisions on their work. Give much positive recognition for partners who worked well together.

Learning Disabled

Whether they choose sandwiches or cakes, the learning disabled students need to examine the idea of layering. Both the sandwich and cake start at the base and are built up from there. You can illustrate this principle by using your hands and the students' hands—stacking them all up together (you know that old trick!). Once students start building the layers, they should catch on to this concept.

Physically Handicapped

You may want to assign some student to create sandwich "parts" on smaller paper such as pickles, olives, tomatoes, meats, and onions. This gives students with limited physical reach an opportunity to work independently. When completed, gather all garnishes and mount vertically on butcher paper.

A suggestion for students who want control of the full project is to drape butcher paper over work surface. Paper can be moved forward as students complete each layer.

Sensory Losses

Hearing impaired—Try this fun approach: Each student has his or her own brown paper panel for either sandwich or cake. Allot a given time to student per layer, say, ten minutes. When time is reached, student passes his or her paper to the next student. This process is repeated until determined number of layers is reached. Divide time according to number of layers and time allotment. The results will be an amusing mixture of everyone's efforts, and lots of exchange will have taken place.

Visually handicapped—Your visually handicapped students might use textural materials to represent various parts of the sandwich or cake. For example, green tissue can become lettuce, and red circles can be pepperoni. For cake, fabric trim and lace doilies can be added for decorations.

To make the idea of layering more understandable to blind students, try accordion-folding the brown paper. Open and lay flat. Lines provided by folds will cue students on the layers' boundaries. Take students' hands; lead them from bottom "up the ladder" to the top.

Gifted

Use the cake activity (since it most closely resembles architectural facades) for a "cake-tower" theme. The theme could be a city, country, or period of history. For example, if the theme were "New Orleans," the cake could have a layer of mardi-gras mask faces, a layer of jazz instruments, a layer of iron grill work, etc.

Students might need to research themes. When projects are completed, students should not reveal the theme's identity—other students must guess!

Stamp It, Print It!

MATERIALS

- Plasticene
- Tongue depressors
- Orange sticks (manicure sticks)
- Poster paint
- Brushes
- Paper
- Paper towels

TEACHER PREPARATION

Plasticene should be soft enough to manipulate. Placing platicene in a sunny spot or on a radiator before the activity should help. You may want to collect—and then offer—objects that can be pressed into the platicene to make prints more interesting, such as bottle caps, combs, forks, etc.

Figure 156

DIRECTIONS

1. Give students a chunk of plasticene about the size of an apple.

2. Grip the tongue depressor at both ends (they tend to break otherwise); then divide the oily clay into two or more pieces. Roll plasticene into stubby cylinders.

3. With the tongue depressors or orange sticks, students dig out a design that they will print.

4. Using brush, apply paint to the "business end" of the plasticene stumps.

5. Press plasticene firmly on the paper but not *too* hard or you will dull the stamp. (See Figure 156.)

6. Give thought to the overall design. (See Figure 157.) Plasticene stamps can be wiped or rinsed lightly in order to apply other paint colors. Patterns can be recut.

Figure 157

SUGGESTIONS

You might want to show the class some real rubber stamps and explain the difference between the stamp print and the block print. Some other methods for stamp print activities are vegetable prints (potato, carrot, onion, etc.), corks, and rubber erasers. You could probably add a few more to the list. Figure 158 shows a carrot print.

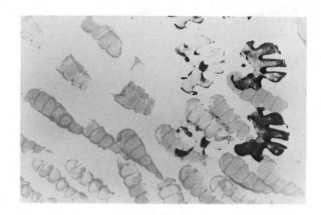

Figure 158

adaptations

Stamp It, Print It!

Mentally Retarded

This is an excellent activity for all levels of mentally retarded students. The severely retarded will enjoy rolling the plasticene into a cylinder. Teacher assistance will be needed for students to create simple stamps. Cut away enough plasticene to give stamps some definition—one stamp per student is fine.

In a hand-over-hand method, student can be instructed in the printing technique. (You "fade away" as student gets the idea.) Stamps can be "dipped" into prepared shallow cups of poster paint before printing. You may want to stay with a small range of colors that are bright and contrast with paper.

The mildly retarded student should be able to accomplish this activity once it is clearly understood.

Socially and Emotionally Disturbed

Prints and greeting cards go well together. Make lots of construction paper available in assorted colors to be used for cards. Students create their stamps and design their own hand-crafted cards from them. Each student will produce a stack of cards, varying their stamp cuts and colors. Prompt students to experiment with each other's stamps.

When cards are completed, students may want to keep them to send to others or "package" them (a bow works wonders) to give as a gift. Also, cards make a good sale item for school fairs. Make sure students put their own logo on the back of the card. This emphasizes personal pride in one's own creative product, while supporting a positive interchange of ideas between students.

Learning Disabled

Ask students to create a border print. Select two or three colors. Ask that students vary their prints in some way, either by overlapping or by alternating colors. Think about the shape of the border. Students decide whether they want a "free form" or a geometric border. Of course, leave center blank. After printed border dries, either write poem or draw picture inside the border "frame."

This approach will help with learning to follow directions, visual closure, and fine-motor control.

Physically Handicapped

The physically handicapped student will benefit from the rolling of the plasticene, so even if arm movement is limited, try to get them to do it (but don't force it). The carving of the plasticene does require some fine-motor ability, so students who lack it will need assistance. The press and print part of this activity is achievable for most physically handicapped students.

Sensory Losses

Hearing impaired—Let's create "wallpaper" for the classroom. This is a group activity that will encourage communication and interplay between students. Demonstrate the rolling out of the plasticene and the carving, etc. Print on brown mural paper. Cover a substantial area in the classroom for display.

Visually handicapped—Assist your blind students in rolling the plasticene and carving the stamps. You might want to use acrylic paint to print stamps, which is thicker than poster paint, or add sand to poster paint for texture. By doing this, blind students can feel their designs when they are dry.

When a blind student prints, it may be of a random nature. If printed impressions overlap excessively, you might suggest that the student start printing on a new page. Finished (and dry) prints should have a slightly "embossed" quality that blind students can appreciate tactually. You might want to offer the original plasticene stamp to students with their finished prints, so that they can explore both paper and plas-ticene surfaces to understand their relationship better.

Gifted

Students can recreate symbols and signs of historical significance, such as fleur de lis, Egyptian hieroglyphics, Roman numerals, etc. Another stimulation can be reproductions of the work of artists whose strong yet simple designs would translate well into stamps, e.g., Matisse, Miro, Calder. Remember, gifted students are capable of producing fine details as well as incisive line work.

Stitchscapes

MATERIALS

- Felt scraps (assorted colors and sizes)
- Yarn and/or embroidery thread
- Sewing needles
- Scissors
- Printed cotton fabric
- Canvas stretchers, embroidery hoops, pins (optional)

TEACHER PREPARATION

Gather print fabrics that suggest "sky" backgrounds, such as stripes and dots. Felt will be difficult for many students to cut, so you might want to precut simple shapes that easily could be made into trees, houses, clouds, etc.

Refer to "Adaptive Aids" for sewing aids that you might want to use with your students.

DIRECTIONS

1. Ask students to describe what is outside their windows, either at home or at school. Get students thinking about outdoor environments.

2. Students select print fabrics for their backgrounds and felt for houses, trees.

3. Cut and arrange elements on the background fabric. Taping fabric to work surface will keep it from slipping around, but students will probably need to remove tape to sew freely.

4. Before they begin to sew, students may want to tape the felt parts on the fabric, pulling tape away as they stitch. (Pins may be used if appropriate for students.)

5. Stitching directly on the fabric should be fine as long as students don't *pull* on the thread (embroidery hoops or stretchers may be used). Stitches may be practiced on scrap fabric. (See Figure 159.) Encourage variety and experimentation.

6. Finished product (see Figure 160) can be framed or mounted on posterboard, leaving a 1-to-3-inch border.

SUGGESTIONS FOR FURTHER DEVELOPMENT

Themes such as "The Four Seasons" or "The Time of Day" (day, night, stars, sunsets, etc.) will extend this lesson into an activity of more than one appliqué. You can create "sets" that have sequence.

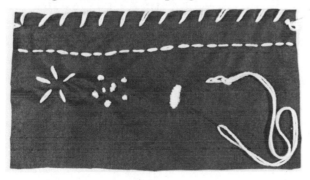

Figure 159

Figure 160

adaptations

Stitchscapes

Mentally Retarded

The severely retarded student might need to work on the appropriate motor coordination needed for stitching.

See "Adaptive Aids" to assist student's hand in moving tools in and out of holes. Once the proper motion has been mastered, try the hand-over-hand method with a large needle and thick yarn through oaktag. For the mildly retarded, punch holes in oaktag; prompt students to sew through holes for practice.

Socially and Emotionally Disturbed

When your students achieve a task, it is very gratifying—but frustration should be avoided. Be certain that the technical aspects of sewing are understood before launching the project.

At the finish, have students make a quilt by stitching pictures together. A quilt is tangible evidence of a cooperative effort.

Learning Disabled

This is an excellent activity for learning disabled students. Sewing will reinforce eye-hand coordination as well as understanding of directionality. To help students who are having difficulty, draw marker lines of felt to illustrate where stitches should go. Make sure that students know where to begin and that they leave enough thread at the end to knot easily.

Physically Handicapped

It may be worthwhile to secure fabric in embroidery hoops or canvas stretchers so that the physically handicapped student can manage. Offer assistance on threading needles, cutting felt, etc., as you see the need appear. If sewing is really impossible, use glue. See "Sewing Aids."

Sensory Losses

Hearing impaired—Show students reproductions of landscapes (or outdoor scenes), city scapes, or any related appropriate subjects. Then present a sample stitchery picture of any of these subjects so that students understand that they will be translating "scapes" into fabric stitch pictures.

Make sure to demonstrate the variety of stitches, such as running stitch, saddle stitch, etc.

Visually handicapped—Blind students can sew with help. Fabric should be taped to indicate where stitches will go, along with hand-over-hand instructions ("in-out," verbal cues). Visually handicapped students need needles with large eyes for threading. (You may need to help.) Precut felt may also be used.

Gifted

Gifted students can play patterns and prints against each other within their fabric pictures, creating rich designs. You might show them American quilt patterns for inspiration. They should be able to experiment with many varieties of stitches and should have excellent technical control of the materials.

A Stroke of the Brush

MATERIALS

- Acrylic paints
- Palettes (substitute Bristol boards or cardboard squares)
- Oil painting brushes (stiff)
- Water containers
- Canvas boards (canvas paper or white illustration boards)
- Paper towels
- White construction paper

HINT: Old shirts make good smocks to keep street clothes paint-free.

TEACHER PREPARATION

You may want to have palettes ready for students' arrival, but do demonstrate setting up a sample palette. Although there is much debate on the "correct" way, going from warm to cool colors clockwise (with white and black on either end) is a safe arrangement. Coffee cans are perfect water containers; plastic containers are too. You can have palettes ready for students.

Try to get reproductions or postcards (from the museum) that illustrate painters' work that is "brushstroke" oriented; e.g., the Impressionists (Manet, Monet, Renoir, Cezanne, and of course, Van Gogh).

DIRECTIONS

1. Show students how to use paint, mixing in the middle of the palette and cleaning brushes in water. (See Figure 161.) Remind them to use their "paint rags" (paper towels).

2. Show students reproductions. (See Figure 162.) Discuss various paint applications.

3. Students will want to practice their brushstrokes. Fold white paper three or four times. In each square, paint a different brush stroke pattern (dots, swirls, slashes, etc.). This will become the "brushstroke reference chart."

4. Ready to paint your canvas? The choices are yours for subjects; just remember to use those brushes creatively! (See Figures 163, 164, and 165.)

5. When dry, consider framing work with simple wood strips. (See Figure 166.) You can hang works with braided picture wire and screw eyes (available from the hardware store).

6. Display your students' masterpieces with pride!

NOTE: Palettes that require cleaning (the nonthrowaway type) should be cleaned immediately after use. Acrylic paints will dry hard and very quickly.

Figure 161

Figure 162

Figure 163

Figure 164

Figure 165

Figure 166

adaptations

A Stroke of the Brush

Mentally Retarded

The severely retarded student can have a full sensory experience with paint using the hands as "brushes" and a variety of other unconventional painting tools. First, collect the Styrofoam trays that meat comes in (the bigger the better). Apply finger to tray and let the student paint (with fingers and hands) directly in the tray. Use poster paint or soap paint. You can assist student in moving hands to create whirls, swirls, and patterns. When finished with "finger and hand" painting, wash hands. Experiment with other brushstroke effects in paint by using shaving cream brushes, toothbrushes, sponges, and combs. Let painting dry and display.

The mildly retarded student can paint with brushes and palettes, but keep palettes simple by not including too many color choices. It might make sense to skip the brush stroke chart (Step 3 in the directions) if students appear to have a very limited understanding of the concept of "brushstrokes." In that case, just demonstrate a few samples of lines—curly, squiggly, straight—then let them paint directly on canvas. However, if your students show curiosity about reproductions and interest in the discussion, proceed with the core lesson as indicated.

Socially and Emotionally Disturbed

Painting has long been recognized as a therapeutic activity, so this is a good one for your socially and emotionally disturbed students. It combines self-expression with structure (the organization of the materials, the brushstrokes).

Why not suggest that students do self-portraits? This is certainly an ideal vehicle for it. If you are more interested in positive social interaction, students can do a portrait of a fellow student who will model for the class (voluntarily).

Learning Disabled

Try to leave enough time to allow your students to set up their own palettes. You will demonstrate first and keep a sample palette available for students' reference. Having students focus on this important task may help get their attention properly fixed on the activity, besides helping them to learn the technical process of painting in a "professional" way.

Make sure students practice the brush stroke movements on paper before proceeding to the canvas.

Physically Handicapped

There are many physical disabilities. Check the "Adaptive Aids" section to see if any suggestions will help your physically handicapped students to paint with greater ease (e.g., head gear, foam brush grip, shortened brush).

It is important that the surface be accessible to the student. This is where the easel—a mainstay of studio work—can be a great help, because it is adjustable. Also, boxes stacked on surface to raise the canvas board may help certain students; you might even try a reading stand. Of course, drawing tables, if available, are helpful to most students.

Sensory Losses

Hearing impaired—Prepare a sample chart of different brushstrokes in advance of lesson. When introducing the activity, demonstrate the steps outlined in the core but show students your prepared brushstroke chart (on Step 3). Indicate that you want them to create "matching" brushstroke patterns. Cut the papers when dry, shuffle them, and have students match the cards to your chart "lotto" style. This should increase understanding and interest in activity and encourage good social interplay.

NOTE: The colors in the sign language guide should help with palette arrangement instructions.

Visually handicapped—Provide your visually handicapped students with a magnifying glass so that they can examine brushstroke postcards and samples with greater visual understanding. The textural richness of painting should be tactually gratifying for your visually handicapped students.

Blind students will also enjoy the sensory quality of the paint. You may want to prepare brushstroke sample chart for students using extra thick paint (load it on) and leave time for paint to dry so students can feel the patterns. Students can create patterns on canvas, adding sand to paint. This will increase the tactile experience. When paint is dry, students can feel their visual statements.

NOTE: Never underestimate the visual ability of a blind student. The painting of the boat in Figure 166 was created by a blind boy. If you observe it, you will notice that it is a dark mass against a light background, which is how he probably sees the world (called "light perception"). You may be surprised, but this boy uses a white cane and braille; yes, he is blind! The painting, you'll agree, is most expressive and pleasing to the eye.

Gifted

The brushstroke lesson presented here is very simple to follow, but painting can be clearly more complex if you take it further. Your gifted students should develop technique and carry out their ideas in paint to the fullest extent. Students should be encouraged to mix "new" colors on their palette and to use a full variety of surface textures on canvas.

You might want students to bring in "props" from home: fruits for still life, musical instruments, clothing effects (hats, gloves, shawls), etc. Students arrange their own setups and practice by sketching on paper. When ready, they will select one color from the palette to first block out the composition. Before students begin to build the surface, ask them to think about what the actual brushstrokes can represent, i.e., flowing water, reflected light, snowfall, etc., when painted in a particular way. Good examples are in the work of Manet, Monet, and Van Gogh.

"Paint away," leaving a few class periods or sessions in order to fully develop their paintings.

Thanksgiving Feast

MATERIALS

- Paper plates (*not* waxed)
- Plastic utensils
- Colored paper (12 by 18 inches)
- Tissue paper (various colors)
- Crayons
- Markers
- Paste
- White glue
- Wallpaper samples
- Scissors

TEACHER PREPARATION

You will need enough plastic spoons, forks, and knives to go around your class. Provide paper plates unless you want to cut large paper circles as a substitute. Wallpaper samples can be acquired, as many resourceful teachers know, by approaching wallpaper and paint stores for outdated books. You can precut food shapes if you wish, such as corncobs, drumsticks, asparagus, etc. For students who will be drawing and cutting their own food, precut squares work well.

DIRECTIONS

1. Talk about the meaning of Thanksgiving—how it started and why we have big dinners to celebrate it.

2. Offer students the paper, crayons, scissors, and paper plates. They can create their turkey drumsticks, potatoes, or whatever their tummies tell them to do. Student might also crumple up tissue paper and glue the pieces to the paper plates. (See Figures 167 and 168.)

3. Paste food to the paper plate.

4. For placemats and napkins, use wallpaper in combination with construction paper.

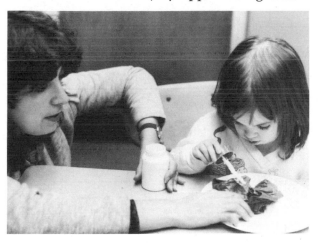

Figure 167

Figure 168

5. Glue all parts of the setting on the placemat. (See Figure 169.) The plastic ware will require the white glue.

SUGGESTIONS FOR FURTHER DEVELOPMENT

This lesson has very strong motivation before Thanksgiving but could also be used as a picnic lesson in the spring.

Figure 169

adaptations

Thanksgiving Feast

Mentally Retarded

Severely retarded students often put inedible objects in their mouths. Because the place setting is suggestive of meal times, avoid confusion by skipping the food part of the lesson. Concentrate on decorating the plate. Students will rip colored paper by holding the paper stationary with one hand and pulling paper with the other hand. Help students to glue down colored tissue on plate. With physical and verbal prompting, guide students in the gluing and placement of plate and utensils.

Let your mildly retarded students draw their own interpretations of Thanksgiving dinner food (even scribbling can be cut out for "spaghetti"). Place food on plate. Major emphasis will be on placing setting in proper location on wallpaper (or construction paper) placemat. To help students toward independence in this task, outline in marker the plate and utensils on the placemat. Students will then match the objects to their outlines.

Socially and Emotionally Disturbed

Thanksgiving is a good occasion to discuss the art of "getting along," as in the case of the pilgrim settlers and the native American Indians.

Create your own "togetherness" banquet in the classroom; have students mount their individual settings on a length of brown paper representing a table top. Have everyone sign a "place card" and glue it in place with student work. The table top (of brown paper) can be a replication of wood, created by two or more students.

Learning Disabled

Provide the learning disabled students with magazines that they can search through for food pictures. Have students tear out as many pages as they think have the appropriate food items, then decide those items which best reflect Thanksgiving. Cut out items and paste on plate. When setting the places, make sure students understand which utensils go on the left and on the right.

Physically Handicapped

Rather than cutting out the food, you might want your physically handicapped students to paint food directly on the paper plate. Painting will allow more freedom of expression when muscular control is limited. Try to get students to choose colors that relate to the food (green for vegetables, brown for meat, etc.) The placemat as well as the napkin can be painted also. If you want students to practice cutting, use the wallpaper (not the coated kind). Paste down the scraps on the painted placemats when paint is dry.

Sensory Losses

Hearing impaired—The spirit of Thanksgiving is sharing and communicating. Students will do both with this approach: assign partners to a specific part of the banquet preparation— "cooking" (drawing) vegetables, meat, etc.; "designing"—plates, napkins, table settings. When all work is complete, everyone joins in to contribute and exchange their specialties.

Have pictures that illustrate Thanksgiving on hand and samples of finished products before beginning lesson.

Visually handicapped—It's very difficult for blind students to cut the precise shapes representing the food. Give students freedom to do it their way without imposing standards (e.g., vegetables might be represented by shredded paper). You might want students to color the plates; the borders often have a ribbed texture that's tactually interesting. For the wallpaper placemat, try to find flocked wallpaper samples (embossed texture). Students may enjoy them more than the regular paper type.

Gifted

Students can develop plate and silver designs by looking at traditional and contemporary patterns. Department store catalogues will provide reference material for ideas. When students design plate patterns, they can use paper plates but they will want to design flatware out of oaktag (no plasticware needed). Napkin rings can also be created out of cardboard rolls (cut from the paper rolls inside foil wrap).

The Total Totem

MATERIALS

- Brown butcher wrap paper
- Manila paper, 9 by 12 inches
- Crayons (and/or oil pastels)
- Markers
- Poster paint
- Feathers
- White glue

TEACHER PREPARATION

You may want to provide some background on totems—their history and the legends that surround them. Encyclopedias provide quick reference material for you and your students.

Cut brown paper into desired lengths. Fold paper in half lengthwise and cut in half (if paper exceeds 20 to 24 inches in width). This provides two panels, approximately 12 inches wide, for each totem pole.

If you wish to include the "wings," cut a 2½-to-3-foot length of brown paper. Precut the wings by folding and cutting to produce symmetrical design. Staple or glue wings across the back of the long panel.

DIRECTIONS

1. Explain that totem poles are decorative birds, animals, and faces stacked on top of each other. (See Figure 170.) Try to include arms and legs (in seated positions) along with the heads. Creatures can also be holding other animals or objects.

2. Practice faces and bodies on 9-by-12 inch paper, holding all papers in the same direction so that they will match when stacked together. (See Figure 171.)

Figure 170

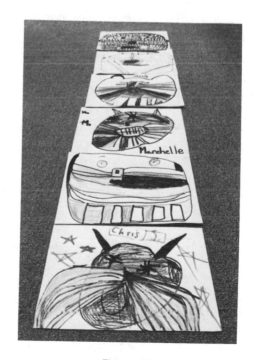

Figure 171

3. When completed, place group of pictures end-to-end on table top or floor. This helps students to understand the essential nature of the project.

4. Place butcher paper lengths across desks, three or four students to a panel. (See Figure 172.) Suggestion: Students face in the same direction when designing totems to avoid unintentionally drawing faces sideways or upside down.

Figure 172

5. Work directly on butcher paper with markers, oils, pastels, crayons, etc. Remind students to *connect* their figures with their neighbors' work by line and by color fusion. (See Figure 173.)

6. Add feathers—not just "anywhere" but where they accentuate or add to drawing—e.g., as crowns, around wings, to represent whiskers, etc.

Figure 173

7. Does it all stack up? If so, your totem is total!

SUGGESTIONS FOR FURTHER DEVELOPMENT

The totems here are dynamic, but you may want a three-dimensional totem pole. This is easily accomplished by saving paper rolls (from wrap paper, aluminum foil, paper towels, etc.). Using papier-mâché, build surface details (nose, eyes, etc.). Paint. When dry, varnish with acrylic medium (either matte or gloss finish).

adaptations

The Total Totem

Mentally Retarded

The severely retarded student is not likely to understand the nature of totem poles or be concerned with its origins. However, the manner in which elements are stacked on top of each other can be your point of focus. Create a texture totem pole with sandpaper, fabric scraps, doilies, and so on. Help students to paste the tactual materials onto 9-by-12-inch papers. When work is complete, glue work "totem-style" onto butcher wrap panel. Assist students with the gluing, verbally prompting students as to location of work (e.g., "We're putting John's work in the middle of the tall paper"). Display texture totems where students can touch them and use as a reference for tactile discrimination.

The mildly retarded student may comprehend the basic character of totem poles once a clear demonstration has taken place. The basic point is that totems are a series of shapes in a vertical arrangement. Building blocks (or books) stacked up and illustrations of totem poles will be helpful. You could also ask students to "make fists" (and imagine that their fists are totem faces and bodies); then tell students to "stack up" their fists from floor to as high as they can go.

Once the concept is understood, proceed with core lesson.

Socially and Emotionally Disturbed

Creating successful totem poles is the result of a cooperative group effort—an excellent exercise in productive social interaction. Once the working rules are clear and student interest is fixed, students should do well with this activity.

Try to draw students' attention to the facial expression of totem faces: are they angry, happy, indifferent, proud? Ask students to create totems with expressions that say something about an emotion. When work is completed, class discussion should follow to see if students can "read" each other's totem faces.

Learning Disabled

After completing step 2 of the directions, ask your learning disabled students to cut out the shapes of the totem pole elements. Students will then exchange their cutouts with their neighbors and trace this acquired shape onto paper panel. The newly acquired totem shape will be replicated by the student, but a new part will be designed to complete it. For example, a student receives a cat face shape. He or she outlines it and recreates the features (adding in his or her own details). The student will then add a new part—say, the cat's paws, holding a fish.

This approach exercises concentration, ability to replicate configurations, and closure skills, while provoking the student's own inventiveness.

Physically Handicapped

Students with restricted physical movement may have trouble positioning themselves to required postures for mural (see step 4). Make adjustment by cutting out the section of the totem that the physically handicapped student is designing. Place on accessible surface, such as an elevated drawing board. (See "Adaptive Aids.") Try to keep student seated with the rest of the group, so that he or she can interact with in planning and developing the project. When work is completed, glue or tape it into place. NOTE: Make sure that paper is vertically proportioned to fit into the rest of the totem panel.

Sensory Losses

Hearing impaired—Demonstrate totems to your hearing impaired students with as many reference materials as you can provide—photos, books, souvenirs, if possible. Most important, show how the elements will be arranged before work begins. Making up samples of Steps 3 and 4 (of Directions) and presenting them would be of considerable value.

When totems are complete, why not have students bring totems to life? Students can mime totem facial expressions; see if other students can guess which face they are emulating!

Visually handicapped—Tactual models of totem poles would be ideal for introducing this lesson. Verbally explain totem poles: they are carved wood, they are often very tall, they are much like treetrunks with faces.

Visually handicapped students may want to incorporate fluorescent materials with other materials suggested in core lesson. (See "Adaptive Aids.") Blind students can work on the group project by slipping a screenboard under their part of the brown mural paper. They will need some directions on placement of features. The feathers will provide both fun and a sensory enrichment to project. Blind students may also wish to add paper strips and circles that describe features and provide further tactual interest.

Gifted

Gifted students may enjoy departing from the expected array of totem elements to create their own special totem themes. To accomplish this, each group of three or four students should decide on a topic to be carried out and plan on assigning various parts. For instance, a theme could be "the Middle Ages," and each student could create a different element, e.g., a gargoyle, a dragon head, a knight, a damsel, etc.

The possibilities for themes are endless, but here are some suggestions: circus, fairy-tale characters, masks of different cultures, space age faces, monsters, famous people, and many more.

Up, Up, and Away!

MATERIALS

- Brown butcher paper (on roll)
- Markers
- Crayons
- Poster or acrylic paint
- Scissors
- Glue
- Wide brushes
- String
- Construction paper

TEACHER PREPARATION

The emphasis is on *big* and *bold*. For huge balloons, you need to precut shapes in parts (balloon, basket). The net part can be cut as part of basket or of balloon. (See Figure 174.) Otherwise, cut in one piece; fold for symmetry.

Figure 174

DIRECTIONS

1. What are hot air balloons? Where and when can you see them? How are they different from party balloons? Talk about their monumental size.

2. Roll out the paper. With a crayon or pencil, sketch out the balloon shape freely (or design half on fold). Cut out.

3. Outline bands of color or design for balloon body. Paint with bright colors.

4. Now for the basket—talk about basket weave patterns and basket shapes.

5. Add details—sand bags, people, etc. Assemble with glue and staple parts. (See Figures 175 and 176.)

Figure 175

Figure 176

201

adaptations

Up, Up, and Away!

Mentally Retarded

Make the largest work surface in your room accessible to your severely retarded students. Guide your student's arm, using a thick crayon in broad circular motions over brown paper. Decorate surface with bright, strong colors. When cutting out balloon, include gondola (carrier basket) in overall contour—special attention does not need to be given to gondola's design.

The mildly retarded can use the same basic approach as the severely retarded. However, some interest can be given to the texture of the carrier basket and people may be added.

Socially and Emotionally Disturbed

Once the main part of this lesson is accomplished, you might want to stress the "people" part. Students can create figure groups for balloon to carry in the basket. They can be based on self-portraits and friends, or just from students' imaginations.

Learning Disabled

The sheer size of the balloons lends to exploring the concepts of *big* and *little*. Talk about the differences between the scale of real hot air balloons and the ones that you are making out of paper. Awareness of the size of the surface they are required to cover will bring the "wholeness" of the project into focus—remind students to paint surfaces fully. It's also important to follow the contour of the shape.

Physically Handicapped

You may want to use a one-piece balloon for manageability. Tape brown paper to large work surfce—use either paint or markers. To extend lesson into the people for the basket, use "You're a Doll" adaptations for basic instructions.

Sensory Losses

Hearing impaired—Do some movement exercises that say "UP!" Stretch, reach, jump. Then make a circular shape with arms. Show pictures of all kinds of balloons in motion, point out the hot air balloons, then launch lesson!

Visually handicapped—Try to bring some party balloons to class. Blow them up; let children feel their elastic surfaces. If possible, take the children outside and let the balloons go! Talk abut "aerodynamics" and the shapes. In class, give students large precut paper balloons. Let them use yarn and white glue to outline contours of balloon. Use textured paint.

Gifted

Students should be able to cut balloon parts on their own. Perhaps they can paper weave the basket part. If they make people, you might suggest a "period" theme, e.g., "The Gay Nineties," to create corresponding styles and costumes.

Students might enjoy designing their own air ships—blimps, zeppelins, etc.—from streamlined to ornate.

Weave-a-Turtle

MATERIALS

- Construction paper (assorted colors)
- Scissors
- Crayons

TEACHER PREPARATION

Students will need to understand the concept of weaving to do this activity. Precut the turtle shape for students lacking in scissors skills. The paper cutter will help with preparing the paper strips you will need for weaving.

DIRECTIONS

1. Demonstrate the basic weaving movement to students who do not know how to weave. (See Figure 177.) The easiest explanation is to start one line with *under*, over, under, etc.; begin the next with *over*, under, over, etc. (or vice-versa) with paper strips through paper.

Figure 178

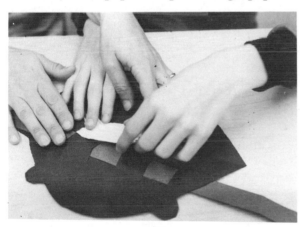

Figure 177

2. Student cut turtle shell shapes on a fold as indicated. Cut either wavy or straight lines to weave paper through.

3. Weave in paper strips. (See Figure 178.) Trim ends. Draw turtle's face. (See Figure 179.)

Figure 179

SUGGESTIONS FOR FURTHER DEVELOPMENT

This is a good introductory activity to weaving. It's simple to move from paper weaving to fiber weaving. To create other creatures for paper weaving, consider snails, fish, and butterflies.

adaptations

Weave-a-Turtle

Mentally Retarded

Students draw with crayons on precut turtles. Cut four to six straight slits. Use oversized paper strips. In a hand-over-hand method, weave paper strips into turtle shape. Use verbal cues of "under-over-under-over" to reinforce weaving movement.

Mildly retarded students may be able to cut the outline of the turtle. They may not require precut turtles. These students should also be able to learn to weave. Severely retarded students will probably benefit the most from the motion of weaving, but may not get the "how to" knowledge.

Socially and Emotionally Disturbed

Weaving is an absorbing activity that requires concentration. To work students into involvement with weaving, treat paper weaving as a first step to many other projects. You might want to present examples of the many forms of weaving, from paper to fabric.

For a group activity, think about a paper weaving "bee." Students can weave individual components of a larger subject such as a woven paper cityscape. Students will weave their own skyscrapers, storefronts, building facades, etc. (How about yellow or white strips into dark buildings to represent windows?)

Learning Disabled

Turtle shape may be outlined from a template created by you or drawn free-hand. Assist student if necessary before cutting.

Weaving is an excellent activity for the learning disabled student. The weaving process exercises directionality: left-to-right, over-and-under. Students may have trouble understanding the sequence and alternation of weaving. Try this: Use *two* colors *only* for the paper strips, say, orange for *over* and green for *under*. The turtle should, of course, be a contrasting color. Make sure strips are woven into the turtle in the proper order.

Physically Handicapped

Many physically handicapped students may benefit from weaving both the front and back of their work—one hand helps the other work strips through. Use oaktag to weave strips into it, because it is more rigid.

Sensory Losses

Hearing impaired—Using the turtle shape, demonstrate the *over* and *under* movement of the paper strips to students. See the Sign Language Chart for these terms.

Visually handicapped—You can try teaching paper weaving to the blind by using corrugated paper and fine sandpaper strips. Students can more easily alternate strips in correct sequence if they can discriminate between "over" and "under" tactually (i.e., the sandpaper can be "over," the corrugated paper becomes "under").

For the visually handicapped, make sure you use highly contrasting colors to make visual discrimination clearer.

Gifted

Students should be encouraged to cut a variety of paper strip sizes. Smaller strips should produce more intricate designs. Students might also want to use magazines and newspapers for strips—don't overlook the cartoon section!

What's the Scoop?

MATERIALS

- Oaktag
- Scissors
- Glue
- Markers (scented type)

TEACHER PREPARATION

Precut triangles for cone shapes and circles for ice cream scoops.

DIRECTIONS

1. What is your favorite ice cream flavor? Ask students to name as many flavors as they can—think about the multiple choices at the ice cream store.

2. Give students the materials and let them create their own ice creams—single and double deckers, super scoops, whatever! (See Figures 180, 181, and 182.)

3. Add jimmies (sprinkles), cherries, or whatever the heart desires.

Figure 180

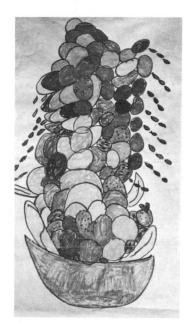

Figure 181

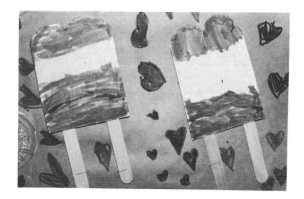

Figure 182

SUGGESTIONS FOR FURTHER DEVELOPMENT

This activity would appear to be more suited to the younger child but don't be fooled, the subject has broad appeal for all ages. Ice cream cones are ideal subjects for graphic art design projects. For instance, a fold-out, flip-down ice cream cone would work beautifully. Also, consider the ice popsicle as a project. Popsicles can be made out of oaktag and scented markers and mounted on real popsicle sticks (or tongue depressors). Consider the ice popsicle in a "paper doll" format—what fun!

Also, 3-D ice cream cones may be made from baker's clay and real cones! (See Figure 183.) (Baker's clay recipe on page 244.)

Figure 183

adaptations

What's the Scoop?

Mentally Retarded

For the severely retarded students, assist in making circles in brightly colored or fluorescent markers or crayons on paper. Paper plates may be used to trace the circle representing scoops or they can be decorated directly. Cut two or three large triangles for cones out of corrugated paper, then cut the circles that students have drawn on paper. You staple circles together vertically and attach cones (triangles) at bottom. Multiscooped cones can be hung with string through top scoop.

For your mildly retarded students, you can bring actual cones (no ice cream necessary) to class. Present precut flat paper triangles; point out the relationship between the real cone and the paper triangle. Students can color the cones on a screenboard for a texture that is similar to a real cone. Use flavored paints for ice cream scoops. Glue or staple cone and scoop together; paste on colored paper and sign names. Display.

Socially and Emotionally Disturbed

Pair students as "business partners" in an ice cream store. The assignments will be creating a store front, making a sign, designing a counter, etc. They will need to use large mural-sized paper for each part of assignment.

All the students will be asked to create ice cream flavors with original names that encourage use of imagination. Encourage students to use their own names; i.e., Terry's tiger stripe fudge, Wendy's wonderful watermelon mint, etc. Flavors can be illustrated in a way that best suits their part of the project. Display all store parts together.

Learning Disabled

Write ice cream flavors on 3-by-5-inch cards to distribute to students. Demonstrate how to illustrate the flavor based on the descriptive names; i.e., chocolate swirl mint would suggest brown swirly patterns. Students might want to do more than one flavor. When all scoops are completed, cut cone shapes (or sundae dish) and mount scoops on brown paper. Discuss the similarities and differences between flavors and the patterns they create.

Physically Handicapped

Your physically handicapped students can accent the scoops by printing the nuts, mints, jimmies (sprinkles), strawberries, etc. The brush itself can be used as a printing tool by gently pressing paint onto paper in a back and forth motion. Sponges, corks, bottle caps, and oil based clay can be used for printing.

Sensory Losses

Hearing impaired—Describe steps of lesson, using samples to illustrate. Present any relevant reference material that you can: photos, even food containers such as ice cream cartons, ice cream cone boxes, etc. Otherwise, follow core lesson.

Visually handicapped—Let your students use precut circle scoops and cone shapes. Use flavored paints for ice cream.

Do cones on screenboards. Remember, lightweight paper works best. You may also want to use scented markers.

Gifted

Students can make a flip book, containing a bite-by-bite sequence describing the inevitable fate of all ice cream cones. Starting with a drawing of the full cone, students will show scoops and cone being eaten page by page. Students can think about facial expression of the person eating the ice cream cone. Since this is an animation project, students may want to use the style of cartoon characterization.

Windows

MATERIALS

- Construction paper, 11 by 18 (use light color for background, black for house)
- Scissors
- Paste
- Crayons
- Fabric scraps

TEACHER PREPARATION

Some children will need house and window openings precut. To simplify cutting of windows, fold paper and cut half of the window.

DIRECTIONS

1. Spend some time discussing how houses have their own styles and shapes.

2. Have students draw the outline of their house to the edge of their paper, using a bright crayon.

3. Cut out windows and house shape. Glue down on background paper.

4. Students create objects and faces for window, and compose area around the house. (See Figures 184 and 185.) What time of day is it? What's the weather?

5. Add fabric curtains or any other detail.

Figure 184

Figure 185

SUGGESTIONS

Magazines can be used to provide faces and objects for windows. (See Figure 186.) The houses can be anything from simple squares with triangle roofs to Victorian style castles, depending on student levels. This lesson can be expanded to a whole "village" of larger houses, cut from brown wrap, later to be displayed as a group project.

Figure 186

adaptations

Windows

Mentally Retarded

Precut simple house shape from white paper and cut spaces for at least two windows. The severely retarded student will decorate the house with fluorescent (or brightly colored) crayons or paints. Colored tissue or colored acetate can be glued into windows with your assistance. Your "mobile homes" can be hung in the real windows to catch the light and visually stimulate students.

Mildly retarded students might have difficulty in cutting out windows. They may want to use squares and rectangles for windows and doors, then decorate and paste them down. Remind students of where doors and windows belong and why.

Socially and Emotionally Disturbed

A way to get students involved could be through suggestions of themes (for windows) such as your friends, your family and your pets, people you know, etc. Emotions can be represented by faces in various windows, i.e., happy face, sad face, angry face, and so on.

Learning Disabled

This activity centers on the relationship between the houses' exterior shapes to each other and to the houses' interiors. Students need to think about the functional placement of windows and doors. Eye-hand coordination and the concept of closure will be exercised through drawing and cutting window shapes.

Physically Handicapped

Students can practice their scissors skills by cutting squares for windows and rec-tangles for doors. If you have wallpaper samples, these make great windows—especially if students cut up lace doilies and use them as curtains. People, plants, and animals can be added to windows, but this requires fine-motor skills.

Sensory Losses

Hearing impaired—Show students a sample of the finished product first. Demonstrate methods for cutting windows out of house front. Follow core lesson. NOTE: For those who can read, a little dialogue can be created between the faces in the windows using "talking balloons."

Visually handicapped—Guide your blind students to a real available window and door so that they can explore the overall shape and perimeters. Blind students have difficulty in understanding the dimensions of a given area.

Another introduction to the activity is to present a doll house or other 3-D model of a house. This offers understanding of the *whole* concept, which blindness has limited.

Window and door decoration can be done with paper squares on the screen-board. If you have embossed wallpaper samples, cut for window curtains and add them—or use fabric scraps instead.

Gifted

This can be a gateway lesson to the study of historical architectural styles. Have students research and select a specific style for their houses. Make sure that all details agree with that style, e.g., a Southern mansion should have appropriate columns, porticos, etc., as well as "Southern belles" and so on in the windows.

Working Wet with Watercolors

MATERIALS

- White paper
- Watercolor paints
- Brushes
- Watercolor cups or containers
- Paper towels
- Tissue paper
- Sponges
- Kosher salt (optional)
- Eyedropper (optional)

TEACHER PREPARATION

Since this activity depends on keeping the paper wet (and it evaporates quickly), have all supplies on hand to begin lesson. A bucket of clear water nearby might be more convenient than running to the sink repeatedly. Also, you might want to cut sponges into various shapes and sizes to use for added design details.

Before diving into their work, students should be instructed on the proper use of materials. First, get plenty of water on your brush to dip into the paints. Use individual colors and mix the colors inside the open lid. Each time you change colors, dip lightly in water and wipe brush on paper towel. (The paper towel is your "paint rag"; using it frequently will keep water fresh.) Paint boxes should be left in a clean and orderly way for future use. Paper towel corners can help clean between colors.

DIRECTIONS

1. With painting materials in front of them, students begin by wetting the

Figure 187

Figure 188

Figure 189

paper thoroughly with sponge. (See Figure 187.)

2. Experiment. Wet paper will respond to the touch of the paint brush with bursts of patterns. (See Figure 188.)

3. Blot the tissue, dab the sponge, and sprinkle the salt on the wet paint.

4. When a harmony of visual patterns and textures has been reached, the work is complete. (See Figure 189.)

SUGGESTIONS FOR FURTHER DEVELOPMENT

Watercolor is a medium that lends itself to experimentation. Here are two techniques you could try for interesting effects:

- Watercolor and Kosher Salt: Kosher salt is recommended because it is coarser than regular table salt and will create a more grainy texture. Using *watercolor paper,* wet down area to be painted. Apply color heavily. Throw in pinches of salt where texture is desired. Let dry thoroughly. Brush off salt. (See Figure 190.)

- Eyedropper Painting: Create a splashy pattern by filling eyedropper with water mixed with watercolor. Wet paper and drop paint on it. Watercolor paper and rice paper work very well because of their absorbency.

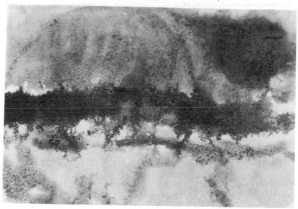

Figure 190

adaptations

Working Wet with Watercolors

Mentally Retarded

Try creating "paint splatter patterns" with your severely retarded students. Load the brush with plenty of paint. You will guide student's hand and, holding the brush together, you will flick paint onto the paper. Change colors as directed; repeat until paper is covered with bursts of color. This activity should be suitable for your students because of its use of both kinesthetics and the visually stimulating results.

Mildly retarded students should be able to follow the core lesson. But demonstrating how to use watercolors as well as showing students possibilities of the experimental materials is critical. Once students seem to grasp that information, proceed.

Socially and Emotionally Disturbed

You may want students to build a composition based on their fantasy and imagination. Take a good-sized brush and load with paint. Squeeze the end of the brush over the wet paper so that a blob of paint falls on it. Ask the students to create a picture based on what the paint splatter suggests to them. Talk about work in group discussion when completed.

NOTE: Often, direct watercolor painting has a calming effect. There is something about the experience that will completely absorb students and have a positive effect on behavior while activity takes place.

Learning Disabled

Tell your learning disabled students to leave room on all sides for a border. Demonstrate to them what you mean. When painting starts to develop, ask students to select a design element of their painting to use as a motif for paper's edges (i.e., printed sponge pattern).

In using this approach, you are asking students to plan ahead and to create their own spatial boundary, which lends a clear framework to the activity.

Physically Handicapped

If students do not have the physical movement required to dip sponge into water and wet their papers, you will need to help by keeping paper wet for them. However, the motion of dipping and squeezing sponges and wiping the paper is an excellent movement exercise. If students are willing to try it, encourage them.

For another worthwhile movement experience, you can create a rolling "paint printer." In advance of lesson, glue bits of sponges and yarn on a paper cardboard roll (paper towel or tinfoil dispenser type). Students will cover their paper with paint either by sponging colored water on or by painting directly with brush. Now roll or press the roller on the wet surface. The result is an interesting printed surface.

Sensory Losses

Hearing impaired—Students should enjoy doing the activity as outlined in the core. For a variation that will encourage class interaction, students can do "monoprints" of each others' work. Students should do contour paintings (line painting) of any subject desired. While wet, students will carefully place a blank paper on top of a "buddy's" work. Slowly remove, "pulling" from the corner of the top of the paper.

A print will appear! Students should then go on to develop the watercolor print with their own details.

Make sure you demonstrate this activity and aid in pulling prints when needed.

Visually handicapped—Visually handicapped students should love using fluorescent paints, which are water soluble and quite compatible with watercolors. A natural subject for "working wet" is undersea life—the fluorescent colors can be used to represent that iridiscence of sea creatures and fish.

Blind students need to use their unengaged hands to feel what part of their papers have been wet with paint. When they do direct watercolor you may want to skip wetting the whole paper. Watch for blind students reworking the same areas; they need to *rotate* their papers. Avoid over-rubbing with brush; it "pills" paper into brush and creates holes in paper. Guide each student's hand so he or she knows where cup and paints are located.

Stabilize water cup with rolled masking tape at the bottom.

Blind students enjoy the sensory experience of watercolor. As they become familiar with the medium, they appear to refine the balance of their compositions based on where they feel water on the page. Water, not color, seems to be the element on which the experience is built.

Gifted

Gifted students should be encouraged to use as many available objects as they can think of to create unusual patterns in the wet paint. Rags, folded paper, corks, erasers, spools, etc., are some possibilities.

You might also want to challenge imaginations by setting up a given theme, such as telling students to paint portholes into their compositions and then describe (in paint) what they see through them. This theme can include diving bells, aquariums, a hole in the frozen lake, etc.

You're a Doll!

MATERIALS

- Yarn
- Scissors
- Heavyweight paper or oaktag, 9 by 12 inches or 11 by 14 inches
- Buttons, lace, trim, doilies, etc.

TEACHER PREPARATION

Gather little goodies that will add textural interest—sequins, fabric scraps, ribbon, jewelry, etc. You may want to precut dolls and/or demonstrate.

DIRECTIONS

1. This is actually a self-portrait, so discuss individual physical characteristics. Is your hair curly or straight? Are you tall or short? Do you have a dark or a light complexion?

2. Give students paper to design a doll that is based on their features, their favorite outfits, or "fantasy" ones. Encourage students to use the whole paper for dolls' contours. (See Figure 191.)

3. Cut dolls out. (See Figures 192 and 193.) Backs may be designed, too.

4. Add lace, trim, and other details. (See Figure 194.)

SUGGESTIONS FOR FURTHER DEVELOPMENT

A cutout wardrobe can be developed for dolls, which will require some accuracy in fitting. For group projects, students can create a 3-D indoor and outdoor environment for figures out of cardboard or shoeboxes (i.e., parks, neighborhoods). Another idea: Mount several dolls in a row on length of paper to create a "chorus line."

Figure 191

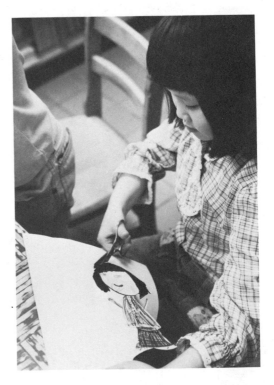

Figure 192

Figure 193

Figure 194

adaptations

You're a Doll!

Mentally Retarded

Severely retarded students can paint the precut dolls with teacher assistance. Students can be helped in gluing a variety of fabric scraps to their dolls. Fabric offers an association with students' own clothing—an everyday tactile experience that should have meaning for students.

For the mildly retarded student, this lesson will reinforce body awareness. In a physically demonstrative way, identify arms, legs, faces; e.g., "This is your hand." Show students corresponding parts on the precut dolls. Explaining facial features is a lesson in itself, so to tackle entire lesson you need to break into steps: (1) face, (2) body, front, (3) body, back. Pasting should be done in hand-over-hand method.

Socially and Emotionally Disturbed

Discuss "body language"—what body postures say about moods and attitudes. Have students assume different poses that "say" proud, cheerful, relaxed, tense, etc. Students use that exercise to make dolls to express a particular mood. When dolls are completed, students should guess what each other's poses were intended to be. NOTE: Some students may object to making "dolls," saying that they're too babyish, too silly, etc. If you think your students might be put off by the word "doll," then call them "cutout figures" or anything else that will be better received.

Learning Disabled

Stress body parts relationships. "The arm is connected to the body by the shoulder," etc. Do warm-up exercises with instructions like "touch your right leg with your right hand," etc. To further understand body movement, you may want students to design dolls with moving parts, using paper fasteners for joints.

Physically Handicapped

Self-image can be difficult for the physically handicapped. Take your cues from the students—if they want to create a more perfect self, support their ideas. Realistic self-interpretation should also be respected. Adaptive aids and help with cutting may be needed.

Sensory Losses

Hearing impaired—Dolls may be used to "speak" for the students in informal dramatizations created for interplay. The movement of dolls can be a "mime" type performance. Dolls can be mounted on popsicle sticks for this type of activity.

Visually handicapped—Body shape of precut dolls should be compared to real anatomical information. Placement of facial features will require assistance. The textures of fabric, buttons, etc., should be incorporated into this lesson for sensory experience.

Gifted

Use dolls as an anatomy lesson. Give students a choice: Show dolls as "X-rayed," revealing anatomy (skeletal, muscular, etc.) with accuracy, or let students try to improve upon the design!

A different approach would be to use dolls for career development. Students create dolls as they might see themselves in the future. Give attention to details, e.g., what would you carry? A briefcase? A tool box? What hat would you wear? And so on.

A BLUEPRINT FOR THEMES

Here are some suggestions for additional subjects that students will find enjoyable. All the themes listed are recommended for general student use, though some subjects may be particularly suited for the special needs groups as indicated in the chart: Mentally Retarded (M.R.), Socially and Emotionally Disturbed (S.E.D.), Learning Disabled (L.D.), Physically Handicapped (P.H.), Hearing Impaired (H.I.), Visually Handicapped (V.H.), and Gifted.

A check mark in the column indicates the activity is especially geared for that particular special interest group. The column "Good Flat Design Theme" refers to subjects with simple, solid, flat designs. For example, "ABCs" represents an arrangement of alphabetical letters in an interesting two-dimensional format.

Figures 195-200 illustrate the art that can be done for some of these themes.

	M.R.	S.E.D.	L.D.	P.H.	H.I.	V.H.	Gifted	Good Flat Design Theme
ABCs: The Alphabet	✔		✔		✔			★
Airplanes and Airports		✔			✔		✔	
Animal Babies and Their Parents	✔		✔				✔	
Biggest, Smallest	✔		✔			✔	✔	★
Birds in Trees			✔	✔			✔	
Bubbles	✔		✔	✔				★
Buildings	✔	✔	✔	✔		✔	✔	★
Bridges		✔	✔	✔			✔	★
Celebrities		✔					✔	
Clowns and the Circus	✔				✔	✔		
Dinosaurs	✔		✔				✔	
Dragons and Monsters		✔		✔	✔		✔	
Fans			✔	✔			✔	★
Families	✔	✔			✔			
Fantastic Animals		✔				✔	✔	
Fitness and Exercise	✔	✔	✔	✔		✔		
* Free Choice (anything goes)	✔	✔	✔	✔	✔	✔	✔	★
Friends	✔	✔			✔	✔	✔	
Industry	✔		✔	✔	✔	✔	✔	★
Jungle Creatures	✔	✔	✔	✔				
Kaleidoscope		✔			✔	✔	✔	★
Kites	✔		✔	✔		✔	✔	★
Knights		✔	✔	✔			✔	

*Free choice is important to everyone for learning, self-structuring, and developing individual styles.

219

	M.R.	S.E.D.	L.D.	P.H.	H.I.	V.H.	Gifted	Good Flat Design Theme
Magic Crystal Ball		✔			✔		✔	
Neighborhoods	✔	✔	✔	✔	✔	✔	✔	
Nuts and Bolts		✔	✔		✔		✔	★
Parks	✔	✔	✔	✔	✔	✔		
Patterns of Animals' Skins			✔	✔		✔	✔	★
Pets	✔	✔		✔	✔	✔		
Playing Card Portraits		✔	✔				✔	
Poetry and Prose		✔			✔	✔	✔	
Roots of Growing Things	✔		✔				✔	
Shadows			✔		✔	✔	✔	★
Shoes and Stockings	✔		✔			✔	✔	★
Ships at Sea	✔	✔		✔	✔	✔	✔	
Spider Web		✔	✔			✔	✔	★
Sports	✔	✔		✔	✔			
Subways			✔				✔	★
Things That Fly	✔		✔		✔	✔		
Twins			✔		✔	✔	✔	
Umbrellas	✔		✔				✔	★
Weather	✔	✔	✔	✔	✔	✔		
Wheels	✔		✔	✔	✔			★

Figure 195
Animal Babies

Figure 196
Dragons and Monsters

Figure 197
Industry

Figure 198
Jungle Creatures

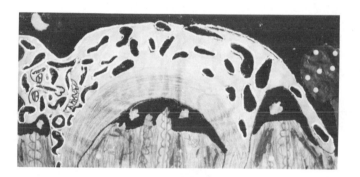

Figure 199
Patterns on Animals

Figure 200
Playing Cards

MATERIALS LAB

Mixed Media

Try various media to carry out selected themes. Experiment! Many materials create sensational effects when mixed. Oil pastels and wax crayons will create *wax resist* when combined with waterbased paints, such as watercolors and poster paints. The result is a batik-like, beaded surface with a rich textural appearance. This method works best when painting is done *on top* of the waxy design or picture.

Other materials can form productive partnerships. Look at the list:

- markers
- watercolors
- poster paints
- acrylic paints

- chalks
- oil pastels
- crayons
- colored pencils

Mix them, then see what happens! Discover your own dynamic combos.

Painting Without Brushes

When you want to draw or paint, you start looking for your pens and brushes. For a change of pace, try dipping some less likely objects into the paint. You might start by collecting from nature—twigs, branches, ferns, dry grass, etc. There are more possibilities indoors—in kitchen drawers, the office desk, the bathroom counter. Try drawing with chopsticks, broken combs, toothbrushes, cotton swabs, eraser ends of pencils, crochet needles, eyedroppers, and hair pins. (See Figure 201.) Start a collection; try your new drawing and painting tools with various paints and different papers. You will achieve one kind of an effect with rice paper, another with Bristol board.

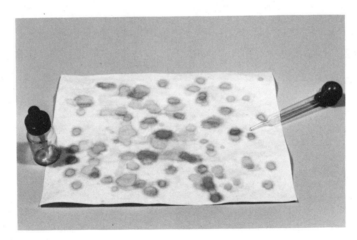

Figure 201

Have We Lost Our Marbles?

If we have, they are in the paint, too. You will need plastic containers and spoons, and box lids (gift box or shoebox) if you want to paint with marbles. Here's how: Fill containers with various colored paint, place a handful of marbles

Figure 202

into each one, along with a spoon. Scoop desired colors with spoons into box lid. Paint by moving box lid with hands on either side. The movement controls the painting. Finished painting is in the box lid. (See Figure 202.) If you wish to reuse the lid, first insert paper for other marble paintings; remove when finished. This is fun for all ages but will be perfect for some physically handicapped, as well as retarded students.

See "Adaptive Aids" for additional suggestions for drawing and painting tools.

HINTS

Holidays and Seasons

Do not underestimate the impact of holidays on a child's life. Birthdays, Christmas or Hanukkah, and Thanksgiving are some of the marker events that are anticipated and remembered. Students are often intense about them. Give students the opportunity to express their involvement through their art.

Seasons also bring excitement and memories of past experiences. They also provide a logical framework in time. Changes in seasons have strong associations—summer may represent freedom, fall brings school and all that goes with it (renewed friendships and responsibilities), etc. It is a subject that students already have definite feelings about, but they may need some help with the sequence of seasons. Keep in mind, too, that special students should be kept aware of the world outside and the environment, so activities dealing with holidays, seasons, and weather are very useful.

Although holiday art activities have been included in this book, many others can easily be converted into holiday themes. "Face It" is perfect to present around the time of Halloween. "Personality Plus Puppets" can easily yield witches and goblins, but could also produce elves and angels. "Stuffed Pretzels" can change into stuffed pumpkins. "Windows" is a perfect haunted house lesson, as is "Silhouettes" (how about a "street of tricks or treats"?) Hearts for Valentine's Day can be printed or stitched. And, of course, "Feat of Clay" and "Apples and Oranges" can become goblins and ghosts or cornucopias.

Preshaped Paper

You may have noticed that many lessons include paper cut in the shape of an object, often with suggestions for precutting. Shaped paper can be very helpful to many students—visually impaired, physically handicapped, learning disabled, and retarded. Why? Because a shape is a *concrete* expression of an object or concept, whether it is a pizza, a guitar, or a portrait. (See Figure 203.) The shape represents the real thing and becomes more manageable. Students are given boundaries and a framework within which they can structure their ideas and designs. Of course, you would not want students to overuse the shaped paper, but it is a solid way to introduce concepts to students who may be somewhat unclear about them.

Figure 203

Point of Reference

Sometimes getting started on a composition or idea can be overwhelming. The blank paper can stare you in the face, offering little support. Special students, particularly learning disabled and retarded, can be especially disconcerted by the

Figure 204

Figure 205

challenge. You can help students organize their thoughts on paper by starting them off with a *part* of the whole picture. This can be done simply by placing a meaningful mark or a shape on the paper. Or you can provide an element around which students can "build a picture." Here are a few suggestions: stickers (animals, boats, flowers), rubber-stamp images, a cutout picture from a magazine (see Figure 204)—even a Band-Aid (see Figure 205) can inspire a picture that will "grow" around it.

ADAPTIVE AIDS AND MATERIALS

- **Brushes, Pencils, and Other Drawing Tools**
    Solving Manual Grasp Difficulties
- **Painting and Drawing Without Arm Movement**
- **Aids for Organization**
- **Sewing and Cutting**
- **Adaptive Aids for Visually Handicapped and Blind Students in Art**
    Recipe File

THREE

Brushes, Pencils, and Other Drawing Tools

SOLVING MANUAL GRASP DIFFICULTIES

Many handicapped students have a hard time with gripping narrow tools. Here are some suggestions that may help physically handicapped as well as other special students:

• **Foam hair curlers**—Store-bought foam hair curlers can be slipped over brushes or pencils. (See Figure 206.) *Foam*, purchased in a fabric store, may be cut to size and wrapped around tool, then secured with rubber hands or wires. Flexible rubber tubing can also be used to build up tool's thickness.

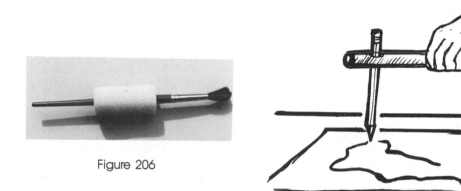

Figure 206

Figure 207

• **Dowels**—Brushes can be cut down and a short dowel taped across the end in a "T" shape. Use electrical duct tape to secure the cross bar; it's stronger than most tapes. Students may find the full hand grasping the cross bar to be easier than holding brushes in conventional manner.

Here's another use for dowels when movement is restricted: Cut dowel to length for student to grasp fully. Drill a hole into the end of the dowel so that pencils or brushes can be slipped into it. (See Figure 207.) The dowel becomes a tool holder that students can manipulate with a grosser grasp than holding the drawing tool itself would allow. (This dowel method can also work as a mouth stick.)

• **Velcro**—Velcro dots or strips can be applied to brush handles. A velcro strap or band can be glued to a cutdown cotton glove and slipped over student's working hand. This can help to prevent brushes from slipping out of hands when grasp is weak or limited.

• **Shaving brushes**—The stubby shape of shaving brushes makes them ideal for use in painting with some students. (see Figure 208.) The brush handle is

Figure 208

much easier to grip than conventional paint brushes. You can also try other wide handle brushes that are sold in paint and hardware stores. Small paint rollers are worth experimenting with also—not to replace brushes, but to supplement painting experiences.

• **Deodorant roll-on applicators**—Roll-on deodorant containers with removable caps can be filled with paint and used for "brushless" painting (see Figure 209.) Pry off ball cap, rinse out bottle, and fill with poster paint. Be sure that paint is not too thick or it will clog ball action. Dipping the paint end of the applicator into water as you work can help to keep the end lubricated and paint flowing. Applicators are thicker than markers and therefore easier for some students to grasp. Rolling paint out is also a good arm and upper body exercise. (See Figure 210.)

Figure 209

230

Figure 210

• **Squeeze bottles**—Plastic squeeze bottles can be purchased at housewares departments. Containers that dispense mustard and ketchup or hair dye squeeze bottles are perfect. You could also save empty plastic shampoo bottles. Fill bottles with paint or Goopi (see page 244); be sure that paint is not *too* thick or it will clog the hole. (You may need to adjust opening.) Remember to label the bottle.

Apply paint directly onto paper by squeezing bottle and moving bottle around surface. The design or composition will be affected by the squeezing action. The movement that squeezing the bottle requires is also an excellent motor activity for building hand strength.

Sponge-tipped, squeezable bottles (see Figure 211) and self-contained paint dispensers (see Figure 212) that regulate paint flow are available commercially.

Figure 211

Figure 212

231

• **Chalk holders**—Rigid plastic chalk holders for single sticks of chalk are designed primarily for teachers to use on blackboards. Some students might find chalk holders helpful in gripping fragile chalk sticks and chalk stubs. Holders are available at educational supply stores and some stationery stores.

• **Trim brushes from the hardware store, long-handled sponges from the bath shop**—There are sponge wedge brushes used for house painting, suited for reaching into corners, that your students may want to try. You can also find some possibilities at the bath shop such as long-handled sponges that would be great for art projects. Other sponges worth trying for easier grip are natural sponges or thick synthetic sponges.

• **Tool handle shapes and triangular crayons considered**—If gripping tools is a problem, you may want to explore various available materials at the well-stocked art supply store. Markers come in flat, wide shapes, brushes come with wide handles, even crayons can be purchased in chunks or triangular, wedge-like forms. You may need to ask around for other-than-regular shaped tools (some "special shaped" products are imported) but a surprising number of varieties are available.

Painting and Drawing Without Arm Movement

Some truly remarkable paintings have been created by artists, many of whom are quadriplegics who hold their brushes between their teeth. The great artist Renoir, when physically limited by arthritis in his later years, strapped his brushes to his arms. He once remarked during an interview that he could continue painting his canvases because he did not paint with hands. That remark sums up the creative spirit.

• **Mouth-held tools**—Many students without use of their arms find painting and drawing by mouth to be a most convenient method. It is absolutely imperative that materials be water-soluble and fume-free, and that handles be cleaned for repeated use. Watercolor markers are ideal for freestyle drawing. Use acrylic paints, poster paints, and watercolors for other works. Long-handled oil painting brushes work well, but avoid chipping paint from the brush handle into the mouth—taping the end might solve the problem.

You could also experiment with cigarette and cigar holders for crayons and colored pencils. You might need to add tape or tubing to secure tools to holders. Mouth stick may be made from a dowel—the dowel has a hole drilled into it and the tool is then inserted.

In mouth painting and drawing, the work surface must be accessible. Easels, reading stands, or papers tacked to a wall will help. Tools should be easy to reach, too.

• **Headbands**—When student's arm movement is restricted, another alternative is using head gear to paint and draw. (See Figure 213.) Headbands can be constructed in a number of ways. One style of headband can be made from foam

Figure 213

with velcro closures. A chin strap may be added to secure it. The drawing tool is attached to center front and is usually angled downward so that the student can work on a flat surface, but the tool can be attached as a projectile part for easel painting. Attaching the drawing or painting tool may take a little experimentation with available materials. You can use foam pipe insulating tubing. Or, you might want to contact an occupational therapist for suggestions.

Just as there are a number of artists who have learned to use their heads and mouths for painting, so also are there many who paint with their feet. In fact, there is an Association of Mouth and Foot Painting Artists, whose membership consists of disabled professional artists. Their works are of a high quality and are truly impressive.

• **"Feet forward"**—If you have ever strolled along the beach, you may remember pausing by the water's edge and digging a line into the wet sand with your pointed toe. In essence, you drew with your feet. Students who have leg and foot control may want to explore these possibilities. Have students try taking off shoes and using feet to draw with a length of butcher paper. You can do this in an upright or seated position; just make sure surface is accessible to feet.

It's tough to draw with a tool between your toes if you're not used to it (you could practice), but big movements and patterns can be easily made by dipping front of foot into shallow container of poster paint. Use bucket and paper towels for cleaning off feet.

You could also print with bottoms of feet and soles of shoes—sneakers make fabulous prints! Simply roll paint onto soles with brayer, or brush paint on (you can also "step" carefully into shallow trays of paint). As long as the lesson is well organized, giving time for setting up and cleaning up, there is no reason why your students cannot jump into their art activity with both feet!

NOTE: Occupational therapy departments are often stocked with various materials that can give you some help and ideas for adapting tools. Foams, flexible rubber tubing, stick-on tapes, no-skid materials, etc., are part of their stock-in-trade. If you want some extra suggestions on developing tools and aids for physically limited students, your added resources are with the occupational therapist. If you do not know an occupational therapist, rehabilitation hospitals (or any general hospital) should be be able to assist you.

Aids for Organization

Good organization can be very helpful to many special students. Physically handicapped students who cannot easily pick up a pencil from a flat desk top will appreciate pencils stored in upright positions. Learning disabled students (and many retarded students) become overwhelmed by confusing mixtures of materials. It helps to have them sorted. Visually handicapped and blind students may want objects stabilized on their work surfaces so that they do not knock them over—especially water-filled cups. Look over the following list to see if your students would appreciate a little extra organizational aid with materials:

• **Trays**—Foil baking pans and plastic bins can be used for materials storage and be brought forward for lessons. Labeling is a good idea. Students will know what to expect and can become familiar with materials. Smaller items can be stored in egg cartons or TV dinner trays.

Visually handicapped and blind students can actually work inside shallow trays (wooden trays are good). The tray should be the approximate size of the desk top. Materials are placed within the tray. This creates a boundary for the student and prevents materials from falling off the desk.

• **Grips and stationary stands**—Vice grips, and C-clamps that attach to a desk can be useful for securing various projects for physically handicapped students. Reading stands can also be used for sketchbooks and other drawing activities.

• **Rotating stands**—Lazy susan stands can make reaching objects easier for physically limited students. Desk caddies, available from art and office supply stores, can bring drawing tools to physically handicapped students with less effort. Clay stands that rotate are recommended for ceramic work and will help with other three-dimensional assemblages.

• **Bench hook (or holding jig)**—Although this device is primarily used in block printmaking, it may be used to secure other materials in place. For example, various constructions, carvings, assemblages of wood, clay, cardboard, etc., can use this bench hook effectively. The bench hook is particularly useful for physically handicapped students, and in some instances, the severely retarded. (See Figure 214.)

To construct the bench hook, you will need two pieces of 1-by-2-inch wood, and a piece of Masonite large enough to leave about a 2-inch space around the linoleum block. Nail or glue the 1-by-2-inch pieces to the larger piece—one on the top end, the other on the bottom end as in the illustration. (NOTE: This device may also be made from flexible sheet metal.)

• **Securing objects to surface**—The simplest way to secure paper or water cups to desk top is to roll masking tape and place under the object. However, nonskid products help to keep objects in place. You might even find some suction cups will work. You could also place nonskid tub strips on a surface where you

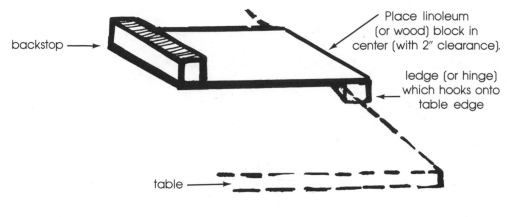

backstop →

Place linoleum (or wood) block in center (with 2″ clearance).

ledge (or hinge) which hooks onto table edge

table →

Figure 214

regularly place objects—the rubber disks used for jar opening will also work for securing replacement of cups, jars, etc., on a slick desk top.

Opening Jars

If you want students to be independent in their material selection, this may include opening jars. Using a rubber disk or sponge mat intended for that purpose can help. Another method is to place the jar on top of a second rubber mat for more pressure and turn with a palm grip. There are also jar opening devices available in housewares stores that you could purchase.

Tools and Materials Storage

Styrofoam blocks and florist blocks can be used for upright storage of pencils and brushes—and make picking them up and working with them much easier for students with limited movement. Of course, blocks do break down after a while. Again, desk caddies can be handy for both storage and ongoing materials usage.

Students may want to store their tools in fish tackle boxes, shoeboxes, cigar boxes, or even in containers used for silverware storage (the rubber kind).

yarn dispenser

Figure 215

If students use yarn or string for activities, yarn may be stored in a cardboard box. (See Figure 215.) Punch out a hole through the top of the closed box, through which a length of yarn is pulled (one hole per spool). This eliminates the difficulties many students encounter when they have to find the end of the yarn on the spool.

Reaching for Materials

If you want to encourage independence in students seeking out their working materials, you could purchase the gripping poles that grocers use to retrieve stock from high shelves. These are not only good for wheelchair-bound students, they can help everybody with those out-of-reach items.

Sewing and Cutting

Sewing and cutting are skills that many special students can achieve once they have found the tool, method, or training that works best for them.

• **Large sewing needles**—Larger needles with bigger eyes (the embroidery and tapestry type) are recommended for many special students. They are easier to thread and to grasp. Once students learn to sew with larger needles, you may be able to wean them into finer needles.

• **Threading needles**—There are many devices that can help students to thread needles. One popular aid is a coin-sized threader with a flexible wire loop. The loop is inserted through the needle's eye, thread is drawn through loop, then pulled through the needle's eye. The loop is much larger and simpler to thread than the actual needle.

You can also avoid threading the needle by purchasing the self-threading needle. This needle appears to have two eyes, and the eye has a slot above it. The thread can be pulled down through the slit for sewing. Many other threading aids are available. Ask about them at the sewing notions departments.

• **Thimbles**—Sturdy thimbles can give students hand leverage when pushing needles through thick fabrics. Sometimes needles can be slippery. Leather thimbles are flexible, but some students may be just as comfortable with thimbles made of metal or other materials.

• **Lacing boards and stitching cards**—Wooden lacing boards are available through educational supply outlets. They aid eye-hand coordination and help to develop sewing skills. They consist of several large holes and pegs attached to a cord, which represents the thread and the needle. Students should be directed in a hand-over-hand manner to understand the movement required for stitching. Lacing boards are good for introducing students to sewing and are excellent for practicing stitchery. You can make your own introductory sewing aids in the form of stitching cards. All you need is oaktag paper, a hole puncher, and shoestrings. Punch out holes along the edges, about 1 ½ inches apart. As in the lacing boards, direct students' hands in sewing movement when using shoestrings. To make it easier for some students to find the holes, you can cut centers out of fluorescent (Day-Glo) stickers and apply them around holes. Also, paper reinforcements will keep the holes in stiching cards from tearing.

Scissors

Learning to use the scissors will help students both inside and outside of school. But scissors can be more than devices that simply cut paper and cloth. Scissors can be used much like paintbrushes and pencils—sensitively and expressively. (See Figure 216.) When doing direct cutting, your scissors in effect become your drawing tool. French painter Henri Matisse, when physically

Figure 216

weakened by illness, turned his attention away from easel painting to paper cutting. His choice of the scissors appeared to be Matisse's adaptive alternative to the more strenuous act of painting. Out of this endeavor grew the original and famous Matisse papercut series. Matisse's cut paper shapes and design art represent a truly unique use of the scissors.

Spring scissors—Spring-type scissors have regular cutting blades but do not have conventional handles. Instead, the scissors have a looped plastic handle with a spring action (like some hedge clippers). This means that less manual strength and coordination are needed to cut with them. Spring scissors are available through educational resource and supply companies and usually come with either blunt or pointed cutting edges.

Double-handed scissors—Some teachers find these scissors, which are made with two sets of handles and one set of blades, to be a good introductory aid to cutting. The principle is for instructor to cut at the same time as the child cuts, and in so doing, teach the required movement.

You may find these scissors quite useful, or you might not be too impressed with them—the opinions vary. They are also available through educational supply stores.

Hints

There are exercises that can help students to develop scissors skills. You can begin cutting in small clips. For example, start by making fringe on the paper. Small movements are easier to manage than large ones. As students progress, you might want to have them cut along lines that have been drawn on paper for them. Cutting curves is perhaps the most demanding cutting activity. A student may better accomplish this task by using his or her nonworking hand to rotate the paper as the student cuts. Some visually handicapped and physically disabled students may find that moving the paper in desired directions may be simpler than manipulating the scissors for cutting. Sometimes resting the elbow of the scissors-holding hand on a surface helps with leverage.

Several factors may contribute to the successful use of scissors. Some papers are easier to cut than others. Papers that are too thin and floppy or too thick might cause students some problems. Cutting fabric effectively is more likely to be achieved once paper cutting skills can be managed.

Scissors should be in working order. When students report that "this scissors won't cut," it just may be the case. The type of scissors you use should be suited to the task at hand. Scissors that are very stiff or too loose will understandably discourage students. Check out the scissors actions and cutting ability and try different kinds of scissors. Don't forget about left-handed scissors either!

Adaptive Aids
for Visually Handicapped
and Blind Students in Art

Contrary to popular misconceptions, blind and visually handicapped students *can* learn and grow visually. The aids listed below are designed to help students with sight losses to develop their own visual imagery and style.

• **Screenboard**—This *easy-to-construct* object makes it possible for blind students to draw on paper with a better understanding of their work. (See Figure 217.) Screenboards are exactly what their name implies—a piece of cardboard with a section of window screen taped on top of it. To make one, you will need heavy cardboard (approximately 15 by 18 inches and a piece of window screen fitted to the size of cardboard. Use cloth bookbinding tape or duct tape, attach window screen to board, then tape around the edges. Fold tape under the board. (See Figure 218.)

Houses and Trees
line drawing on screenboard
by a young blind child

Figure 217

screenboard

Figure 218

Figure 219

Here's how they work: Blind students draw on paper placed on top of the screenboard. (See Figure 219.) Wherever paper is marked by crayons (or similar material) the screen texture will emerge. Delineations on the screenboard become raised lines that students can feel.

- **Tracing wheels**—A tracing wheel is actually a sewing notion that is used in paper pattern tracing. Tracing wheels come in various sizes. They have some use as drawing tools for severely visually handicapped and blind students. Use lightweight paper (braille paper is fine, if available) and wad of newspaper (or rubber mat). Students draw on paper on top of newspaper with tracing wheels, which will make embossed lines that students can touch. Tracing wheels are fun to use, but they are not as plastic as other drawing tools; it is difficult to make curves with them.

- **Magnifiers**—It isn't a bad idea to have some magnifiers on hand for visuallly handicapped students. There are many types, but the conventional hand-held kind is generally useful in the classroom. Bar magnifiers, which are placed directly on the printed page, are also good. Magnifiers can aid students in examining reference materials and in helping with visual details in art.

- **Yarn**—Blind students can draw with yarn and string. The technique is simple: students create linear configurations by gluing yarn directly onto paper or boards. When yarn is dry, students develop the areas within the yarn lines in any way they choose with crayons, fabric scraps, paint, etc.

- **Repoussé methods**—Copper and aluminum foil repoussé techniques can be worthwhile trying with your blind (and severely visually limited) students. Repoussé has been a popular project in arts and crafts programs and art rooms for ages, but it may have a particular appeal for the visually limited student because of the embossed lines and textures it offers.

242

To do repoussé, you will need foil (copper, aluminum, or brass) of an appropriate gauge that is intended for this type of activity. NOTE: Aluminum household foil will not work. Cut foil into suitable sizes with heavy shears. Place foil on wad of newspaper or sponge rubber mat. Designs and line figures will be incised by pressing into foil with stylus or manicure stick (dried out ballpoint pens will also work). Turn foil over and rub stick around the raised lines to further accentuate them. Tongue depressors also help to press out flat foil surfaces. Turn foil piece back to continue work; repeat (flip over) process as often as needed. Finished products can be "antiqued" by rubbing ink into them with a soft cloth.

RECIPE FILE

When students have sensory losses, it becomes important to provide activities and materials that engage other senses. The addition of scents to materials helps many special students (especially blind students) to learn color through association with fragrance. Materials with added scents also tend to engage students actively and enthusiastically in their art activities. Actually, all students will likely find the following materials "scent-sational"!*

SHOPPING LIST

Flavorings	Color
orange essence	= orange
banana or lemon	= yellow
cherry or strawberry	= red
blueberry	= blue
peppermint	= green
grape	= violet
cinnamon	= brown
vanilla essence	= white
anise (licorice)	= black

Food coloring set (to add color)

Flour (all purpose, not self-rising)

Salt

Sugar

Soap flakes (Ivory Snow is good)

---

*A word of caution: Many severely retarded students put materials into their mouths and try to ingest them. Although the following recipes are basically nontoxic, the materials are to be treated as *art materials—not as food*. If the flavorful smell proves to be extra enticing for your severely retarded students, you may want to skip the use of scented materials.

Baker's Clay (basic recipe)

2 cups flour
1 cup salt
1 cup water

Mix flour and salt together in a bowl or coffee can. Add water gradually, mixing until ingredients stiffen to form a ball. Remove ball and knead for a few minutes. Add more flour if it is too sticky. Dust work surface and hands with flour for easier handling. You may want to work on wax or foil paper. Store clay in a plastic bag and refrigerate; it will last a little longer. The amount of clay suggested will "serve" four to six students.

To make scented clay, simply add a few spoonfuls of the essence and coloring of your choice to the water. To itensify color, use larger amounts of essence, plus appropriate food coloring. For pastel colors, use less.

Clay may be used to make small items such as ornaments (remember to put the hanging holes in when wet), sculpture, and jewelry. You can make magnetic posting pieces for your refrigerator door by attaching magnetic tape to little clay works! Avoid larger, top-heavy pieces—baker's clay does not have the body to support them.

When work is finished, it will *air harden*, although you can bake it on a cookie sheet, in a 325° to 350° oven, about a half-hour on each side. To air dry, set pieces where air can best circulate around both sides. You can stretch some *window screen* across the top of an empty box (staple sides), place clay on top. Clay will need 24 to 48 hours to dry.

If you have used the flavorings and colorings, you won't need to paint it. If clay is plain, paint with watercolor, poster paint, or acrylics. Acrylic gloss medium can be brushed on all dry pieces for a protective finish.

Goopi

2 cups flour
½ cup salt
½ cup sugar
1½ cups water
essences and flavorings, if desired

Sift all dry ingredients into a bowl, plastic pitcher, or coffee can. Add water, then color (artificial food coloring or paint) and essence gradually. Mixture may be poured into a *squeeze bottle* or used as *fingerpaint*. Stiff paper such as oaktag or lightweight board should be used. (See Figure 220.)

The two previous recipes lend themselves well to the addition of scents. However, essences can also be added to poster paint, matching scent to color.

Fragrance markers should be mentioned too, as a commercially available supply that provides a scent. The principle of these water-soluble markers is that of our "shopping list"—match a color with a flavor. Fragrance markers can be purchased in art and hobby stores, stationery stores, and in some toy stores.

Figure 220

NOTE: Adding the dimension of smell is extremely helpful to the severely visually impaired, who can certainly have difficulty with the concept of color. Flavorings represent natural associations with color. Students will know when they are using a color if it has a distinct aroma. Of course, in using several colors at once, scents will blend together. But generally the added olfactory experience can be instructional as well as stimulating.

All students should be reminded that materials are to create art with, not to eat. The majority of your students are unlikely to have problems with that information.

Tactual Enrichment

Art materials are, by their very nature, tactual. However, you can even add to the tactile, sensory character of paint (and in some instances, clay) by incorporating the following:

Sand Paint

Texture can be added to paint, which increases its tactile quality. Textured paint has a different feel while it is being painted and invites touching when dry. To create textured paint, you need only to add sand. Another good textural ingredient for paint is *vermiculite.*

Soap Paint

1 cup Ivory Flakes

1 cup water

Food coloring or paint (optional)

Mix Ivory Flakes and water in a bowl. Blend until creamy with whisk or beater. Add food coloring or paint if desired.

245

Figure 221

Soap paint is applied directly onto stiff paper with hands. (See Figure 221.) When using with retarded students, use hand-over-hand methods. It has a pleasant and distinctive feel to it.

Papier-Mâché

Although there are many recipes for papier-mâché, this one is recommended for its simplicity and purity of ingredients.

1 cup flour

1 cup water

black and white newspaper

white glue (optional)

Mix flour and water a little at a time in a bowl. Some people prefer adding flour to water, believing that it makes a smoother paste. Add white glue if desired. Avoid "puffs" of flour in air by sifting it directly into water. Tear newspaper into strips. Cover work surface with newspapers. When lumps in mixture have disappeared, dip strips in. Slip excess paste of strips by pulling them through two fingers.

Apply strips to cardboard shape (as in "Mirror, Mirror"). Add dry paper strips between very wet ones to absorb extra wetness. Wrap strips in overlapping manner with respect to original form. Squeeze and manipulate to control shape if needed. When complete, let dry where both sides can be exposed to air (see wire and box suggestion under Baker's Clay). Paint, decorate, let dry. Seal with acrylic gloss medium.

Visual Stimulation

Some materials are visually stimulating because of their bright colors or their fluorescence—their ability to reflect light. There is reason to use these

246

materials beyond the dazzling effects. Retarded students, particularly the severely retarded, are often drawn into activities mainly because of the visually exciting aspects of the medium. Visually handicapped students will be encouraged to use their residual vision when they are presented with fluorescent and bright materials. Many students will find it exciting to work with materials that are not ordinary and will become involved with their work as a result of this attraction.

Fluorescent Materials

Fluorescent materials are extremely bright. They can be used in combination with other materials or on their own. To further intensify their appearance, try using them with black paper. *Here are some of the available fluorescent media:*

Crayons, thick and thin

Chalk (pastels)

Paper and posterboards

Paint

Clay

Stickers

Tape

"Color Aid" Paper

These are bright and richly colored papers that are made through a silkscreen process and often used in advertising art. They can be enjoyed in the classroom. When certain colors are played against each other, they "vibrate." These contrasts produce highly visually stimulating works. However, these papers are expensive, so use accordingly.

Light, playing off surfaces, can be a medium in its own right. Glistening light can catch your students' attention and keep it going!

Foil Paper

Besides the popular silver, foil paper comes in a variety of colors. Foil paper is worthwhile for many design projects and for collages, mobiles, decorations, etc. You can also use tinfoil. Foil paper sticks to surfaces well with white glue.

Glitter

Sparkles or glitter should be considered for activities outside of the holiday season. Glitter will compliment many designs and compositions. Again, use white glue. Supervise students who may not know how to sprinkle glitter properly.

Metallic-Look Paints

Use only waterbased. Acrylic paints come in gold, copper, bronze, and silver. Students will love these paints. Watercolors also come in metallic tones but are not as visually strong as the acrylics.

Colored Acetate and Cellophane

Both materials are excellent for mobiles and window hanging projects. They are able to transmit and spread colored light, much like stained glass windows. There's another activity for you—use black construction paper for your framework, the acetate for the "glass," to create mock stained glass. Again, there is expense involved with acetate purchases, so keep that in mind for the planning of amounts to be used.

Reflective Tapes and Strips

Used for traffic visibility (on bikes and equipment), these unlikely materials are worth experimentation in the art room. They would be most effective for use with the severely retarded and visually handicapped student. There are other materials to explore of the Day-Glo, high visibility types. See about various safety stickers, too.

Figure 222

THE ART CLASSROOM

FOUR

Rooms where teaching and activities take place are more than places to line up desks and bookshelves in rows. Countless studies have been done on the effects of the immediate environment. The observations and theories may vary, but one aspect remains constant—the environment does have considerable impact on individual development and function. Students spend a large percentage of their lives inside the school, so it is worthwhile taking a good look at the surroundings provided for them. Teachers have little or no say in the selection of the architectural styles or the building sites of the schools where they work, but much can be done to use the physical spaces within to the students' benefit.

This section is directed toward using the teaching environment to its maximum potential. Many elements are examined, from using lighting for influencing behavior to art classroom safety.

ACCOMMODATIONS FOR SPECIAL STUDENTS

Severely Retarded

Furniture—Students may need "soft" furniture such as beanbag chairs, mats, and cots. Sometimes working on the floor is more suitable for students. Make sure that furniture is stable and work is secured because students may not be able to navigate the environment with real control. Watch out for sharp corners.

Lighting—Because it is often difficult for students to focus attention, lighting should be directed on work whenever possible. If possible, general lighting should be average to above average because severely retarded students are often visually limited as well.

Tools, Equipment, and Storage—Stay with simple, basic art room supplies. Avoid sharp tools. See "Adaptive Aids" for suggestions on adapting existing tools to students with limited grasp. Many tools and materials adaptations that are recommended for the physically handicapped also apply for severely retarded.

There is little place (or space) for elaborate art process equipment in most art school and classroom programs (such as standing looms, printing presses, etc.). Clearly, these installations would be inappropriate for severely retarded students.

Make sure that all materials are kept out of students' reach when *not* in use. It is not uncommon for severely retarded students to attempt the ingesting of art materials. As pointed out on page 269, "nontoxic" does not mean edible. You could, however, keep materials stored within students' view, particularly if they are of a colorful and appealing nature. Rigid plastic cartons (milk carriers are great) and plastic laundry bins can often be set up on their sides to reveal the items within them, such as yarn and poster paints.

Other Considerations—Because severely retarded students do often spend a lot of their time on the floor, general housekeeping needs to be attended. Floors should be kept reasonably clear and trashcans free of potentially dangerous waste. You might also look after electrical wiring and exposed outlets. Many of the same safety concerns parents have with preschool children in the home apply to severely retarded students in school. The term "childproofing" is used to describe making the home safe for the very young child—this is a very similar situation.

Many severely retarded students are multiply handicapped, and there are often health complications. Students can be on strong medication, which will sometimes affect behaviors. There may be a general picture of poor health that includes allergies and asthma. This is another good reason to avoid dusts and aerosol sprays.

It is a good idea to have some information on students' health so that you are aware of special problems. One of the most disconcerting and frightening health difficulties to the uninformed teacher is the *seizure*. Seizures are often present in the multiply handicapped and severely retarded student, but they do occur in other populations as well. General information and first-aid for seizures are discussed on page 270—become familiar with it if you have special students, particularly the severely retarded. Knowing what to do can make a big difference if your students should have a seizure in the classroom.

Mildly Retarded

Furniture—Arrange desks and tables in a way that allows for easy passage and movement within the class. Many mildly retarded students are poorly coordinated and have some difficulty getting around. Once students can make their own way with ease, avoid frequent repositioning of furniture. It may present new obstacles to overcome. Also, retarded students often appreciate a certain predictability in their environment.

Lighting—Average (to better than average) light.

Tools, Equipment, and Storage—Materials should be organized and kept in specific areas. If students learn where they can find something, it allows them some confidence in knowing where they can go to retrieve it. It's a good idea to store materials in movable bins or trays, so that students can have access to them. Identifying bins and trays with bold, simple labels is also recommended. This not only encourages independence, but it also reinforces reading skills.

Other considerations—Mildly retarded students are capable of doing uncomplicated tasks and enjoy the recognition that doing well brings. Enlist retarded students in sorting and matching jobs in the room. Organizing picture files by category, sorting crayons, paints, etc., would be beneficial to students and to you. Students can also run filmstrip projectors, record players, and be class messengers if they know the building.

Socially and Emotionally Disturbed

Furniture—Seating arrangements can be extremely important. Students should be seated so that they are able to work cooperatively as a group. However, take care *not* to seat students together who agitate each other. When a student's actions are inappropriate for group work, set a place aside for the student away from the group. The student may be asked to go to the "time out" space for a specified amount of time. This should be a separate desk reserved for this reason only, primarily to give the student a chance to calm down.

Providing a special area away from the group can have other purposes. Occasionally a student will be granted time to work independently if he or she has finished an art project, or if the student has a legitimate reason to want to work alone. Again, a table can be put aside for the "quiet" work or independent activities.

The amount of freedom you give your socially and emotionally disturbed students in moving about the room will depend on the way that they handle it. If they abuse the privileges you grant them, then they should earn classroom rights by demonstrating more positive behaviors. Definite guidelines (sometimes even written contracts between teacher and student) may need to be set. Socially and emotionally disturbed students often need structure. They also need some predictability in their environment—from the design of the room to behavioral expectations.

Lighting—It is a fact that lighting is used to create mood and atmosphere in interior design. If your classroom lighting is harsh (or light bulbs exposed), it is possible that your students could react negatively to it. Glaring light, like loud music, can assault the senses. It is safer to have softer lighting, but certainly have enough illumination for students to work comfortably.

Don't forget that light can be used to influence behavior, especially with younger students. When noise levels are rising and your admonishments go unheeded, try turning lights down or flicking them off entirely (if room still has some natural light). Flicking light can get students' attention, but sometimes working (or resting) in low light temporarily is just what is needed to bring students back on an even keel.

Tools, Equipment, and Storage—Socially and emotionally disturbed students often need to learn respect for classroom tools and equipment. Their skill and ability to manipulate them are probably intact. But students must treat materials properly—for the purposes for which the tools were intended. If materials are abused, this should not be taken lightly. A temporary suspension of privilege would be reasonable. When sharp tools are to be used, great care must be taken beforehand to impart the proper attitude to students. You must feel assured that students can handle them! Even classroom scissors can be regarded as sharp tools. You will want to impart a strong basic attitude and rules for using tools correctly.

For safety's sake, store your sharp and potentially threatening objects well away from students. If you have students who might get into trouble with them, a locked cabinet is not a bad idea. However, *whenever it is possible*, give students your trust and let them exercise some freedom in borrowing materials.

Other Considerations—Socially and emotionally disturbed students are often at odds with both themselves and the world. Ideally, the art room is a place where success can be experienced and accomplishments made. The atmosphere should be supportive, unreasonable expectations avoided.

Learning Disabled

Furniture—Because many learning disabled students are distracted quite frequently, it is a good idea to provide an area in the room where they might go occasionally to focus on a particular task. You can call this a study area or learning center, but its main function is to separate the student from the background noise. You might want to bracket the desk (or table) on the front or sides with cardboard or pegboard. You can even fit some desks into cutdown refrigerator cartons. Be sure that work surfaces are not in shadow.

Some learning disabled students may be poorly coordinated. If your students show these traits, design your room in an obstacle-free manner, leaving plenty of room to move about with ease.

Lighting—Normal, moderate lighting is fine for general classroom use. For concentration on specific projects, high-intensity lights or desk lamps may be desired.

Tools, Equipment, and Storage—Proper use of tools and equipment will need to be clearly demonstrated. Students may have to be reminded of what they were previously instructed; information may bear reinforcement. Visual aids can help students with finding materials and carrying out tasks. For example, a poster or a chart can be a constant reminder when properly placed. Labeling drawers that contain materials or color coding can also help.

Other Considerations—A major difficulty for learning disabled students is organization. Organizing their thoughts, their movements, and their lives in general is so often a real challenge. Art activities can be multileveled. Learning disabled students will have a head start if the room and the materials are in order before they begin their strategies for accomplishing the task at hand.

Physically Handicapped

Furniture—The key concept in planning for the physically handicapped is a barrier-free environment. Classroom arrangement should allow for easy passage of your physically disabled students. If the student is on braces or other orthopedic equipment, or is in a wheelchair, you will have to assess the spaces that the student needs to be able to move about freely. Allow as much clearance as you can to give students independence of movement.

Another concern is the level of the work surface. Some levels will have to be elevated; sturdy boxes, stacked on the desk, may work. Often students will be able to place a board across their wheelchairs, although some adjustment might be needed. Some students will work better on a horizontal rather than a vertical plane. Try to provide easels or adjustable drawing boards for these students. (See "Adaptive Aids" for stationary stands.)

While it is ideal for furniture generally to be scaled to the student's size, this idea becomes more important in the case of the physically handicapped child. A chair height that permits the child to place both feet on the floor (instead of having them dangle) is recommended. This gives the student better leverage. Young children's desks should be small enough for them to "clear" the top with room for movement. A student who may already be physically disabled does not need to be further limited by the furniture.

Lighting—Normal lighting is fine.

Tools, Equipment, and Storage—In order to encourage physically handicapped students to be independent, you have to make it possible for them to do things for themselves. Drawers with handles that are easy to grip and shelf tracks that slide out easily help to accomplish this. Try carts with wheels so that disabled students can transport materials that they cannot carry. Work aprons with big pockets can help too!

If you are working with older students and want them to use studio (or other) equipment, such as a potter's wheel, inquire about adaptations from the manufacturing company. Potter's wheels can be made suitable for the wheelchair bound. If you have a sewing machine, the foot pedal can be placed on the top of the sewing surface. The pedal can be controlled by the elbow when legs are not able to manage it. Many appliances can be adapted to the handicapped with a little ingenuity and by asking the manufacturer questions.

Remember, place tools and equipment within students' reach. Tape things down, especially paper, to secure to surface.

Other Considerations—The physical handicap is clearly not a "hidden" handicap. It is a fact that the disabled person must confront daily in order to function. If the person is wheelchair bound, there are seemingly endless obstacles to overcome. Although government regulations have somewhat helped the physically handicapped (see page 263 describing "Section 504"), many challenges remain.

On a physical level, the problem is one of access. To get a wheelchair up a set of steps when no ramp is near represents the kind of perplexities that face the handicapped.

When setting up your classroom to accommodate your students, try negotiating your planned space by getting into a wheelchair. You will quickly develop an appreciation for the problem, and test your room design at the same time.

Hearing Impaired

Furniture—Position furniture so that students can *see your face*. Try to seat hearing impaired students so that they see not only you, but can see the faces of their classmates. It is easier for hearing impaired students to understand you if they are within a close visual range.

Keep in mind that students should be given freedom of movement in the classroom. Students need to move around to read lips and to attract your attention. Since deafness can create a great sense of isolation, it is a good idea to avoid always seating students in a manner that will separate them. Desk clusters or group tables should be incorporated in planning your room.

Lighting—Light is extremely important in communicating with hearing impaired students. In order to be understood, light should be on your face. If you are in shadows, it will be hard to see your lips and expressions. Also, avoid standing in front of windows. It creates a glare that reduces visibility.

When you want your hearing impaired students' attention, simply signal by flicking the lights off and on!

Tools, Equipment, and Storage—Use visual aids whenever you can; it will help students to identify supplies and understand instructions. Demonstrate how to use tools and equipment, and where to put them when you are finished with them. Make sure students understand; let them show you in response to your directions.

Other Considerations—Unlike the physically handicapped, the deaf student cannot always be easily distinguished from others. Yet, it is just as important that the needs arising from hearing loss be recognized. You must develop a consciousness about your hearing impaired students. Remember to communicate ideas and processes in every way possible, i.e., facial clarity, body language, aids, and demonstration. Make sure the layout of your room supports your efforts.

Visually Handicapped/Blind

Furniture—Chairs, files, desks, and other furniture should be placed in the room in an uncluttered manner. Once furniture arrangement is established, keep it that way! Sight impaired students can get bruised by unexpected objects. If you intend to move things around, inform your students and show them in a physical way.

If your student is blind, you can help him or her become familiar with the surroundings by using a simple sighted guide technique. Have student place his hand on your upper arm right above your elbow. Lead him to his destination. If the student does not know you very well, identify yourself and verbally describe what you are doing and where you are going (e.g., "Hi, Jane, it's Mrs. Collins. I'll take you to your seat. We're going around the supply closet now," etc.).

Be sure to assign seats to visually handicapped students with respect to their functional vision. Many visual impairments will affect either the left or right sides of the visual field (or both) or reduce vision in other ways. Check out from which angles your students can best see the board and demonstrations. It is generally a good practice to seat visually impaired students close to you. However, if you are certain that a student is completely blind, it is sometimes better to seat him or her in an accessible place, often nearer to the exit. When you want to seat the blind student, you can *knock* on his or her desk while you verbally address the student. You may also want to identify the student's desk with a Braille name tag or a tactile clue, such as a felt circle.

Lighting—If a student has some residual vision, good lighting becomes crucial. Lights should fully illuminate students' desk activities; high intensity lights can be used for close work. You should also watch for glare on objects from light. Avoid giving demonstrations in front of the window. Generally, make sure that enough light is on you so that your sight impaired students can see you better.

One exception to the rule is the light-sensitive visually impaired student. Very often this condition is part of albinism. Students with albinism often wear tinted glasses to protect their eyes, and may want to avoid direct sunlight as well as strong artificial light.

Tools, Equipment, and Storage—Students with severe sight losses will need hand-over-hand demonstration of tools and equipment. Make sure when you show your class a technique or process that you are in their full view. Remember, some sight impairments affect only certain angles in the visual field.

Attempt to keep materials in specified places. It will aid students when they look for supplies. This is particularly important for blind students. You may even want to label materials and storage bins in Braille, or affix an identifying tactual clue on them (such as gluing the letter "S" in felt on the sewing supply box), or use an actual sample of the material within.

Be careful to *shut* drawers and cabinet doors. Doors that are left slightly ajar can injure a blind student!

Other Considerations—The world can be hard to negotiate when your sight is impaired. If you have ever worn a blindfold or had drops in your eyes, you may remember how disoriented you could become. Of course, blind students have probably adapted to their environment—unlike the sighted person who covers his eyes and tries to find his way. Yet there are still many pitfalls to avoid. By providing your severely sight impaired students with organized, familiar surroundings, you can reduce or eliminate much confusion and apprehension.

Gifted

Furniture—Students should have something to say about where things go and why. They can even submit room specifications or "blueprints."

Special space can be set aside as an independent work area where students can develop their own ideas. It would be wonderful to build a loft space into the classroom if at all possible. There are many how-to-do-it books on construction and it could make a great project for the right students and teacher. The idea of incorporating different levels and perspectives could be very stimulating for gifted students. At least, have some high stools, low benches, and furniture of miscellaneous heights around the room to provide students with variety, rather than regimentation.

Lighting—Changeable lighting (an adjustable system) is ideal for adding interest to the room, but most classroom lighting is not installed by the teacher. So, be happy with moderate, normal lighting.

Tools, Equipment, and Storage—Students should be quite capable of proper treatment and care of tools and equipment, unless they are very young children. They should be given almost full responsibility in handling them (with some teacher supervision, of course). Students should be encouraged to find their own sense of order and keep it. Maintenance and storage are part of their job. The rewards are the freedom they are given in the classroom. They should be able to make good decisions about what is needed for a specific activity, where to find it, and how to put it away properly.

Other Considerations—Gifted students should be afforded ample opportunity to use their intelligence in organizing their world. They are in an excellent position to be in control of their environment. Gifted students need a chance to develop these skills, and the art classroom is the perfect place to practice!

CAN A ROOM TEACH ART?

There are many ways to use your walls and classroom space for stimulating participation in art and art appreciation.

Exhibits

Displaying work is a dynamic part of the creative cycle. First the idea is born, which may be in direct response to outside stimulation or drawn from images within. Next, the technical process of creating the work. Finally, there is a product that will communicate your own interpretive idea to others. By showing your work, you share your special inner vision and perhaps have an influence on the viewer's way of seeing.

Whether work is informally hung on clothesline or appears in a mini-art gallery on panels, the important thing is that it is being shown! You may want to place work on posterboard or construction paper (or even mat and frame it) on occasion to give it a thoroughly finished and important look.

Bulletin boards and cork strips are the most commonly used display aids in the schools. You can use them for mixed examples of children's work, specific themes, or art reproductions. A "Picture of the Week" display will encourage changing exhibits. Try to give as many students as you can an opportunity to see their "name in lights."

The Four Walls—Blank or Brilliant?

The art/classroom is usually a bustling place that thrives on energy and activity. It is the creative nerve center of the school. The atmosphere should reflect its vitality. This is not to suggest that the room should be decorated like the funhouse at your local amusement park. That would be too distracting, particularly to many special students. On the other hand, if your no-frills style might suggest an examining room, you should be rethinking your room's decor!

How do you strike a happy medium in creating an atmosphere that is not overly stimulating, yet not too sterile? There are some basic considerations. First, if you plan to decorate in an ambitious, lively manner, perhaps you could pick *one* wall or section for your efforts. Leave some "restful" space. Should your displays be of a more conservative nature, it would be fine to spread them around the room in an overall approach.

Use of colors should be regarded for its impact on your environment. If you have control over wall painting decisions, you might want to paint one wall a sunny accent color or a color that will complement your displays, if you are intending a wall for that purpose.

Students should respond favorably to a warm and cheery environment. They will not only appreciate seeing their own work in a pleasant setting, but they will also enjoy posters, art reproductions, and graphics. You will want to identify the work on the walls so that students can become familiar with names and styles. Don't overlook masks, fans, hats, kimonos, souvenirs, and textiles—the list is endless—for "hands-on" wall displays as well.

Recognizing students' efforts through displaying their work does wonders for self-esteem. To add to feelings of success, consider arranging shows for students outside the walls and halls of the school. Community centers, banks, libraries, and local businesses are usually quite receptive to student exhibits. Such events promote good feelings and celebrate accomplishments.

Discovery and Appreciation

The art classroom can be a place not only to create art, but to develop appreciation for art, too. Observation and discovery are very effective methods for teaching art appreciation. Why not set up an *appreciation resource center* in the corner of your room? You could easily stock a bin or nearby shelf with reference materials. Art history and art books, manageably sized reproductions, art postcards, and even a slide viewer with a set of art slides could be provided. Visual devices, such as magnifying glasses and colored lenses, will encourage students to experiment with "ways of seeing." Concepts such as warm and cool color tones are suggested when viewing art through colored filters. Magnifying glasses help students study details.

You may also include task cards—step-by-step teacher-made cards directing students in selected independent activities. Task cards can be kept in folders or files. Even activity *kits* on given subjects, such as landscape, portrait, or still life (or on specific artists), might be made available. These are often kept in labeled gift-type boxes, and have built-in activities for students to accomplish on their own. Teaching about mixing colors as well as patterns lends itself to task cards and kits.

This approach to art appreciation does have potential with many special students who need to learn to concentrate and follow specific directions, or who may need time away from the group. Students may either "earn" their time at centers through positive behaviors, or be given freedom to go to centers when other work is completed. The method by which this is handled and time frame allotted depends on what is appropriate for a particular situation or student.

The severely retarded student may not be the ideal candidate for an art appreciation resource center as described above, but is able to respond to tactual experiences. You can still set up a special place for students to visit in the art classroom. *Sensory shoeboxes* could be kept out on an accessible desk for students to investigate. You might want to tape boxes closed and cut a slot in the lid through which students could insert their hands to touch materials inside. Many materials could be provided, such as fake fur and fabric scraps, pasta and macaroni, cotton, cutup sponges, and so on. You may also wish to include natural objects in your "special" place: seashells, pine cones, dried grasses, etc. Exploration of these materials offers an enrichment experience for retarded students.

MUSEUMS AND SPECIAL STUDENTS

There is no better place to learn art appreciation than in art museums. (Figures 223-228 were done by students in response to art appreciation and museum experiences.) Activities in the classroom that include art reproductions, slides, and books ideally should be used to reinforce museum experiences. Students of all ages will gain a great deal from museum visits—not only information and knowledge, but a sense of the many worlds beyond their own. Early and repeated exposure to art and artists creates a basis for appreciation. As students become familiar and comfortable with museums, they tend to integrate what they have learned into their own form of expression. Appreciation is expansive; it has a way of encouraging respect for the natural and built environment. By developing appreciation skills, students can generally increase their awareness and intellectual curiosity.

Figure 223

Figure 224

261

Figure 225

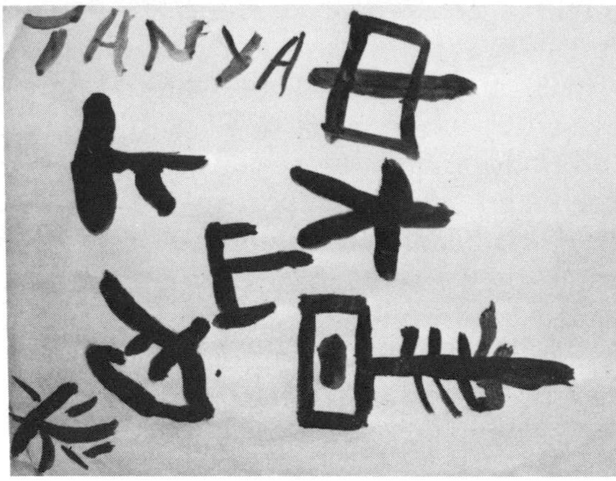

Figure 226

Figure 227

Figure 228

262

Section 504 and the Special Visitor

Section 504 is part of the Federal Rehabilitation Act. It states that no handicapped individual shall be excluded from participation on the basis of his or her handicap. This act affects institutions and programs that receive federal funds, which would certainly include museums.

In compliance with 504, museums have attempted, among other things, to remove architectural barriers, install wheelchair ramps, adjust heights of public facilities for the disabled, and provide handicapped parking spaces. But there is more beyond architectural access; there is program access. Many museums offer clear graphics for the deaf and large print information and catalogues for the visually handicapped, along with other adaptive audio equipment.

A number of museums have appointed a "504 Coordinator," whose main responsibility is to see that the museum follows the 504 guidelines. The coordinator keeps in touch with the handicapped community. He or she may organize training programs for museum guides, as well as volunteers and docents, on learning how they can assist disabled visitors. Tours may be arranged through the 504 Coordinator, as well as special services.

If you are planning a trip to the museum with your special students, it is wise to get in touch with the 504 Coordinator. He or she can help you with your particular requirements. You might be told, for example, what areas are completely accessible to the wheelchair bound, what type of adaptive materials (print, tapes) are available, if you can enlist a deaf signing guide, etc. Some museums will even have a list of "touchable" objects for the blind. Occasionally there will be a special area of the museum that has been set aside as a touchable section for blind visitors. However, this concept is not encouraged under Section 504, whose thrust is to integrate, not segregate, the special visitor.

Inquire about the museum's art programs and accessibility of current exhibits. Sometimes even transportation and special educational programs are offered to the handicapped student. Let the museum know about your students' special needs so that they can be prepared to best meet them.

Children's Museums

In recent years, a number of "hands-on" children's museums have sprung up around the country. Their nature is participatory; they invite interaction between their exhibits and their young visitors. (See Figure 229.)

Because of the sensory, experiential character of children's museums, they are the perfect place for special students. They educate students about their immediate environment and often bring exotic worlds in closer to the students. Exhibitions frequently reinforce concepts. Usually, games, exploration, and activities of direct involvement are offered. (See Figure 230.)

Children's museums are stimulating and educational. (See Figure 231.) Retarded students, who may not be receptive to the more formal atmosphere of art museums, should be excellent candidates for a visit to the children's museum.

Figure 229

Figure 230

Figure 231

264

SAFETY IN THE ART CLASSROOM

On the Safe Side

A considerable amount of attention has been given recently to the safe use of art materials. Books, articles, lectures, and symposiums have become available to artists and teachers on this vital subject. Studio artists and hobbyists have been able to make adjustments in their materials usage accordingly. Usually the changes are very simple. It is often a matter of receiving basic information and developing a sense of safety awareness. Once consciousness about health is attained, it almost works automatically. This section will guide you in the direction of safety in an uncomplicated way.

It is most important that you become informed about health and safety when you work with students. Young children and special students constitute part of what is known as a "high-risk" group. Because children and even older students are still growing, their body metabolism is more rapid than that of an adult, so they can absorb material more quickly through exposures. Their immature body defense systems and smaller body weight also make them more physically vulnerable to hazards.

When special students are exposed to suspicious or unsafe materials, their problems could be even more serious than other students their age. Many special students have health complications that could be worsened by potentially hazardous substances. Health conditions that may include respiratory ailments, allergies, and even physical or organic dysfunction are of particular concern; you would certainly want to avoid any possible threat or aggravation to health!

With a little effort, your art classroom can be reasonably hazard-free. There are very safe, available substitutes for materials containing unhealthy ingredients.

Young students do not have to perform advanced technical processes, and there is no need to expose them. For example, photographic chemicals and darkroom activities can represent health hazards. Glazing, soldering, enameling, and so on are not necessary for high risk groups to chance.

Classroom Art Materials:
A Dozen Do's and Don'ts to Remember

Not *Recommended for Art Classroom Use*	*Safer Alternatives*
1. Permanent markers (may contain powerful solvents)	Watercolor markers, water-based markers (See Figure 232 and 233)
2. Rubber cement, epoxy resins, or other solvent-based glues	White glue or library paste (See Figure 234)
3. Dry tempera powders	Liquid poster paint (or solid poster paint blocks)
4. Oil-based paints, enamel paints	Acrylic paints and other water-based paints
5. Turpentine	Materials requiring soap and water cleanup, e.g., acrylics, (for adult professional studio use, try *turpenoid* instead)
6. Batik and commercial dyes, permanent vat dyes	Natural vegetable dyes; also, water-based fabric paints; fabric crayons (See Figure 235)
7. Oil-based, solvent-based, printing inks	Water-based printing inks
8. Chalk and pastel dust	Wet technique or oil crayons (e.g., Craypas)
9. Aerosol spray	Brush-on technique using acrylic gloss medium (teacher supervised)
10. Instant papier-mâché mixes	Flour and water
11. Unmarked glazes or lead glazes	Paint clay with poster paint or acrylics, seal with acrylic gloss medium
12. Unvented or improperly vented kiln	Air-dry clay work (kiln must be correctly installed with exhaust hood for safe use)

266

Figure 232

Figure 233

Figure 234

Figure 235

Speaking About Safety

Art materials are intended for creative, educational purposes. They should go directly onto the work area—*not* into the body. The ways of entry are inhalation, absorption, and ingestion. Let's look at ways to avoid unintentional exposures.

Clean Air Avoid mixing dusts and powders when you can. They can irritate the respiratory system or worse. Watch for clay flour (it may contain silica), tempera powder, and other dry pigments. If you must mix powder, add water into the container to eliminate dust clouds. Plastic bags are good for mixing because you can enclose your hand with the end of the bag as you mix. It is best to use prepared (premixed) materials in solid or liquid form.

Avoid activities that produce fumes, vapors, and smoke unless you have the correct exhaust fan. This type of activity (enameling, soldering stained glass, etc.) generally would be inappropriate for the classroom.

Aerosol sprays should be used only in a properly vented spray booth, often with user wearing a protective mask. If you use them outside, make sure the wind is blowing the spray away from you or you can injure your eyes. The use of aerosol cans should be discouraged, whether it is fixative, paint, or varnish. Sprays release tiny particles which are absorbed deep into the lungs (and bloodstream). They are not indispensable, so why not eliminate them?

Good ventilation is important. Windows should be opened regularly to circulate fresh air. If your room is on a vent system, be sure to check vents to see if they are functioning properly. Room temperature should be comfortable. A room that is overheated, with stale air, is unhealthy. Rooms that are too cold should be adjusted also.

If you keep the atmosphere free from dusts, fumes, and vapors—and keep the new air coming in—you have reduced your own potential for air pollution. Cross-ventilation can be achieved by opening doors and windows on either side of the room. A word of warning: Simply opening a window does not purify hazardous products. When you do fume- or dust-producing activities, the circulated air will only help to blow the pollutants around the atmosphere! This is why such activities must be left to the advanced professional who will install exhaust fans over the work to avoid hazardous fumes, vapors, etc.

Keeping House A simple and often repeated rule, "wash your hands," takes on new meaning when it comes to the art classroom. Although some activities are intrinsically messy, leave adequate time for washing up students' hands (and faces) thoroughly. Special students may not have the awareness to clean themselves properly and could end up ingesting the art materials via their hands. It is not "cute" or reflective of deep artistic involvement to have paint or clay-covered students. Use smocks and workshirts when necessary and wash them routinely.

Check the lids of containers to see if they have been adequately secured. This is particularly important with solvent-based materials (which students should not use, but which you may want to use with caution). If mostly water-based materials are used as suggested (poster paints, acrylics, etc.), cleanup should be a soap-and-water affair. Students, however, should not be shaking cleanser around. If students do assist in cleaning, handsoap on the sponge will do; at the most, use liquid dishwashing detergents or liquid cleanser. Many household cleaning agents are quite strong with potent chemical ingredients. Do not leave brushes soaking in open cans or bottles filled with powerful cleaners or solvents!

Before you take your broom in hand, for general orderliness, here's a hint that will keep the dust from flying: *plant sprayers.* Fill with water and pump into the atmosphere. It will prevent dry particles from circulating by weighting them down with moisture. This will make your job less irritating—literally.

Remember: No eating or drinking around art materials!

What You Don't Know Can Hurt You Read the labels on your materials. If there is reason to be suspicious of contents, or if a product is insufficiently identified, that may be enough reason to not use it. An example of this would be dry glazes packaged in envelopes, marked by color only. Glaze powders may be composed of lead.

Unfortunately, manufacturers do not always list ingredients accurately. If you want to know more about the product, you can always request a material safety data sheet from the company.

What if a product is labeled "nontoxic"? Does that mean it is 100 percent safe? Not really. "Nontoxic" means that the product is not known to cause acute, short-term health effects. This is *not* to speak of long-term, chronic disease or conditions that the product might cause. "Nontoxic" still requires consumer awareness.

Plain old common sense is basic to safety. Your nose can sometimes serve you well. For instance, if you are overwhelmed by a strong odor that is the byproduct of a craft activity, don't wait until you get acclimated to the smell; check it out! If a paint jar has a rancid or peculiar smell, it may have developed a mold and gone bad. Discard it. Art materials have a fixed shelf life and don't last forever. Update your inventory from time to time. Resist bringing outside articles and products into the art classroom if they are of dubious origins; for example, surplus products or "treasures" from the junk heap. One "found object" sculptor became quite sick from the fumes of his junk yard assemblage when he soldered it together. It was later determined—unbeknownst to the ill artist—that some old bicycle parts that he used contained lead and produced poisonous fumes.

Finally, while you are teaching art, teach safety. Give students information on proper product usage, cleanup, and general awareness. You might even want to do a class project on safety, creating reminders in the form of posters and graphics. Display them in prominent places!

What You Do Not Need
in Your Art Classroom

The following products are extremely hazardous. Beside having known devastating effects on health, some are flammable as well. They should never be used for art or classroom activities.

Asbestos This is a possible cancer-causing agent and lung disease producer (asbestosis). No known exposure level is safe. Some art products that may contain asbestos are papier-mâché mixes, and certain clay and modeling powders.

Lead Lead poisoning is one of the oldest recognized hazards known. Its capacity for damage to the body is well documented. Lead may be found in lead glazes, lead frits, lead solder (toxic fumes), and lead paint. It may also be found in some printers' inks.

Benzene, Carbon Tetrachloride, Toluene, and Xylene All solvents, these chemicals are highly hazardous. Some are found in the form of cleaning fluids and paint and varnish removers. Toluene is often an ingredient in permanent markers, although it may not be listed on the label. Do not use products that contain any of these chemicals.

First-Aid for Seizures

Generally, when a student has a scraped knee or sprained ankle, there is ample time to take him or her to the nurse for care. But seizures happen so suddenly that you must handle the matter on the spot. The way that the seizure is dealt with will not only affect the seizuring student, but the other students in the class as well. A reassuring teacher will calm the class; a panicked teacher will further upset them. The first step to dealing with a seizure effectively is learning about them and what to do when they occur.

The most dramatic seizure is the *grand mal* (generalized tonic-clonic). The student may become stiff and start to fall. Jerking movements will begin. Skin may turn pale or take on a bluish complexion because of reduced breathing. Saliva may escape from the mouth. Here's what you can do:

- Without leaving student, notify nurse or office.
- Ease the student to the floor. Do not try to restrain him. The seizure must run its course.
- Do *not* force any objects into his mouth.
- Clear the area of sharp objects which could injure him.
- Place something soft and flat under his head. Turn him on one side to release saliva.
- Loosen any tight clothing. Remove glasses.
- You cannot stop the seizure. It should be over in a few minutes.

You will want to notify the school nurse that a seizure has taken place. If the seizure follows the usual course and the student gains consciousness, there is no harm. Rarely, one seizure follows another without student gaining consciousness; this indicates the need for emergency medical assistance.

After the seizure, the student will be disoriented and confused. Do not offer him anything to eat or drink unless he is fully awake. After it is all over, the student will probably want to rest for a while.

There are other seizures. The *petit mal* (generalized absence seizure) is most common in children and usually lasts for less than a minute. The child may stare blankly and appear to be daydreaming. Finally, the *complex partial seizure* (temporal lobe, psychomotor) may include complex behaviors. The student may walk around aimlessly, make unusual chewing sounds and act generally confused. This seizure may last anywhere from a minute to several hours.

There is nothing that you can do for petit mal (absence) seizures. You may want to reassure the students' classmates that everything is all right, however. In the complex partial seizure, the child *may* respond to calm and gently spoken directions. Do not try to restrain; move harmful objects out of the way. Notify the school nurse.

Of all the seizures, the grand mal seizure can be the most frightening for children. Among other things, the loss of consciousness distinguishes this seizure from the others. *A prepared and informed teacher can make all the difference in the art classroom.*

Glossary

Albinism. A lack of pigmentation occurring primarily in skin, hair, and eyes. May include light sensitivity (photophobia). Often visual impairment accompanies albinism.

Athetosis (athetoid). Form of cerebral palsy marked by slow, involuntary movement.

Audiologist. Specialist who evaluates hearing disorders.

Autism. Sometimes referred to as "childhood schizophrenia." A serious personality disorder that can include severe behavioral aberrations; most commonly marked by a withdrawal from reality.

Bilateral. Refers to two sides.

Blindism(s). A set of behaviors that are often engaged in by blind children, such as rocking back and forth, flicking fingers in front of eyes, rubbing hands in eyes, looking into lights, etc.

Body parts. Refers to arms, legs, head, and torso and their relationships to one another.

Brain damage. Congenital or acquired injury or disease that impairs a part of the brain causing learning disability, retardation, or neurological dysfunction.

Cerebral palsy. A central nervous system disorder often marked by erratic movement, awkward stumbling gait, and slurred speech.

Closure (visual closure). A contour that is defined by an unbroken line; defining a shape by completing an outline.

Cognitive. An intellectual thought process yielding awareness and knowledge.

Concepts. Characteristics that describe an idea; an abstract idea; a theme. Concepts include big/little, in/out, up/down.

Congenital. A characteristic or condition existing since birth.

Contracted muscles. Shortened muscles, reducing body movement.

Desensitize. A process in which materials or methods are gradually introduced to those who may have an aversion to them. As acceptance begins, quantity and exposure time are increased. This technique is useful in art with tactually defensive students.

Developmental level. Stage at which certain skills would normally be present or acquired.

Directionality. Orientation of the body to space around it; awareness of left/right, up/down, diagonals, etc.

Discrimination. The ability to recognize differences and act upon that knowledge, as in sorting out information or materials.

Down's Syndrome. Formerly referred to as Mongolism, a chromosomal abnormality that includes retardation. Recognizable physical characteristics include a definite slant to the eyes, rounded features, soft body shape, and childlike appearance into adulthood.

Dyslexia. Lack of ability to read. Often characterized by "reversals." Printed page may appear as a scramble of incoherent data. A common learning disability.

Ecolalia. A speech aberration in which "parroting" takes place. Ecolalic patterns are often a verbal "playback" of the words and spoken phrases of others.

Eye-hand coordination. Movement of the hand as directed by the eye and brain.

Field loss. Reduced visual range due to injury or disease, i.e., tunnel vision.

Fine motor. Small movements with hands.

Gross motor. Refers to larger movements of the body.

Hand-over-hand. Technique in which teacher places his or her hand over the student's hand to teach a skill manually.

Homebound. Refers to a situation where students are unable to attend school due to short- or long-term illness or injury. *Homebound teachers* visit students in their homes or in their hospital placements to instruct them during their absence from school.

Hyperactive. Excess of energy, restless, easily distracted, i.e., unable to sit still.

Hypoactive. Absence of energy; lethargic, listless, very quiet.

Individualized Education Program (IEP). An educational prescription, designed by teachers and other related professionals, recommending services and programs to meet students' special needs.

Kinesthetic (kinesthetic sense). The sensory experience of the body's movement; physical awareness of the body's position in space.

Laterality. Awareness of one side of the body in relationship to space around it; a directional sense.

Light perception. Discrimination between light and dark.

"Left brain." Theory that holds the left brain responsible for reading and verbal tasks.

Legally blind. By definition, 20/200 vision or less in the better eye with glasses or lenses; a severe field loss, such as tunnel vision.

Mainstreaming. The practice of placing exceptional students in nonhandicapped classes.

Midline. The imaginary middle line of the body that defines the right and left halves.

Multiply handicapped. A combination of two or more disabilities, often involving retardation; physical and/or motor dysfunction.

Multisensory. Involving several or all senses.

Neurological. Of or referring to the nervous system

Occupational therapist. Specialist in providing activities designed to improve skills and movement.

Olfactory. Sense of smell.

Paralysis. Loss of function and/or movement of a part of the body, often involving sensation. *Hemiplegia* refers to paralysis affecting one side; *Paraplegia* refers to paralysis below the waist; *Quadraplegia* is a paralysis of both arms and legs.

Parts-whole relationship. Understanding the connections between a given part to the whole volume.

Perceptual handicap. Impairment in the ability to accurately process and interpret written, auditory, sensorial or visual information.

Perseverate. Difficulty in shifting from one activity to the next; repetition of language, action, or visual image.

Physical therapist. Rehabilitative specialist who provides exercises and techniques to improve health, skills, and physical abilities.

Pincer grasp. Grasp utilizing the thumb and index finger, i.e., the small finger movement needed to pick up a bead.

Palmer grasp. Grasp that does not utilize the thumb; objects are "raked in," using four fingers in a palm-down motion.

Prosthesis. An artificial part used to replace a body defect or amputation.

Range of motion. Extent to which a limb can move in all directions.

Reversals. Perceiving, reading, and writing words and letters backwards. For example, "was" appears as "saw"; "b" as "d." A common trait among dyslexics.

"Right brain." The theory that the right side of the brain is the creative side, responsible for art and spatial comprehension.

Rote learning. Memorization through repetition, not dependent on intellectual process.

Schizophrenia. Serious personality disorder characterized by a psychotic break with reality.

Seizure. Also epileptic convulsion—an attack involving a series of contractions of the muscles. *Grand mal* (clonic-tonic) is a violent, jerking disturbance where muscular control and consciousness are lost. *Petit mal* may involve some twitching or loss of awareness, but is not usually violent in nature.

Sensorial, sensory. Of or pertaining to the senses.

Sequencing. Placement of materials, events, or information in logical progressive order.

Sheltered workshop. An employment setting for individuals whose disabilities prevent them from entering the job mainstream. Workshop participants are usually paid modest salaries. Work often includes simple tasks.

Spastic (spasticity). Contracted, restricted, and stiff muscular movement.

Tactile defensiveness. Strong aversion to textures, materials, or even human touch. In art, common aversions include clay and paste.

Verbal cueing (also prompting). Helping student to perform an activity through teacher's talking, giving directions, and offering praise for correct responses. Reinforcement and repetition often required.

Index